汽车检修一学通丛书

图解汽车维修英语
第 2 版

文艳玲　陈宏昌　谭克诚　林世明　**编著**

机械工业出版社

本书分为 5 章共 27 个单元。内容涵盖了汽车大部分系统或总成的结构特点、工作原理、零部件名称，并介绍了新能源汽车技术。每个单元包括课文、难句理解、词汇和短语、习题等多个环节，书后还附有一些汽车常用缩略词和科技英语知识，可以帮助读者学习科技英语翻译技巧。

本书可作为汽车维修技术人员和工程技术人员的培训用书，也可作为职业院校、应用型本科汽车类专业群中的汽车专业英语教学用书。

图书在版编目（CIP）数据

图解汽车维修英语/文艳玲等编著. —2 版. —北京：机械工业出版社，2023.11
（汽车检修一学通丛书）
ISBN 978-7-111-73888-6

Ⅰ.①图… Ⅱ.①文… Ⅲ.①汽车-车辆修理-英语-图解 Ⅳ.①U472-64

中国国家版本馆 CIP 数据核字（2023）第 171444 号

机械工业出版社（北京市百万庄大街 22 号　邮政编码 100037）
策划编辑：谢　元　　责任编辑：谢　元
责任校对：赵海青　　责任印制：常天培
北京宝隆世纪印刷有限公司印刷

2023 年 11 月第 2 版第 1 次印刷
184mm×260mm · 13.5 印张 · 334 千字
标准书号：ISBN 978-7-111-73888-6
定价：65.00 元

电话服务　　　　　　　　　网络服务
客服电话：010-88361066　　机　工　官　网：www.cmpbook.com
　　　　　010-88379833　　机　工　官　博：weibo.com/cmp1952
　　　　　010-68326294　　金　书　网：www.golden-book.com
封底无防伪标均为盗版　机工教育服务网：www.cmpedu.com

前　言

2010年编写的《图解汽车维修英语》自出版以来，受到汽车维修技术人员的一致好评，为了能更好地满足职业院校的师生对汽车专业英语学习的需求，编者结合自身的教学改革实践经验以及广大读者提出的宝贵意见，在保留原书特色的基础上进行了全面修订，本次修订的主要内容包括：

1. 对部分章节进行了调整，使其更能紧跟汽车科技的发展。
2. 对新单词部分增加了音标，使学习更加方便。
3. 增加并替换了部分章节中的图片，使其更贴近原文内容。
4. 对课后练习进行了增加和删减，使之更符合语言学习规律。

根据教育部颁布的《高等职业教育专科英语课程标准（2021年版）》，汽车英语是继英语基础模块学习后，根据专业开展的拓展模块，与基础模块形成递进关系，旨在提升学生与职业岗位相关的英语应用能力，是汽车类专业群高技能人才必须掌握的技能，也是汽车类专业群的一门专业核心课程。

本书根据教育部高职高专技术技能型人才培养模式要求，结合汽车类专业群实际需要和教学经验进行修订，以直观性和通俗性为特点，遵循"学用结合"的原则，旨在使学生熟悉本专业的英语词汇及用法，培养汽车维修技术人员和汽车类专业群学生的英文阅读理解、翻译和资料查询能力，从而了解汽车领域科技文章结构及体裁，以便能从国外资料中更好地获取先进的汽车科技信息和知识。

本书实用性更强，选材更新颖，更贴近企业，重点突出，篇章力求精而专。每个单元都图文并茂地把各部件的组成、结构和原理、当前的设备、零部件和系统等内容直观地呈现出来，还有配套练习来辅助教学内容，以便强化对整篇课文内容的理解。

本书分为5章，共27个单元。内容涵盖了汽车大部分系统或总成的结构特点、工作原理、零部件名称。第1章为汽车的基本构造，包括汽车基本结构、汽车的分类以及一些技术参数共3个单元；第2章为发动机，内容包括发动机的基本术语、分类、工作原理及两大机构和五大系统共10个单元；第3章为底盘，内容包括传动系统、制动系统、转向系统和悬架系统共4个单元；第4章内容包括车身和电气系统共7个单元；第5章为电动汽车简介，共3个单元。每个单元包括课文、难句理解、词汇和短语、习题等多个环节，书后还附有一些汽车常用缩略词和科技英语知识。

通过对本书的学习，读者可以进一步巩固已掌握的词汇和语法知识，扩大专业词汇量，熟悉专业英语的表达方式，掌握阅读专业英语的方法，为获取相关的专业知识打下良好的基础。本书可作为汽车维修技术人员和工程技术人员的培训用书，也可作为职业院校、应用型本科汽车类专业群中的汽车专业英语教学用书。

本书第 1 章由林世明编写，第 2、3 章及附录由文艳玲编写，第 4 章由陈宏昌编写，第 5 章由谭克诚编写。在编写本书的过程中，得到了上汽通用五菱汽车股份有限公司员工的大力支持，他们提出了许多汽车专业技术方面的宝贵意见和建议，编者在此深表谢意。

由于编者水平有限，书中难免出现不足之处，恳请广大读者批评指正，编者在此表示衷心的感谢。

编　者

目 录

前 言

Chapter 1 Automotive Fundamentals / 001

Unit 1 Basic Structure of Automobile / 001
Unit 2 The Automobile Classification / 005
Unit 3 The Vehicle Technical Parameters / 008

Chapter 2 Engine / 015

Unit 1 Engine Overview / 015
Unit 2 Engine Construction / 018
Unit 3 Kinds of Engine / 025
Unit 4 Engine Operating Principles / 030
Unit 5 Electronic Fuel Injection System / 035
Unit 6 Valve Train / 044
Unit 7 Engine Ignition System / 053
Unit 8 Engine Starting System / 061
Unit 9 Engine Lubrication System / 067
Unit 10 Engine Cooling System / 076

Chapter 3 Chassis / 084

Unit 1 Power Train System / 084
Unit 2 Braking System / 094
Unit 3 Steering System / 102
Unit 4 Suspension System / 110

Chapter 4 Body and Electrical System / 118

Unit 1 Body / 118
Unit 2 Instrument Panel / 123
Unit 3 Air Conditioning System / 132

V

Unit 4	Automobile Sensors	/ 138
Unit 5	Anti-Lock Braking System	/ 145
Unit 6	Safety Airbag System	/ 151
Unit 7	Cruise Control System	/ 156

Chapter 5 Electric Vehicles / 160

Unit 1	Introducing Electric Vehicles	/ 160
Unit 2	Technology of Electric Vehicles	/ 167
Unit 3	Hybrid Electric Vehicles	/ 172

Appendix Ⅰ	English Abbreviations for Automobile	/ 177
Appendix Ⅱ	科技英语知识	/ 185
	一　科技英语词汇的来源及特点	/ 185
	二　科技英语词汇的分类及构成	/ 187
	三　科技英语的句法特点	/ 191
	四　科技英语的翻译 1	/ 196
	五　科技英语的翻译 2	/ 202
Appendix Ⅲ	新能源汽车专业术语	/ 207

References / 210

Chapter 1

Automotive Fundamentals

Unit 1 Basic Structure of Automobile

An automobile is a kind of road vehicle usually with four wheels which is driven by an engine.

In 1886, a German engineer, Gottlieb Daimler, invented the first quadric cycle automobile, which means that the car industry came into being. Nowadays the car industry around the world has tremendous development, and it has been the major industry, especially in the developed countries, which are famous for BMW, Benz and Volkswagen in Germany, GM, Ford and Chrysler in America, Toyota, Nissan, Mitsubishi and Honda in Japan. With the rapid development of technology, the automobile has become an important symbol of modern science and technology.

Automobiles are the same in structure, although they are quite different in style and design. In other words, any automobile is composed of four sections, such as engine, chassis, body and electrical system. See Fig.1-1-1.

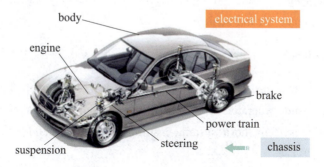

Fig.1-1-1 Layout of an automobile

1 Engine

The engine is the heart of an automobile. The purpose of an automotive engine is to convert fuel into energy that moves the automobile. Currently, the easiest way to create motion from fuel is to burn the fuel inside an engine. Therefore, an automotive engine is an internal combustion engine, which burns fuel within the cylinders and converts the expanding force of the combustion into the rotary force used to drive the automobile. See Fig.1-1-2.

Fig.1-1-2 Engine

2 Chassis

The chassis consists of the power train or transmission system, the suspension system, the steering system and the braking system. The function of the chassis is to receive the power of the engine and make the car move normally. See Fig.1-1-3.

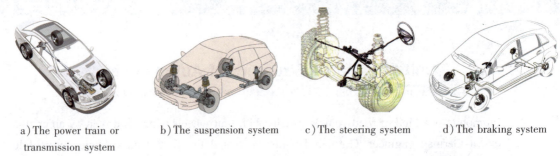

a) The power train or transmission system   b) The suspension system   c) The steering system   d) The braking system

Fig.1-1-3　Chassis assembly map

3 Body

The body is equipped on the chassis. It serves the obvious purpose of holding the driver, passengers and goods, providing shelter, comfort and protection for the occupants. The body provides three-quarters of the vehicle's total rigidity in bending and torsion. In the case of collision, it is intended to resist and minimize intrusions into the occupant space. The body is designed to keep passengers safe and comfortable. The body styling provides an attractive, colorful, modern appearance for the vehicle.

4 Electrical System

The electrical system consists of power and electrical equipment. The power equipment consists of the battery and generator. The electrical equipment consists of the starting system, ignition system, lighting system, horn system, instrumentation, air conditioner, audio, wiper and other devices. See Fig.1-1-4.

Fig.1-1-4　Electrical system

New Words and Expressions

automobile	/ˈɔːtəməubiːl/	n.	汽车
engine	/ˈendʒin/	n.	发动机
structure	/ˈstrʌktʃə/	n.	构造
chassis	/ˈʃæsi/	n.	底盘
electrical	/iˈlektrikəl/	adj.	电的
rotary	/ˈrəutəri/	adj.	旋转的
transmission	/trænzˈmiʃn/	n.	变速器，传动装置
shelter	/ˈʃeltə/	n./v.	保护，庇护
occupant	/ˈɔkjupənt/	n.	乘员
ignition	/igˈniʃn/	n.	点燃，点火
suspension	/səˈspenʃn/	n.	悬挂
equipment	/iˈkwipmənt/	n.	设备
battery	/ˈbætəri/	n.	蓄电池
generator	/ˈdʒenəreitə/	n.	发电机
obvious	/ˈɔbviəs/	adj.	明显的
protection	/prəˈtekʃn/	n.	保护

internal combustion engine	内燃机
air conditioner	空调
consist of	由……组成
power train, transmission system	传动系统
suspension system	悬架系统
braking system	制动系统
steering system	转向系统
occupant space	承载空间

Notes to the Text

1. With the rapid development of technology, the automobile has become an important symbol of modern science and technology.
   随着汽车技术的高度发展，汽车已经成为现代科技发展水平的一个重要标志。

2. Therefore, an automotive engine is an internal combustion engine, which burns fuel within the cylinders and converts the expanding force of the combustion into the rotary force used to drive the automobile.
   因此，汽车发动机是内燃机，它将燃油在气缸中燃烧，把燃烧产生的膨胀推力转变成旋转力，用来驱动汽车。

3. The function of the chassis is to receive the power of the engine and make the car move normally.
   底盘的作用是接收发动机产生的动力，并保证汽车正常行驶。

Exercises

Ⅰ. Answer the following questions according to the text.

1. What are the four basic sections of an automobile?
2. What's the function of the engine?
3. How many systems does the chassis include?
4. What's the function of the body?

Ⅱ. Write out the terms according to the picture.

1. _____ 2. _____ 3. _____ 4. _____

Ⅲ. Choose the correct answer to fill in the blanks.

1. The purpose of an automotive _____ is to convert fuel into energy that moves the automobile.
   A. engine   B. chassis   C. body   D. electrical system
2. The function of the _____ is receiving the power of the engine and making the car move normally.
   A. engine   B. chassis   C. body   D. electrical system
3. The _____ provides three-quarters of the vehicle's total rigidity in bending and torsion.
   A. engine   B. chassis   C. body   D. electrical system
4. The _____ consists of the starting system, ignition system, lighting system, horn system, instrumentation, air conditioner, audio, wiper and other devices.
   A. engine   B. chassis   C. body   D. electrical system

Ⅳ. Translate the following sentences into English.

1. 虽然汽车在设计方面有所不同，但在构造上是基本相同的。
2. 底盘包括传动系统、悬架系统、转向系统和制动系统。
3. 任何汽车都是由四部分组成的，如发动机、底盘、车身以及电气系统。
4. 发动机的类型有多种，但最常见的是内燃机。

Chapter 1 Automotive Fundamentals

Unit 2 The Automobile Classification

The automobile can be classified according to vehicle types, engine position and drive types, drive power types and vehicle body types.

1 Classified by the Vehicle Types (Fig.1-2-1)

a) Sedan b) Coach c) Truck

d) Off-road vehicle e) Right-hand drive truck f) Dump truck

g) Stock car h) Agriculture vehicle i) Special vehicle

Fig.1-2-1 Classified by the vehicle types

2 Classified by the Engine Position and Drive Types

According to the engine position and drive types, cars can be classified into front engine front drive (FF), front engine rear drive (FR), rear engine rear drive (RR), middle engine rear drive (MR) and full wheel drive (nWD). See Fig.1-2-2.

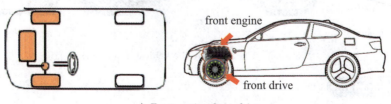

a) Front engine front drive

Fig.1-2-2 Classified by the engine position and drive types (continued)

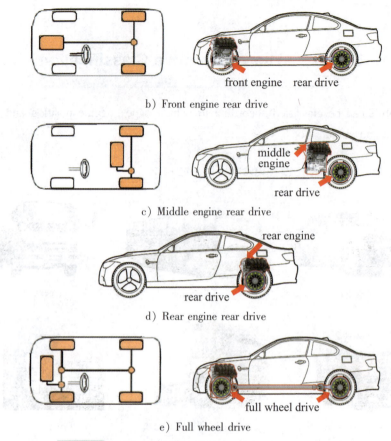

b) Front engine rear drive

c) Middle engine rear drive

d) Rear engine rear drive

e) Full wheel drive

Fig.1-2-2　Classified by the engine position and drive types

3 Classified by the Drive Power Types

According to the drive power types, cars can be classified into gasoline engine vehicles, diesel engine vehicles, hybrid vehicles, electric vehicles and fuel cell vehicles.

4 Classified by the Vehicle Body Types

According to the vehicle body types, cars can be classified into three-box vehicles, two-box vehicles, coupes and convertible sedans. See Fig.1-2-3.

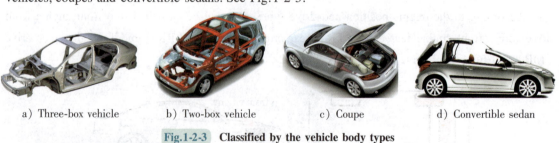

a) Three-box vehicle　　b) Two-box vehicle　　c) Coupe　　d) Convertible sedan

Fig.1-2-3　Classified by the vehicle body types

Notes to the Text

1. The automobile can be classified according to vehicle types, engine position and drive types, drive power types and vehicle body types.

汽车可按车辆类型、发动机位置和驱动类型、驱动动力类型和车身类型进行分类。

2. According to the drive power types, cars can be classified into gasoline engine vehicles, diesel engine vehicles, hybrid vehicles, electric vehicles and fuel cell vehicles.

按驱动动力类型划分,汽车可分为汽油车、柴油车、混合动力汽车、电动汽车和燃料电池复合动力汽车。

New Words and Expressions

classify	/ˈklæsiˌfai/	v.	分类
vehicle	/ˈviːəkl/	n.	车辆
sedan	/siˈdæn/	n.	私家轿车,轿车
fuel	/ˈfjuəl/	n.	燃料
gasoline	/ˈɡæsəliːn/	n.	汽油
wheel	/wiːl/	n.	车轮
agriculture	/ˈæɡrikʌltʃə/	n.	农学,农业
tractor	/ˈtræktə/	n.	拖拉机,牵引机

off-road vehicle	越野车
front engine front drive (FF)	前置发动机前轮驱动
front engine rear drive (FR)	前置发动机后轮驱动
middle engine rear drive (MR)	中置发动机后轮驱动
rear engine rear drive (RR)	后置发动机后轮驱动
full wheel drive (nWD)	四轮驱动
dump truck	自卸车
gasoline engine	汽油机
diesel engine	柴油机
electric vehicle	电动汽车

Exercises

I. Answer the following questions according to the text.

1. What types can we classify cars into according to the engine position and drive types?
2. What types can we classify cars into according to the vehicle body types?
3. What does FF stand for?
4. What does FR stand for?

II. Write out the terms according to the pictures.

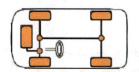   

1. _____   2. _____   3. _____   4. _____

Ⅲ. **Choose the correct answer to fill in the blanks.**

1. According to the _____, cars can be classified into FF, FR, RR, MR and nWD.
   A. engine position and drive types   B. drive power types
   C. vehicle types   D. vehicle body types
2. According to the _____, cars can be classified into sedans, coaches, trucks and so on.
   A. engine position and drive types   B. drive power types
   C. vehicle types   D. vehicle body types
3. According to the drive power types, cars can be classified into _____.
   A. gasoline engine vehicles   B. diesel engine vehicles
   C. hybrid vehicles   D. all of the above
4. The abbreviation RR refers to _____.
   A. front engine front drive   B. front engine rear drive
   C. middle engine rear drive   D. rear engine rear drive

Unit 3 The Vehicle Technical Parameters

On the vehicle, there is a nameplate to show the date of manufacture, the plant, the engine, the chassis model, the transaxle, the manufacturer, the color, the trim, the gross vehicle weight rating (GVWR), the vehicle capacity, the size of tires, the tire pressure and so on.

1 The Key Dimension Data of a Vehicle (Fig.1-3-1)

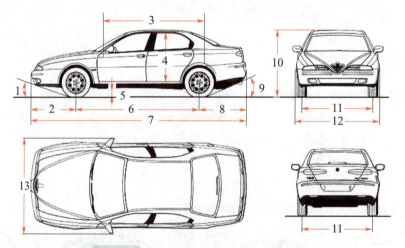

Fig.1-3-1 Key dimension data of a vehicle
1—approach angle 2—front overhang 3—length of body 4—height of body 5—ground clearance
6—wheel base 7—overall length 8—rear overhang 9—departure angle 10—vehicle height
11—wheel tread 12—width of body 13—vehicle width

Chapter 1 Automotive Fundamentals

2 Engine Terms

(1) Top Dead Center (TDC)

TDC stands for top dead center. TDC indicates the position of the crank and piston when the piston is farthest away from the crankshaft. When the piston is at the top of its travel, it is at TDC.

(2) Bottom Dead Center (BDC)

BDC stands for bottom dead center. BDC indicates the position of the crank and piston when the piston is closest to the crankshaft. When the piston is at the bottom of its travel, it is at BDC.

TDC and BDC can be seen in Fig.1-3-2.

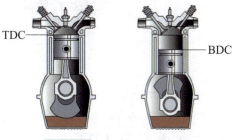

Fig.1-3-2　TDC and BDC

(3) Bore and Stroke

The bore and stroke of an engine help identify its size. The bore of the engine is defined as the diameter of the cylinder. The stroke of the engine is a measurement of the distance the piston travels from the top to the bottom. It is the distance from TDC to BDC.

(4) Crank Throw

The stroke is determined by the design of the crankshaft. The distance from the center of the crankshaft to the center of the crankpin is called the crank throw. If multiplied by 2, this dimension will be the same distance as the stroke. If the stroke changes on the engine, the crankshaft will have a different length of throw. See Fig.1-3-3.

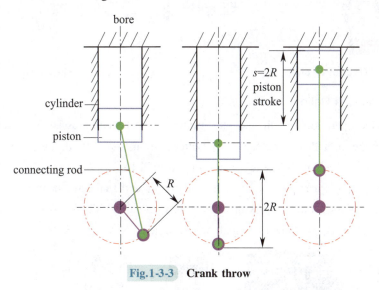

Fig.1-3-3　Crank throw

(5) Swept Volume

Swept volume is also called cylinder displacement. It is the volume of the cylinder from BDC to TDC. See Fig.1-3-4.

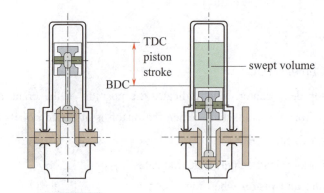

Fig.1-3-4　Piston stroke and swept volume

（6）Clearance Volume

Clearance volume, also called combustion chamber volume, refers to the volume of space above the piston when it is at TDC. See Fig.1-3-5.

（7）Total Cylinder Volume

When the piston is at BDC, the volume of the entire space above the top of the piston is called the total cylinder volume. It is equal to the sum of the cylinder working volume and the combustion chamber volume. See Fig.1-3-6.

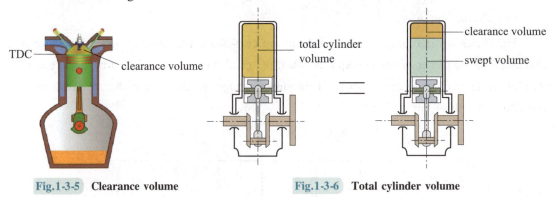

Fig.1-3-5　Clearance volume　　　　　　Fig.1-3-6　Total cylinder volume

（8）Compression Ratio

During engine operation, the air and fuel mixture must be compressed. This compression helps squeeze and mix the air and fuel molecules for better combustion. Actually, the more the air and fuel are compressed, the better the efficiency of the engine will be.

Compression ratio is a measure of how much the air and fuel have been compressed. It means that the piston compresses the gas mixture which is made from air and fuel. Compression ratio = (swept volume + clearance volume) / (clearance volume). See Fig.1-3-7.

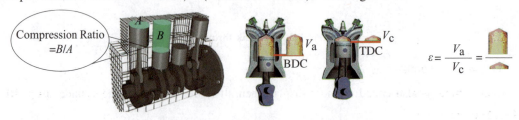

Fig.1-3-7　Compression ratio

(9) Engine Capacity

Engine capacity is also called engine stroke volume. It is the swept volume of all cylinders. Each cylinder has a certain displacement. If there is more than one cylinder, the total displacement would be multiplied by the number of cylinders. (That is to say, engine capacity = 1 bore × the number of cylinders.) Generally speaking, the larger the engine capacity is, the higher the engine power is. See Fig.1-3-8.

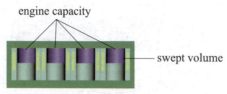

Fig.1-3-8 **Engine capacity**

(10) Engine Torque

Engine torque refers to the torque output by the engine from the crankshaft end. Under the condition of fixed power, it is inversely proportional to the engine speed, i.e. the faster the speed, the smaller the torque, and the greater the vice versa. It reflects the load capacity of the car in a certain range. Its unit is N·m. In the case of the same engine displacement, the greater the torque, the better the engine.

(11) Specific Fuel Consumption

It means the fuel consumption in the given distance.

(12) Engine Power

It means the output of the engine in the given time. The unit of measurement is kW.
Engine terms are shown in Fig.1-3-9.

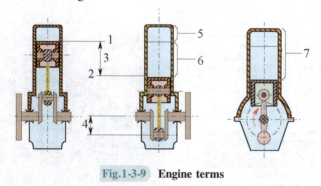

Fig.1-3-9 **Engine terms**

1—TDC   2—BDC   3—piston stroke   4—crank throw
5—clearance volume   6—swept volume   7—total cylinder volume

3 Vehicle Labeling

Each vehicle has labels that tell us the date and plant of the vehicle manufacture, type (model), engine number, chassis number, transmission or axle number, frame number, color, trim, GVWR, gross axle weight rating (GAWR), tire size, tire pressure and so on. These are very important for the vehicle to be used and serviced. See Fig.1-3-10.

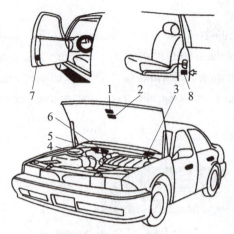

Fig.1-3-10 Vehicle labeling location

1—vehicle emission control information label 2—service points label
3—vehicle identification number (VIN) plate 4—engine serial number 5—chassis number
6—vehicle information code plate 7—tire inflation pressure label 8—certification label

The following are some manufacturers' vehicle labels. See Fig.1-3-11.

BMW 735i Label		
735i VEHICLE TYPE	PASSENGER CAR	
MFD BY BAYERISCHE MOTOREN WERKE AG 02/87		
GVWR	4872 lbs	2210 kg
GAWR FRONT	2337 lbs	1060 kg
GAWR REAR	2646 lbs	1200 kg
This vehicle conforms to all applicable U.S. FEDERAL MOTOR VEHICLE SAFETY, BUMPER AND THEFT PREVENTION STANDARDS in effect on the date of manufacture shown above.		
VIN	WBA GB	3310J1630107
MADE IN GERMANY	2121647	

Fig.1-3-11 Some manufacturers' vehicle labels

Notes to the Text

1. During engine operation, the air and fuel mixture must be compressed. This compression helps squeeze and mix the air and fuel molecules for better combustion.

在发动机运行过程中，燃油混合气必须被压缩。这种压缩有助于燃油混合气更好地燃烧。

Chapter 1 Automotive Fundamentals

2. Engine torque refers to the torque output by the engine from the crankshaft end. Under the condition of fixed power, it is inversely proportional to the engine speed, i.e. the faster the speed, the smaller the torque, and the greater the vice versa. It reflects the load capacity of the car in a certain range. Its unit is N·m. In the case of the same engine displacement, the greater the torque, the better the engine.

发动机转矩是指发动机曲轴端输出的力矩。在功率固定的条件下，它与发动机转速成反比关系，即转速越快，转矩越小，反之越大。它反映了汽车在一定范围内的负载能力。它的单位是牛·米。在发动机排量相同的情况下，转矩越大，说明发动机越好。

3. This vehicle conforms to all applicable U.S. FEDERAL MOTOR VEHICLE SAFETY, BUMPER AND THEFT PREVENTION STANDARDS in effect on the date of manufacture shown above.

该车符合美国各州联邦政府使用的安全、防撞和防盗标准，自上面的出厂日期开始生效。

New Words and Expressions

nameplate	铭牌	ground clearance	离地间隙
approach angle	接近角	top dead center（TDC）	上止点
wheel tread	轮距	bottom dead center（BDC）	下止点
wheel base	轴距	crank throw	曲柄半径
swept volume	有效容积，工作容积	compression ratio	压缩比
clearance volume	燃烧室容积	engine torque	发动机转矩
total cylinder volume	气缸总容积	specific fuel consumption	燃油消耗率
engine capacity	发动机排量	engine power	发动机功率

Exercises

Ⅰ. Answer the following questions according to the text.

1. What does compression ratio mean?
2. What does TDC mean?
3. What does engine capacity mean?
4. What does BDC stand for?

Ⅱ. Choose the correct answer.

1. What does "A" stand for in the following picture? _____.
    A. Length of body
    B. Wheel tread
    C. Wheel base
    D. Overall length

2. Choose the corresponding terms with 1 to 5 from the following terms.
    A. wheel tread   B. vehicle height   C. ground clearance
    D. overall length   E. width of body   F. approach angle

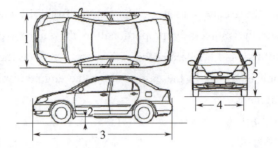

Ⅲ. Write out the terms according to the picture.

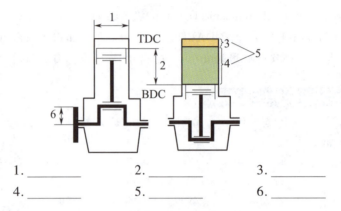

1. _____   2. _____   3. _____
4. _____   5. _____   6. _____

Ⅳ. Translate the following pictures into Chinese or English.

Picture 1

```
                    BMW 735i Label
    735i   VEHICLE TYPE      PASSENGER CAR
    MFD BY BAYERISCHE MOTOREN WERKE AG 02/87
    GVWR                 4872 lbs      2210 kg
    GAWR FRONT           2337 lbs      1060 kg
    GAWR REAR            2646 lbs      1200 kg
    This vehicle conforms to all applicable U.S. FEDERAL MOTOR VEHICLE SAFETY, BUMPER AND
    THEFT PREVENTION STANDARDS in effect on the date of manufacture shown above.
    VIN                  WBA GB        3310J1630107
    MADE IN GERMANY      2121647
```

Picture 2

Chapter 2

Engine

Unit 1 Engine Overview

Automobile engine is the source of power that makes the wheels go around and the car move. The automobile engine is an internal combustion engine because the fuel (gasoline) is burned inside it. The burning of gasoline inside the engine produces high pressure in the engine combustion chamber. This high pressure forces pistons to move, the movement is carried by connecting rods to the engine crankshaft. The crankshaft is thus made to rotate: the rotary motion is carried through the power train to the car wheels so that they rotate and the car moves. The engine's overall structure is as follows. See Fig. 2-1-1, Fig. 2-1-2 and Fig. 2-1-3.

Generally speaking, an engine contains two assemblies and five systems. Two assemblies refer to an engine crankshaft and connecting rod assembly and a valve train. The crank and connecting rod mechanism is composed of the block group, the crankshaft and flywheel assembly and the piston and connecting rod assembly. See Fig. 2-1-4 and Fig. 2-1-5.

Fig.2-1-1 Engine overall structure

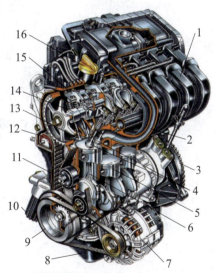

Fig.2-1-2 Engine section view

1,2—intake manifold 3—flywheel 4—intake valve 5—piston
6—connecting rod 7—alternator 8—oil pan 9—crankshaft pulley
10—oil filter 11—timing belt 12—tension pulley 13—exhaust valve
14—camshaft 15—valve rocker arm 16—oil filler

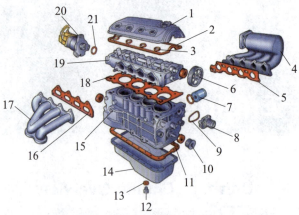

Fig.2-1-3 **Engine decomposition diagram**

1—cylinder head cover 2—cylinder head cover gasket 3—rubber grommets 4—intake manifold
5—intake manifold gasket 6—camshaft pulley 7—oil filter 8—water pump 9—water pump gasket
10—timing belt drive pulley 11—oil pan gasket 12—oil pan drain bolt 13—drain bolt crush washer
14—oil pan 15—engine block 16—exhaust manifold gasket 17—exhaust manifold
18—head gasket 19—cylinder head 20—distributor 21—distributor O-ring

Fig.2-1-4 **Block group**

1—cylinder head cover 2—cylinder head 3—cylinder pillow 4—oil pan 5—cylinder block

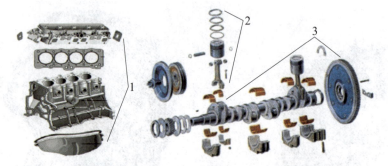

Fig.2-1-5 **Crank and connecting rod mechanism**

1—block group 2—piston and connecting rod assembly 3—crankshaft and flywheel assembly

　　Five systems refer to the fuel supply system, the cooling system, the lubrication system, the ignition system and the starting system. These five systems are discussed briefly in the following units.

Notes to the Text

1. Automobile engine is the source of power that makes the wheels go around and the car move.
发动机是使车轮转动从而驱动汽车行驶的动力来源。

2. The crank and connecting rod mechanism is composed of the block group, the crankshaft and flywheel assembly and the piston and connecting rod assembly.

曲柄连杆机构由机体组、曲轴飞轮组与活塞连杆组组成。

New Words and Expressions

combustion	/kəmˈbʌstʃən/	n.	燃烧
chamber	/ˈtʃeimbə/	n.	室，箱
crankshaft	/ˈkræŋkʃɑːft/	n.	曲轴
rotate	/ˈrəuteit/	vt./vi.	（使）旋转
circulate	/ˈsəːkjuleit/	v.	（使）循环
camshaft	/ˈkæmʃɑːft/	n.	凸轮轴
sprocket	/ˈsprɔkit/	n.	扣链齿（链轮上与链条啮合的齿）
pulley	/ˈpuli/	n.	滑轮
flywheel	/ˈflaiwiːl/	n.	飞轮
assembly	/əˈsembli/	n.	装配，组成

combustion chamber		燃烧室
crank and connecting rod mechanism		曲柄连杆机构
block group		机体组
crankshaft and flywheel assembly		曲轴飞轮组
piston and connecting rod assembly		活塞连杆组

Exercises

Ⅰ. **Answer the following questions according to the text.**

1. What is the crank and connecting rod mechanism composed of?
2. What components does the group block include?
3. How many systems does an engine require? What are they?

Ⅱ. **Choose the correct answer to fill in the blanks.**

1. Generally, the automobile engine is a(n) _____ because the fuel (gasoline) is burned inside it.

   A. external-burning engine   B. electric engine
   C. steam engine   D. internal combustion engine

2. The crank and connecting rod mechanism is composed of _____.

   A. the block group   B. the crankshaft and flywheel assembly
   C. the piston and connecting rod assembly   D. all of the above

3. The cylinder head contains _____ for cooling in the assembled engine.

   A. oil passages   B. water jackets   C. a fan   D. an oil cooler

4. What determines the size and the placement of the engine block? _____.

   A. The number of spark plugs   B. The number of pistons
   C. The number of cylinders   D. The number of valves

Ⅲ. Write out the terms according to the pictures.

1._____ 2._____ 3._____ 4._____

Unit 2 Engine Construction

Complete engine assembly consists of the mechanical components that make up the engine itself and also a number of associated systems. These are the systems that are needed to start the engine and also to control it and keep it running. The mechanical parts of the engine assembly can be broken down into a number of sub-assemblies, or a group of associated components, although these are usually referred to merely as assemblies, for example, cylinder-head assembly and piston assembly. Some parts of an engine are internal, other parts are external. The main components of the engine are as follows.

1 Cylinder Block

Engine block is the main supporting structure to which all other engine parts are attached. It has two main sections: cylinder section and crankcase section. The crankcase section is used to house the crankshaft and oil pan.

Cylinder block is a single machined casting unit. It contains cylinders, cylinder heads, coolant passages and lubrication passages. The cooling passageways are built within the block. These passageways, also known as water jackets, surround the cylinders. They allow coolant to circulate throughout the cylinder area to keep the engine cool. There is also a drilled passageway within some blocks for the camshaft. Many oil holes are drilled internally so that engine parts can be adequately lubricated. Fig.2-2-1 shows a cylinder block.

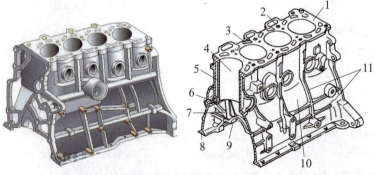

Fig.2-2-1 Cylinder block

1—block top surface 2—coolant hole 3—oil return hole 4—cylinder 5—water jacket 6—main oil passage 7—reinforcing rib 8—block underside 9—main bearing seat 10—block side wall 11—side wall reinforcing rib

2 Cylinder Head

A cylinder head is bolted to the top of each bank of cylinders to seal the individual cylinders and contain the combustion process that takes place inside the cylinder.

The cylinder head is used to hold the valves, and it has ports to allow air, fuel and exhaust to move through the engine. In addition, it has coolant passages. After the cylinder head has been cast, some areas must be machined so that intake and exhaust manifolds can be attached, valves can be seated, spark plugs and injectors can be installed, and a good seal can be provided to the block. Usually, in-line engines have one head, while V-type engines have two. Fig. 2-2-2 shows a cylinder head.

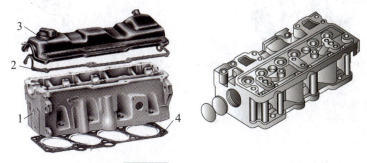

Fig.2-2-2　Cylinder head

1—cylinder head　2—gasket　3—cylinder head cover　4—cylinder head gasket

3 Piston and Connecting Rod Assembly

Piston and connecting rod assembly transmits the power from combustion to the crankshaft. It mainly consists of the piston, compression rings, oil control rings, piston pin and connecting rod. See Fig. 2-2-3.

(1) Piston

Piston fits closely within the engine cylinder. Each cylinder contains a piston that travels up and down inside the cylinder bore. All the pistons in the engine are connected through individual connecting rods to a common crankshaft.

(2) Piston Rings

There are two types of piston rings: compression rings and oil control rings. The compression rings are used to seal the pressures of compression and power. The oil control rings are employed to scrape oil from the cylinder walls.

(3) Piston Pin

The piston pin is used to connect the piston to the connecting rod.

(4) Connecting Rod

The connecting rod is used to connect the piston to the crankshaft. It can rotate at both ends so that its angle can change as the piston moves and the crankshaft rotates. So it can change the reciprocating motion of the piston to the rotary motion of the crankshaft.

It consists of the connecting small end and the big end, shank, rod cap and bolts.

The components of the connecting rod are shown in Fig. 2-2-4.

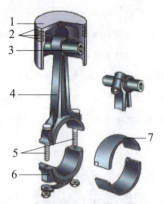
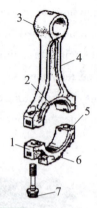

Fig.2-2-3 Piston and connecting rod assembly

1—piston 2—piston rings 3—piston pin
4—connecting rod 5—connecting rod bolts
6—connecting rod cap 7—connecting rod bearing

Fig.2-2-4 Connecting rod

1—oil spray hole 2—big end 3—small end
4—connecting rod shank 5—connecting rod cap
6—forward mark 7—bolt

4 Camshaft Assembly

The camshaft is driven by the crankshaft and used to open and close the valves. Most pistons are made from cast aluminum. The piston, through the connecting rod, transfers the force created by the burning fuel mixture to the crankshaft. This force turns the crankshaft. The camshaft assembly includes the camshaft, camshaft timing gear, camshaft bearing, timing chain and belt（if used）. See Fig. 2-2-5.

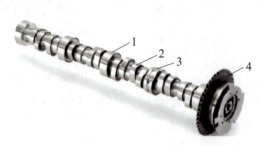

Fig.2-2-5 Camshaft

1—camshaft journal 2—cam 3—oil hole 4—timing gear

5 Crankshaft Assembly

The crankshaft is located below the cylinders on an in-line engine, at the base of the V on a V-type engine and between the cylinder banks on a flat engine. As the pistons move up and down, they turn the crankshaft.

The crankshaft is a one-piece casting or forging of heat-treated alloy steel of considerable mechanical strength. It must be strong enough to take the downward thrust of the pistons during the power strokes without excessive distortion. In addition, it must be carefully balanced to eliminate undue vibrations resulting from the weight of the offset cranks. To provide balance, crankshafts have counterweights opposite the cranks. Crankshafts have drilled oil passages through which oil can flow from the main to the connecting rod bearings. A crankshaft is generally composed of the front end, crankshaft main journal, crank, balance weight, connecting rod journal and rear end. Fig. 2-2-6 shows the crankshaft assembly.

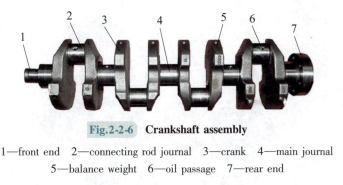

Fig.2-2-6 Crankshaft assembly

1—front end   2—connecting rod journal   3—crank   4—main journal
5—balance weight   6—oil passage   7—rear end

6 Flywheel

The flow of power from the engine cylinder is not smooth. To keep the combustion from generating vibrations, a flywheel is attached to the back of the crankshaft. The flywheel is a disk that is about 12 to 15 inches (30.48 to 38.10 cm) in diameter. The inertia of the flywheel tends to keep it turning at a constant speed and to smooth out the normal engine pulses. Thus, the flywheel absorbs energy as the crankshaft tries to speed up and gives back energy as the crankshaft tries to slow down. In effect, the flywheel absorbs power from the engine during the power stroke (or speedup time) and then gives it to the engine during the other three strokes (or slowdown time) of the cycle.

Fig.2-2-7 shows the flywheel. Fig.2-2-8 shows the crankshaft and flywheel assembly.

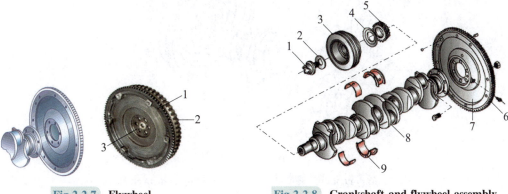

Fig.2-2-7 Flywheel

1—flywheel   2—ring gear
3—mounting to crankshaft

Fig.2-2-8 Crankshaft and flywheel assembly

1—cranking claw   2,4—side ring   3—belt pulley   5—timing gear
6—ring gear   7—flywheel   8—crankshaft   9—main bearing bush

7 Crankshaft and Connecting Rod Mechanism

Crankshaft and connecting rod mechanism is a set of the engine's moving parts. Its function is to transform the piston's reciprocating movement into the crankshaft's rotational movement. At the same time, the crankshaft and connecting rod mechanism changes the press on the pistons into the external output torque of the crankshaft to drive the rotation of the vehicle wheels. See Fig.2-2-9 and Fig.2-2-10.

Fig.2-2-9 Overall structure of crankshaft and connecting rod mechanism

1—piston 2—piston pin 3—connecting rod 4—main bearing cap 5—bolts for attaching to cylinder crankcase
6—big end bearing cap 7—big end bearing 8—connecting rod bushing

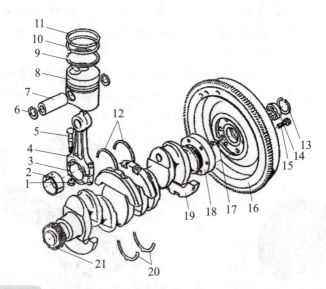

Fig.2-2-10 Components of crankshaft and connecting rod mechanism

1—nut 2—bearing 3—connecting rod cap 4—connecting rod body 5—connecting rod bolt
6—bead flange 7—piston pin 8—piston 9—oil control ring 10—below compression ring
11—submit compression ring 12—submit thrust washers 13—bead flange 14—bearing
15—flywheel bolt 16—flywheel 17—locating pin 18—crankshaft
19—balance weight 20—below thrust washers 21—crankshaft timing gear

New Words and Expressions

drill	/drIl/	v. /n.	钻
crankcase	/ˈkræŋ(k)keIs/	n.	曲轴箱
forging	/ˈfɔːdʒIŋ/	n.	锻件
vibration	/vaIˈbreIʃn/	n.	振动,抖动
strength	/ˈstreŋθ/	n.	强度
distortion	/dIˈstɔːʃn/	n.	扭曲
excessive	/IkˈsesIv/	adj.	过多的,过度的
eliminate	/IˈlImIneIt/	vt.	淘汰,剔除
undue	/ʌnˈdjuː/	adj.	不适当的,过分的
offset	/ˈɔfset/	adj.	偏移的
		vt. /vi.	抵消,补偿
impulse	/ˈImpʌls/	n.	脉冲
overlap	/ˌəuvəˈlæp/	v. /n.	搭接
bolt	/bəult/	v.	用螺栓固定
cylinder block	气缸体	cylinder head	气缸盖
cylinder wall	气缸壁	oil pan	油底壳
piston pin	活塞销	connecting rod	连杆
water jacket	水套	timing gear	正时齿轮
balance weight	平衡重	oil drain hole	回油孔
compression ring	气环	oil control ring	油环
connecting small end	连杆小头	connecting big end	连杆大头
connecting rod journal	连杆轴颈	main bearing journal	主轴颈
balance shaft	平衡轴		

Notes to the Text

1. A cylinder head is bolted to the top of each bank of cylinders to seal the individual cylinders and contain the combustion process that takes place inside the cylinder.
   安装在每列气缸顶部的气缸盖是用来密封气缸的,气缸内的燃烧过程在此发生。

2. A crankshaft is generally composed of the front end, crankshaft main journal, crank, balance weight, connecting rod journal and rear end.
   曲轴一般由前端、主轴颈、曲柄、平衡重、连杆轴颈和后端组成。

3. Each cylinder contains a piston that travels up and down inside the cylinder bore. All the pistons in the engine are connected through individual connecting rods to a common crankshaft.
   每个气缸都含有一个在气缸内上下运动的活塞。发动机里所有的活塞都通过各自的连杆与一个共同的曲轴相连接。

4. The crankshaft is a one-piece casting or forging of heat-treated alloy steel of considerable mechanical strength.
   曲轴是由合金钢铸造或锻造,经过热处理,具有一定机械强度的整体结构。

5. The crankshaft is located below the cylinders on an in-line engine, at the base of the V on a V-type engine and between the cylinder banks on a flat engine.

在直列式发动机里，曲轴位于气缸下面；在 V 型发动机里，位于 V 型底部；在对置式发动机里，曲轴位于两列气缸之间。

6. The flywheel uses inertia to smooth out the normal engine pulses.

飞轮利用惯性来缓和发动机的振动。

Exercises

Ⅰ. Answer the following questions according to the text.

1. What components does a crankshaft generally consist of?
2. There are two types of piston rings. What are they?
3. Which component's function is to transform the piston's reciprocating movement into the crankshaft's rotational movement?

Ⅱ. Choose the correct answer to fill in the blanks.

1. The _____ is the main supporting structure to which all other engine parts are attached.
   A. cylinder head   B. cylinder block   C. crankshaft   D. camshaft

2. The _____ is used to hold the valves, and it has ports to allow air, fuel and exhaust to move through the engine.
   A. cylinder head   B. cylinder block   C. crankshaft   D. camshaft

3. The _____ is used to connect the piston to the connecting rod.
   A. piston   B. piston rings   C. piston pin   D. connecting rod

4. The _____ is used to connect the piston to the crankshaft and changes the reciprocating motion to the rotary motion.
   A. piston   B. piston rings   C. piston pin   D. connecting rod

5. The _____ is driven by the crankshaft and used to open and close the valves.
   A. crankshaft   B. piston   C. flywheel   D. camshaft

6. The crankshaft has large weights, called _____, that balance the weight of the connecting rod.
   A. counterweights   B. crank   C. throws   D. main bearing journal

Ⅲ. Translate the following phrases into Chinese or English.

1. oil pan _____   6. 气缸体 _____
2. ignition distributor _____   7. 活塞环 _____
3. connecting rod _____   8. 排气阀 _____
4. water jacket _____   9. 平衡重 _____
5. spark plug _____   10. 回油孔 _____

Chapter 2 Engine

IV. Write out the terms according to the picture.

1. _____   2. _____   3. _____   4. _____   5. _____
6. _____   7. _____   8. _____   9. _____

Unit 3 Kinds of Engine

There are a variety of engines, and most of them use the petroleum fuel and are known as gasoline engines. The vaporized liquid fuel is mixed up with the air, burns, and expands to produce the power that drives the cars. This kind of engine is also called the internal combustion engine. Nowadays, the cars are mostly equipped with the gasoline engines.

The automobile engine can be classified according to: ①number of cylinders; ②arrangement of cylinders; ③arrangement of valves; ④type of cooling; ⑤number of cycles; ⑥type of fuel burned; ⑦type of ignition.

1 Classified by the Number of Cylinders

According to the number of cylinders, the automobile engine can be classified into single-cylinder engine and multi-cylinder engine. See Fig.2-3-1.

a) Single-cylinder engine   b) Multi-cylinder engine

Fig.2-3-1 Classified by number of cylinders

2 Classified by the Arrangement of Cylinders

The term engine configuration refers to the way that the cylinders of an engine are arranged. According to the arrangement of cylinders, the automobile engine can be classified into in-line engine, V-type engine and horizontal-opposed engine or flat engine. See Fig. 2-3-2. Within these three basic arrangements, there are a number of variations.

（1）In-Line Engine

With in-line engines, the cylinders are arranged in a straight line, one behind the other. Most in-line engines have their cylinders vertical, but some are slanted. That is, the engine is tilted at an angle to reduce the overall height. These engines are sometimes referred to as slanted engines.

Some in-line engines have their cylinders horizontal, so that the engine is more or less on its side. This reduces the overall height mounted under part of the cab. The mechanical arrangement of a four-cylinder in-line for a passenger car is shown in Fig.2-3-2a.

（2）Horizontal-Opposed Engine

This arrangement has its cylinders arranged in two flat banks with the crankshaft between them. The engine shown in Fig.2-3-2b has a short rigid crankshaft with five bearings. A horizontal-opposed engine has even firing impulses and good balance. The movement of a piston in one direction is opposed to the movement of a piston in the opposed direction.

Horizontal-opposed engines, with their flat design, give the engine a low height and also help to keep the center of gravity of the vehicle low. A low center of gravity gives the vehicle stability.

（3）V-Type Engine

With V-type engines, the cylinders are arranged in two banks at an angle. This reduces the length of the engine and makes it more compact. This also reduces the length of the crankshaft, which can be designed to be more rigid than a long shaft. See Fig. 2-3-2c.

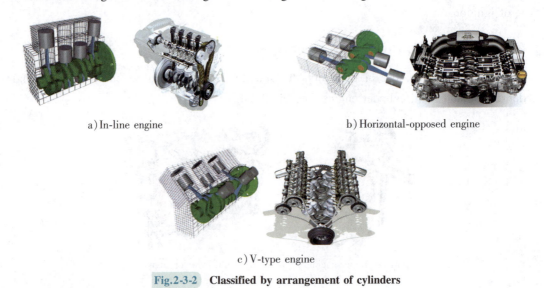

a）In-line engine 　　　　　　　　　　　　　　b）Horizontal-opposed engine

c）V-type engine

Fig.2-3-2　Classified by arrangement of cylinders

3 Classified by the Arrangement of Valves

According to the arrangement of valves, the automobile engine can be classified into two-valve engine, four-valve engine, five-valve engine and so on. See Fig. 2-3-3.

Chapter 2 Engine

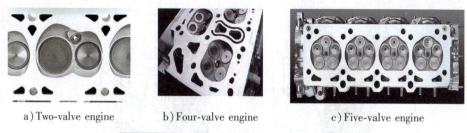

a) Two-valve engine b) Four-valve engine c) Five-valve engine

Fig.2-3-3 Classified by arrangement of valves

4 Classified by the Type of Cooling

According to the type of cooling, the automobile engine can be classified into water-cooled or liquid-cooled engine and air-cooled engine. See Fig.2-3-4.

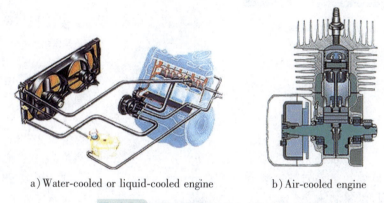

a) Water-cooled or liquid-cooled engine   b) Air-cooled engine

Fig.2-3-4 Classified by type of cooling

5 Classified by the Number of Cycles

According to the number of cycles, the automobile engine can be classified into two-stroke cycle engine and four-stroke cycle engine. See Fig.2-3-5.

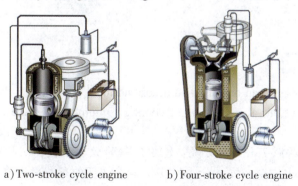

a) Two-stroke cycle engine   b) Four-stroke cycle engine

Fig.2-3-5 Classified by number of cycles

6 Classified by the Type of Fuel Burned

According to the type of fuel burned, the automobile engine can be classified into gasoline engine and diesel engine. See Fig.2-3-6.

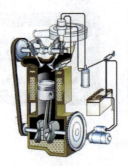 

a) Gasoline engine b) Diesel engine

Fig.2-3-6 Classified by type of fuel burned

New Words and Expressions

petroleum	/pəˈtrəuliəm/	n.	石油
vaporize	/ˈveipəraiz/	v.	(使某物)汽化,蒸发
configuration	/kənˌfigəˈreiʃn/	n.	配置,构造,结构,外形
variation	/ˌveəriˈeiʃn/	n.	变化,变动,变异
arrangement	/əˈreidʒmənt/	n.	排列
compact	/ˈkɔmpækt/	adj.	紧凑的,紧密的
rigid	/ˈridʒid/	adj.	坚硬的,不弯曲的,刚性的
gasoline	/ˈgæsəli:n/	n.	汽油
diesel	/ˈdi:zəl/	n.	柴油

timing belt	正时带	intake valve	进气门
exhaust valve	排气门	spark plug	火花塞
oil pump	机油泵	air filter	空气滤清器
circulating oil	循环机油,润滑油	multi-cylinder engine	多缸发动机
in-line engine	直列式发动机	V-type engine	V型发动机
flat engine	对置式发动机		

Notes to the Text

The automobile engine can be classified according to: ①number of cylinders; ②arrangement of cylinders; ③arrangement of valves; ④type of cooling; ⑤number of cycles; ⑥type of fuel burned; ⑦type of ignition.

汽车发动机可以按照7种情况分类：①按气缸的数量分类；②按气缸排列的方式分类；③按进气方式分类；④按冷却方式分类；⑤按工作循环的行程数分类（二冲程或四冲程）；⑥按所用的燃料分类；⑦按点火方式分类。

Exercises

Ⅰ. Answer the following questions according to the text.

1. What types can engines be classified into according to the type of fuel burned?

2. What types can engines be classified into according to the number of cylinders?

3. What types can engines be classified into according to the type of cooling?

4. What types can engines be classified into according to the arrangement of cylinders?

5. What types can engines be classified into according to the number of cycles?

Ⅱ. Choose the correct answer to fill in the blanks.

1. According to the _____, the automobile engine can be classified into single-cylinder engine and multi-cylinder engine.

    A. arrangement of valves B. number of cylinders

    C. arrangement of cylinders D. type of cooling

2. According to the _____, the automobile engine can be classified into in-line engine, V-type engine and horizontal-opposed engine or flat engine.

    A. arrangement of cylinders B. type of fuel burned

    C. number of cycles D. number of cylinders

3. With _____, the cylinders are arranged in two banks at an angle. This reduces the length of the engine and makes it more compact.

    A. flat engines B. in-line engines

    C. horizontal-opposed engines D. V-type engines

4. With _____, the cylinders are arranged in a straight line, one behind the other.

    A. V-type engines B. flat engines

    C. in-line engines D. horizontal-opposed engines

5. According to the number of cycles, the automobile engine can be classified into _____ engine and four-stroke cycle engine.

    A. one-stroke cycle B. two-stroke cycle

    C. three-stroke cycle D. five-stroke cycle

6. According to the _____, the automobile engine can be classified into gasoline engine and diesel engine.

    A. type of fuel burned B. number of cylinders

    C. number of cycles D. arrangement of cylinders

Ⅲ. Translate the following phrases into Chinese or English.

1. multi-cylinder engine _____
2. internal combustion engine _____
3. combustion chamber _____
4. timing belt _____
5. in-line engine _____
6. four-stroke cycle _____
7. V 型发动机 _____
8. 风冷式发动机 _____
9. 空气滤清器 _____
10. 对置式发动机 _____

Ⅳ. Write out the terms according to the pictures.

1. _____

2. _____

3. _____

4. _____

Unit 4   Engine Operating Principles

The actions taking place in the engine cylinder can be divided into four stages, or strokes. "Stroke" refers to piston movement; a stroke occurs when the piston moves from one limiting position to the other. The upper limit of the piston movement is called TDC (top dead center). The lower limit of the piston movement is called BDC (bottom dead center). A stroke is the piston movement from TDC to BDC or from BDC to TDC. In other words, the piston completes a stroke each time it changes its direction of motion.

Almost all cars currently use a four-stroke combustion cycle to convert gasoline into motion. The power production cycle consists of four strokes of the piston reciprocating motion. That is to say that the intake stroke, compression stroke, power stroke and exhaust stroke are one engine cycle. When the fourth stroke is completed, the cycle begins again. The four-stroke approach is also known as the Otto cycle, in honor of Nikolaus Otto, who invented it in 1867. The four strokes are illustrated in Fig. 2-4-1.

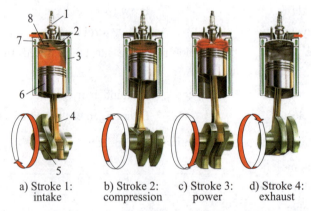

a) Stroke 1: intake   b) Stroke 2: compression   c) Stroke 3: power   d) Stroke 4: exhaust

Fig.2-4-1   Four strokes operating principles

1—spark plug   2—exhaust valve   3—cylinder   4—connecting rod
5—crankshaft   6—piston   7—cylinder head   8—intake valve

1 Intake Stroke

The first stroke is the intake stroke. As the piston starts to move downward, the intake valve opens and the air-fuel mixture enters the cylinder. When the piston reaches the bottom dead center

(BDC), the intake valve closes, trapping the air-fuel mixture in the cylinder. During the stroke, the exhaust valve stays closed. Sometimes, the intake stroke can also be called "induction stroke". Intake stroke is shown in Fig. 2-4-2.

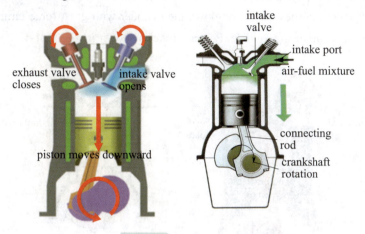

Fig.2-4-2　Intake stroke

2 Compression Stroke

The second stroke is the compression stroke. After the piston reaches the bottom dead center (BDC), it begins to move upward. As this happens, the intake valve closes. The exhaust valve is also closed, so that the cylinder is sealed. As the piston moves upward, it compresses the trapped air-fuel mixture. The amount that the mixture is compressed is determined by the compression ratio of the engine. The compression ratio on the average engine is in the range of 8∶1 to 10∶1. It means that when the piston reaches the top of the cylinder, the air-fuel mixture is squeezed to about one-tenth of its original volume, and the pressure rises. Compression stroke is shown in Fig. 2-4-3.

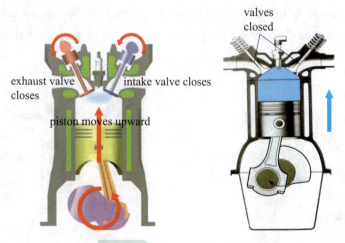

Fig.2-4-3　Compression stroke

3 Power Stroke

The third stroke is the power stroke. With the piston reaches the top dead center (TDC) on the compression stroke, an electric spark is produced at the spark plug. The ignition system delivers a high-tension current to the spark plug, and ignites the compressed air-fuel mixture that produces a powerful explosion. Each spark plug fires at a different time, which is determined by the engine fire order. The power process pushes the piston down the cylinder with great force turning the crankshaft to provide the power to drive the vehicle. Power stroke is shown in Fig. 2-4-4.

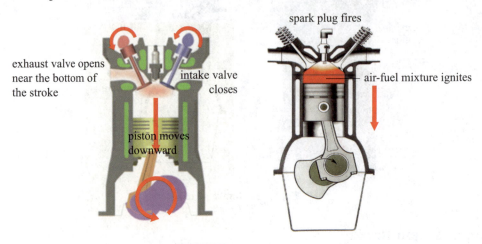

Fig.2-4-4　**Power stroke**

4　Exhaust Stroke

The fourth stroke is the exhaust stroke. With the piston reaches the bottom dead center (BDC) again, the exhaust valve opens, and the piston moves up again and forces the burned gases out of the cylinder through the exhaust-valve port. Since the cylinder contains so much pressure, when the valve opens, the gas is expelled with a violent force. That is why a vehicle without a muffler sounds so loud. The piston travels up to the top of the cylinder pushing all the exhaust out before closing the exhaust valve in preparation for starting the four-stroke process over again. Exhaust stroke is shown in Fig. 2-4-5.

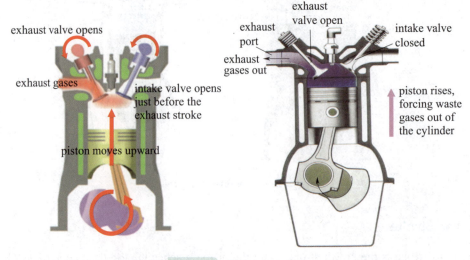

Fig.2-4-5　**Exhaust stroke**

New Words and Expressions

piston	/ˈpistən/	n.	活塞
cylinder	/ˈsilində/	n.	气缸
explosion	/ikˈspləuʒn/	n.	爆裂（声），爆炸（声）
stroke	/strəuk/	n.	行程，冲程
cycle	/ˈsaikl/	n.	循环，周期
approach	/əˈprəutʃ/	n.	方法，步骤
illustrate	/ˈiləstreit/	n.	图解，说明
trap	/træp/	vt.	收集，留住，截留
damper	/ˈdæmpə/	n.	阻尼器，减振器，风门，挡板
induction	/inˈdʌkʃn/	n.	吸入
seal	/siːl/	n./v.	密封
expel	/ikˈspel/	vt.	排除，喷出（空气等）
muffler	/ˈmʌflə/	n.	消声器

take place	发生	compression stroke	压缩行程
divide…into	把……分为	power stroke	做功行程
refer to	涉及，有关系	exhaust stroke	排气行程
in honor of	以纪念……	air-fuel mixture	空气燃油混合气，可燃混合气
intake valve	进气阀	burned/exhaust gas	废气
exhaust valve	排气阀	intake stroke	进气行程

Exercises

Ⅰ. Answer the following questions according to the text.

1. What do TDC and BDC stand for?
2. What does a stroke mean?
3. What do the four strokes refer to?
4. What is the four-stroke approach also known as?

Ⅱ. Choose the correct answer to fill in the blanks.

1. As the piston starts to move downward, the intake valve opens and the air-fuel mixture enters the cylinder. This stroke refers to the _____.

    A. compression stroke　　B. intake stroke　　C. power stroke　　D. exhaust stroke

2. What do almost all cars use to convert gasoline into motion?_____.

    A. One-stroke combustion cycle　　　　B. Two-stroke combustion cycle
    C. Three-stroke combustion cycle　　　D. Four-stroke combustion cycle

3. Near the end of the compression stroke, the spark plug fires, igniting the compressed air-fuel mixture that produces a powerful explosion. This stroke refers to the _____.

    A. intake stroke　　　　　　　　　　　B. compression stroke
    C. power stroke　　　　　　　　　　　D. exhaust stroke

4. A car engine's job is to _____.

   A. convert fuel into heat   B. convert fuel into motion

   C. convert fuel into exhaust   D. convert fuel into electricity

5. The piston moves up in the cylinder with both valves closed and compresses the trapped air-fuel mixture. This stroke refers to the _____.

   A. intake stroke   B. compression stroke

   C. power stroke   D. exhaust stroke

6. With the _____ at the bottom of the cylinder, the exhaust valve opens to allow the burned exhaust gas to be expelled to the exhaust system.

   A. piston   B. valve   C. camshaft   D. crankshaft

Ⅲ. **Fill in the blanks with the suitable words or phrases given below.**

| convert…into | electric motor | diesel engine |
| four-stroke cycle | internal combustion engine | engine |

1. The _____ is generally considered the "heart" of an automobile.

2. The _____ is the one most commonly used in the automotive field.

3. According to the fuel energy used, the internal combustion engines are also divided into gasoline engines and _____.

4. The piston _____ the potential energy of the fuel _____ the kinetic energy.

5. This _____ of the piston within the cylinder is repeated time and again to push the vehicle forward.

6. There are actually various types of engines such as _____, steam engines and internal combustion engines.

Ⅳ. **Write out the strokes according to the pictures.**

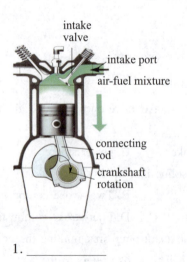

1. _____

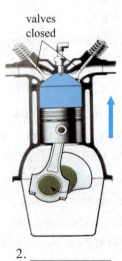

2. _____

Chapter 2 Engine

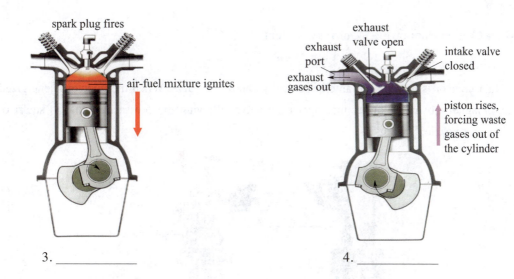

3. _____   4. _____

Unit 5 Electronic Fuel Injection System

Electronic fuel injection (EFI) system collects information through various sensors, the computer controls the operation of fuel injectors based on the information. The electronic fuel injection system has the job of supplying a combustible mixture of air and fuel to the engine and getting a cleaner emission. This system can be divided into three basic sub-systems: fuel delivery system, air induction system and electronic control system.

1 Fuel Delivery System

To ensure the engine works regularly, enough fuel and air are needed. The function of the fuel delivery system is to supply clean fuel to the engine and to control the supplied amount. The fuel delivery systems of all engines are basically the same, mainly composed of the fuel tank, fuel filter, electric fuel pump, fuel distributor pipe, fuel pressure regulator, fuel pulsation damper, connecting tubing and so on. Fuel delivery system is shown in Fig. 2-5-1.

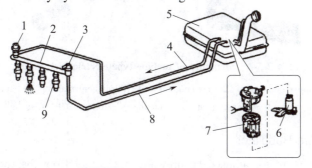

Fig.2-5-1 Fuel delivery system

1—fuel pulsation damper 2—fuel distributor pipe 3—fuel pressure regulator 4—fuel transmission pipe
5—fuel tank 6—electric fuel pump 7—fuel filter 8—fuel return pipe 9—injector

Main Components of Fuel Delivery System

(1) Fuel Injector

A fuel injector is nothing but an electronically controlled valve. When the injector is energized, an electromagnet moves a plunger that opens the valve, allowing the pressurized fuel to squirt out through a tiny nozzle. See Fig. 2-5-2.

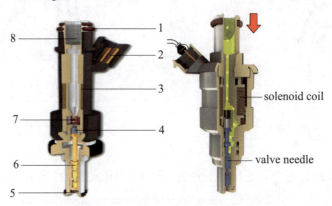

Fig.2-5-2　Structure of fuel injector

1—seal ring　2—connector　3—solenoid coil　4—armature
5—nozzle　6—needle　7—return spring　8—filter

(2) Fuel Pump

An electric fuel pump is inside the fuel tank, which is used to deliver fuel from the tank to the intake manifold or the throttle body. An electric fuel pump can deliver more fuel than the engine requires under maximum operating conditions. Its function is to supply fuel for each injector and cold start injector. See Fig. 2-5-3.

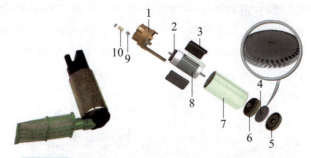

Fig.2-5-3　Structure of turbine-type electric fuel pump

1—upper end cover　2—commutator　3—permanent magnet　4—turbine
5—lower end cover　6—bearing seat　7—housing　8—rotator　9—steel ball　10—spring

(3) Fuel Pressure Regulator

The fuel pressure regulator adjusts the pressure of the fuel from the fuel line (high-pressure side) to a constant pressure higher than the pressure inside the intake manifold, and excess fuel is returned to the fuel tank through the return pipe. See Fig. 2-5-4.

Fig.2-5-4 **Structure of fuel pressure regulator**

1,7—housing   2—fuel return valve seat   3—gasket   4—screen
5,6—seal ring   8—diaphragm   9—spring   10—vacuum tube

Fuel is delivered from the tank to the injector by means of an electric fuel pump. The pump is typically located near the fuel tank. Contaminants are filtered out by a high-capacity in-line fuel filter. Fuel is maintained at a constant pressure by means of a fuel pressure regulator. Any fuel that is not delivered to the intake manifold by the injector is returned to the tank through a fuel return pipe. See Fig.2-5-5.

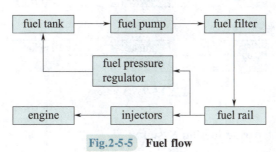

Fig.2-5-5 **Fuel flow**

2 Air Induction System

The function of the intake system is to inhale the air for the gasoline burning. Fig. 2-5-6 shows the structure of the air induction system.

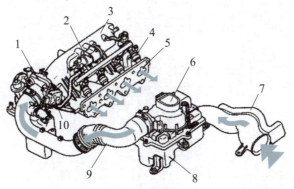

Fig.2-5-6 **Structure of air induction system**

1—throttle body   2—idle air control valve   3—intake pipe   4—injector   5—intake manifold
6—air flow meter   7—resonator   8—air cleaner   9—intake flow pipe   10—throttle position sensor

Air is filtered through the air cleaner and the amount flowing to the air intake chamber is determined according to the throttle valve opening in the throttle body and the engine speed. Intake air controlled by the throttle valve opening is distributed from the air intake chamber to the manifold of each cylinder and is drawn into the combustion chamber.

At low temperatures, the idle air control(IAC)valve opens and the air flows through the IAC valve and the throttle body into the air intake chamber. During engine warming up, even if the throttle valve is completely closed, air flows into the air intake chamber, thereby increasing the idle speed (first idle operation).

When the throttle valve is opened, air flows through the air cleaner (ACL), through the air flow meter (AFM on L-type systems), past the throttle valve, and through a well-tuned intake manifold runner to the intake valve. Air delivered to the engine is a function of driver demand. As the throttle valve is opened further, more air is allowed to enter the engine cylinders. See Fig.2-5-7.

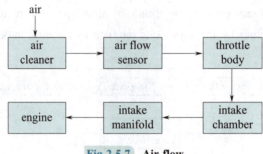

Fig.2-5-7 Air flow

Main Components of Air Induction System

(1) Air Meter or Sensor

An airflow meter is a device that's used in many electronic fuel injection systems for measuring the volume of air entering the engine (see Fig.2-5-8). Some use a spring-loaded vane, while others use a hot wire or heated filament to sense air flow.

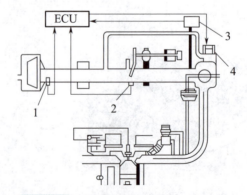

Fig.2-5-8 Air induction system (D-type)
1—air temperature sensor 2—throttle position sensor
3—air pressure sensor 4—idle air control valve

(2) Throttle Valve

The gas pedal in a car is connected to the throttle plate or throttle valve, which is the valve that regulates how much air enters the engine. So the gas pedal is really the air pedal.

(3) Air Intake Chamber

The air intake chamber prevents pulsation of the intake air. It also prevents intake air interference in each cylinder.

3 Electronic Control System

The engine electronic control system consists of various sensors, switches and actuators. The various sensors detect the intake air pressure, engine speed, oxygen density in the exhaust gas, engine coolant temperature, atmospheric pressure, etc., and convert the information into an electrical signal, which is sent to the engine control module (ECM). Based on these signals, the ECM determines the injection volume (timing) and calculates the optimum ignition timing for the current conditions.

The ECM not only controls the fuel injection timing, but also performs the self-diagnostic function which records the occurrence of a malfunction, ignition timing control, idle speed control and exhaust gas recirculation (EGR) control. The electronic control system is shown in Fig. 2-5-9 and Fig. 2-5-10.

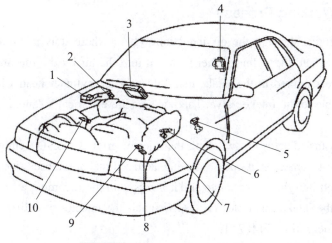

Fig.2-5-9 Electronic control system

1—EFI manifold relay 2—variable resistor 3—engine (& ECT) ECU 4—fuel pump ECU
5—vacuum sensor 6—acoustic control induction system vacuum switching valve (ACIS VSV)
7—No. 2 knock sensor 8—No. 1 knock sensor 9—water temperature sensor
10—intake air temperature sensor

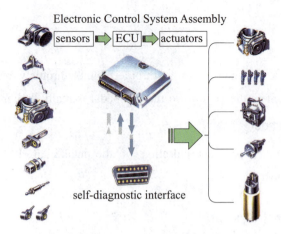

Fig.2-5-10　Sensor, ECU and actuators

4 Types of EFI

There are different types of gasoline fuel injection systems used in automobiles. The two basic arrangements in EFI systems are port fuel injection and throttle body injection(TBI).

The throttle body fuel injection system is also called the single-point fuel injection system. Fuel is injected into the area around the throttle valve, where air velocity is at the maximum, thus ensuring fuel droplets are thoroughly atomized and will be distributed throughout the air mass.

Port fuel injection(also called multi-point fuel injection) systems use a solenoid fuel injector with a coil and a spring to open and close the needle valve in each cylinder. Gasoline is injected into the intake manifold 70 – 100 mm above the intake valve.

5 EFI System Working Process

Air enters the engine through the air induction system where it is measured by the air flow meter. As the air flows into the cylinder, fuel is mixed into the air by the fuel injector.

Fuel injectors are mounted in the intake manifold near the cylinder head where they can inject fuel as close as possible to the intake valve. The injectors are electrical solenoids which are operated by the ECU.

The ECU pulses the injector by switching the injector ground (GND) circuit on and off.

When the injector is turned on, it opens, spraying atomized fuel at the back side of the intake valve.

As fuel is sprayed into the intake airstream, it mixes with the incoming air and vaporizes due to the low pressures in the intake manifold. The ECU signals the injector to deliver just enough fuel to achieve an ideal air-fuel ratio of 14.7∶1.

The ECU determines the basic injection quantity based on measured intake air volume and engine speed.

Depending on engine operating conditions, injection quantity will vary. The engine control unit has to monitor a huge number of input sensors such as coolant temperature sensors, engine speed sensors, throttle position sensors (TPS), oxygen sensors, voltage sensors, manifold absolute pressure (MAP) sensors and make injection corrections which determine final injection quantity.

New Words and Expressions

pump	/pʌmp/	n.	泵
		v.	（用泵）抽水，抽吸
regulator	/ˈregjuleitə/	n.	调节器
sensor	/ˈsensə/	n.	传感器
throttle	/ˈθrɒtl/	n.	节气门
injection	/inˈdʒekʃn/	n.	喷射，注射
injector	/inˈdʒektə/	n.	喷油器
filter	/ˈfiltə/	n.	滤清器
actuator	/ˈæktjueitə/	n.	执行器
oxygen	/ˈɒksidʒən/	n.	氧
atmospheric	/ˌætməsˈferik/	adj.	大气的
calculate	/ˈkælkjuleit/	vt.	计算；预测；认为；打算
signal	/ˈsignəl/	n.	信号
		v.	发信号
optimum	/ˈɒptiməm/	n.	最适宜
		adj.	最适宜的
contaminant	/kənˈtæminənt/	n.	污染物，杂质
electromagnet	/iˌlektrə(ʊ)ˈmægnɪt/	n.	电磁铁，电磁体，电磁
plunger	/ˈplʌn(d)ʒə/	n.	活塞，柱塞
squirt	/skwɜːt/	vt.	喷射
		n.	喷射器
solenoid	/ˈsəʊlənɔid/	n.	螺线管，电磁线圈
oxygen	/ˈɒksidʒ(ə)n/	n.	氧气
airstream	/ˈeəstriːm/	n.	气流，空气射流
armature	/ˈɑːmətʃə(r)/	n.	电枢，衔铁

electronic fuel injection (EFI)			电子控制燃油喷射
fuel delivery system			燃油供给系统
air induction system			进气系统
electronic control system			电子控制系统
air filter			空气滤清器
fuel filter			燃油滤清器
port fuel injection			进气口燃油喷射
throttle body injection			节气门体燃油喷射
air flow meter			空气流量计
air intake chamber			进气歧管室
fuel injector			喷油器
throttle valve			节气门
self-diagnostic function			自诊断功能
fuel pressure regulator			燃油压力调节器
fuel return pipe			回油管
oxygen sensor			氧传感器
coolant temperature sensor			冷却液温度传感器
engine speed sensor			发动机转速传感器
throttle position sensor			节气门位置传感器
solenoid coil			电磁线圈

Notes to the Text

1. The electronic fuel injection system has the job of supplying a combustible mixture of air and fuel to the engine. In order to get a cleaner emission, the electronic fuel injection system is applied.
   电子燃油喷射系统的工作是为发动机提供可燃混合气。为了减少排放，所以应用了电子燃油喷射系统。

2. Fuel systems that have electric fuel pumps and fuel injectors may use a fuel pressure regulator to keep the fuel pressure constant.
   拥有电动燃油泵和喷油器的燃油系统会使用燃油压力调节器来保持燃油压力的稳定。

3. The fuel delivery systems of all engines are basically the same, mainly composed of the fuel tank, fuel filter, electric fuel pump, fuel distributor pipe, fuel pressure regulator, fuel pulsation damper, connecting tubing and so on.
   各种发动机的燃油供给系统基本相同，主要由油箱、燃油滤清器、电动燃油泵、燃油分配管、燃油压力调节器、燃油脉动阻尼器、连接油管等组成。

4. The fuel pressure regulator adjusts the pressure of the fuel from the fuel line (high-pressure side) to a constant pressure higher than the pressure inside the intake manifold, and excess fuel is returned to the fuel tank through the return pipe.
   燃油压力调节器调节从燃油管道（高压端）出来的燃油压力，并使其稳定且高于进气歧管内的燃油压力，同时额外的燃油通过回油管回到油箱中。

5. When the throttle valve is opened, air flows through the air cleaner (ACL), through the air flow meter (AFM on L-type systems), past the throttle valve, and through a well-tuned intake manifold runner to the intake valve.
   当节气门打开时，空气流过空气滤清器，通过空气流量计，流经节气门，并进入设计合理的进气歧管流向进气门。

6. The gas pedal in a car is connected to the throttle plate or throttle valve, which is the valve that regulates how much air enters the engine. So the gas pedal is really the air pedal.
   汽车上的加速踏板连接着节气门，这个阀门可调节进入发动机的空气量，所以加速踏板其实就是空气踏板。

7. The ECU determines the basic injection quantity based on measured intake air volume and engine speed.
   电子控制单元根据测量的进气量和发动机转速确定基本喷油量。

8. Throttle body fuel injection system is also called single point fuel injection system. Fuel is injected into the area around the throttle valve, where air velocity is at the maximum, thus ensuring fuel droplets are thoroughly atomized and will be distributed throughout the air mass.
   节气门体燃油喷射又称单点燃油喷射系统，燃油被喷进空气速度达到最大值的节气门周围，因此能确保油滴被彻底雾化并被分配到空气团各处。

Exercises

I. Answer the following questions according to the text.

1. Which basic sub-systems is the EFI system composed of?
2. What is the function of the intake system?
3. What is the function of the fuel system?
4. Please name the major parts that make up the fuel system.
5. Please describe the working process of the EFI system.

II. Choose the correct answer to fill in the blanks.

1. Electronic fuel injection system collects information through various _____.
   A. throttle valves　　B. ISC valves　　C. sensors　　D. ECUS
2. The computer controls the operation of _____ based on the information.
   A. fuel injectors　　B. sensors　　C. fuel droplets　　D. needle valves
3. For TBI, fuel is injected into the area around the _____.
   A. air mass　　B. throttle valve　　C. intake valve　　D. throttle body
4. For port fuel injection, Gasoline is injected into the _____ 70 – 100 mm above the intake valve.
   A. port　　B. throttle valve shaft　　C. valve　　D. intake manifold
5. In case of checking the water temperature sensor in the water, be careful not to allow _____ to go into the terminals.
   A. water　　B. fuel　　C. fluid　　D. oil
6. Throttle body fuel injection is also called _____.
   A. multi-point injection　　　　B. port fuel injection
   C. single-point fuel injection　　D. solenoid fuel injection
7. The function of the _____ is to supply clean fuel to the engine and to control the supplied amount.
   A. fuel delivery system　　　　B. air induction system
   C. electronic control system　　D. ignition system
8. The abbreviation of single point fuel injection is _____.
   A. MPI　　B. SPI　　C. EFI　　D. TBI
9. Electronic fuel injection system can be divided into _____ basic sub-systems.
   A. two　　B. three　　C. four　　D. five

III. The following picture is the fuel delivery system. Write out the terms according to the picture.

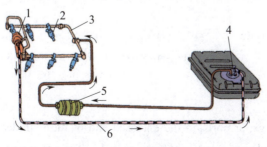

1. _____　2. _____　3. _____　4. _____　5. _____　6. _____

Ⅳ. **Read the following abbreviations and translate them into corresponding Chinese terms.**

1. EFI   electronic fuel injection   _____
2. TV   throttle valve   _____
3. A/F ratio   air/fuel ratio   _____
4. TBI   throttle body injection   _____
5. DFI   direct fuel injection   _____
6. IATS   intake air temperature sensor   _____
7. ACL   air cleaner   _____
8. TPS   throttle position sensor   _____

Unit 6   Valve Train

1 Function and Components of Valve Train

Engine valve train is the other assembly in the engine. The function of the valve train is to open and close the intake and exhaust ports of the cylinders to ensure that the burning mixture can pour into the cylinder and let out the exhaust gas in time. For this purpose, the valves at definite moments open and close the intake and exhaust ports in the cylinder head, through which the cylinders connect to the intake and exhaust manifold.

The valve train consists of the valve assembly and a mechanism that opens and closes them. See Fig. 2-6-1. The valve assembly is composed of the intake valve, exhaust valve, valve guide, valve seat, valve spring, etc. See Fig.2-6-2. A mechanism that opens and closes the valve typically includes the camshaft, rocker shaft, rocker arm, push rod, tappet, timing gear, etc. See Fig.2-6-3.

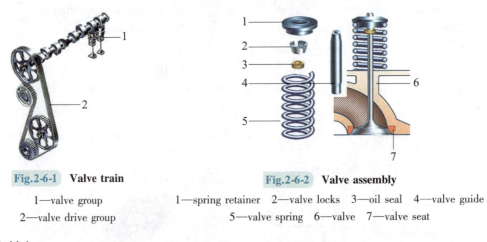

Fig.2-6-1   Valve train
1—valve group
2—valve drive group

Fig.2-6-2   Valve assembly
1—spring retainer   2—valve locks   3—oil seal   4—valve guide
5—valve spring   6—valve   7—valve seat

（1）Valve

There are two openings, or ports, in the enclosed end of the cylinder. One of the ports permits the mixture of air and gasoline vapor to enter the cylinder. The other port permits the burned gases,

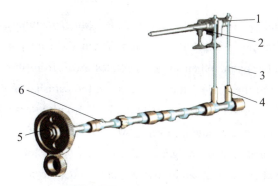

Fig.2-6-3　Valve drive group

1—rocker arm　2—rocker shaft　3—push rod　4—tappet　5—timing gear　6—camshaft

after combustion, to exhaust, or escape, from the cylinder. The two ports have valves assembled into them. These valves close off one or the other port, or both ports, during the various stages of engine operation. That is to say, each cylinder has at least two valves, an intake valve and an exhaust valve. Valves are usually made from a steal alloy such as a mixture of steel and nickel, or steel and silicon. Exhaust valves must withstand extremely high temperatures up to 815℃ (815 degrees Celsius) without damaging the valve. The engine valve is made up of the valve face, valve head and valve stem, see Fig.2-6-4. Sometimes, the angle between its head and face is called margin or chamfer, which is 45° or 30°.

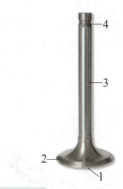

Fig.2-6-4　Components of valve

1—valve head　2—valve face
3—valve stem　4—collect groove

Many newer engines are using multiple intake and exhaust valves per cylinder for increased engine power and efficiency. These engines are sometimes named for the number of valves that they have, such as "24 Valves V6" which indicates a V6 engine with four valves per cylinder. Modern engine designs can use anywhere from 2 to 5 valves per cylinder. See Fig. 2-6-5.

a) Two valves per cylinder

b) Four valves per cylinder

c) Five valves per cylinder

Fig.2-6-5　Multiple valves per cylinder

（2）Camshaft

The camshaft is a rotating shaft that has lobes, called cams, opening and closing the intake and exhaust valves in time with the motion of the piston. When the cam pushes against the lifter, the lifter in turn pushes the valve open. When the cam rotates away from the lifter, the valve is closed by a spring that is attached to the valve. There is a cam on the camshaft for each valve, or two cams per cylinder. The camshaft is driven by gears, or by a chain, from the crankshaft. It turns at one-half crankshaft speed. In the four-cycle engine, every two revolutions of the crankshaft produce one revolution of the camshaft and one opening and closing. The cam lobes are so positioned on the camshaft as to cause the valves to open and close in the cylinders at the proper time with respect to the actions taking place in the cylinder. See Fig.2-6-6.

（3）Valve Spring

Springs return the valves to their closed position after rocker arms press down on the valves, opening them. These springs have to be very strong because, at high engine speeds, the valves are pushed down very quickly, and it is the springs that keep the valves in contact with the rocker arms. If the springs were not strong enough, the valves might come away from the rocker arms and snap back. This is an undesirable situation that would result in extra wear on the cams and rocker arms. See Fig.2-6-7.

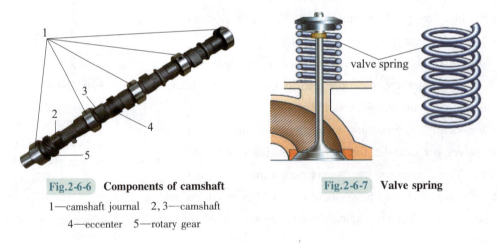

Fig.2-6-6　Components of camshaft
1—camshaft journal　2,3—camshaft
4—eccenter　5—rotary gear

Fig.2-6-7　Valve spring

（4）Push Rod

For an overhead valve (OHV) engine, the push rod is a metal rod that fits between the mechanical tappet and the rocker arm. It transmits lift motion from the camshaft to the rocker arm. Some push rods are hollow which will permit lubricating oil to flow and lubricate the rocker arm. See Fig.2-6-8.

（5）Rocker Arm

In a conventional engine, the rocker arm is nothing but a rocking lever, which is to convert the upward motion of a push rod into the downward motion that compresses the spring and opens the valves. See Fig.2-6-9.

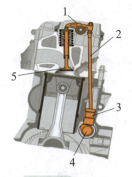
Fig.2-6-8 Push rod

Fig.2-6-9 Rocker arm

1—rocker arm 2—push rod
3—tappet with hydraulic 4—camshaft 5—valve

（6）Timing Belt and Timing Chain

The timing gears, sometimes called timing pulleys, are housed in the front of the engine. A timing belt or timing chain links the crankshaft to the camshaft. See Fig. 2-6-10. They are necessary to transmit rotation from the crankshaft to the camshaft and other mechanisms.

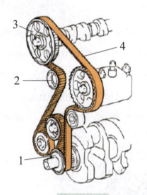

Fig.2-6-10 Timing belt and timing chain

1—crankshaft timing pulley 2—tensioner pulley 3—camshaft timing pulley 4—timing belt

2 Valve Operation

The cam is an egg-shaped piece of metal on a shaft that rotates in coordination with the crankshaft. The metal shaft, called the camshaft, typically has individual cams for each valve in the engine. As the camshaft rotates, the lobe, or high spot of the cam, pushes against parts connected to the stem of the valve. This action forces the valve to move downward. This action could open an inlet valve for an intake stroke, or open an exhaust valve for an exhaust stroke. See Fig. 2-6-11.

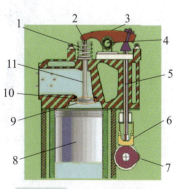
Fig.2-6-11 Valve operation

1—valve spring 2—valve clearances 3—rocker arm
4—rocker shaft 5—push rod 6—tappet 7—camshaft
8—piston 9—valve head 10—valve seat 11—valve stem

3 Types of Valve Train

Some engines have two camshafts on each head, one for the intake valves and one for the exhaust valves. These engines are called double overhead camshaft (DOHC) engines. Engines with the other type are called single overhead camshaft (SOHC) engines. See Fig. 2-6-12. Engines with the camshaft in the block are called overhead valve (OHV) engines.

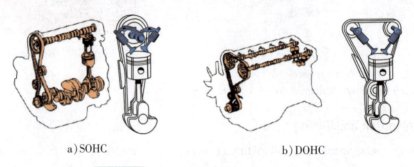

a) SOHC   b) DOHC

Fig.2-6-12   Arrangement ways of valve train

(1) Double Overhead Camshaft

A double overhead camshaft engine has two camshafts per head. So in-line engines have two camshafts, and V-type engines have four. Usually, double overhead camshafts are used on engines with four (or more) valves per cylinder. The main reason to use double overhead camshafts is to allow for more intake and exhaust valves. More valves mean that intake and exhaust gases can flow more freely because there are more openings for them to flow through. This increases the power of the engine. See Fig. 2-6-13.

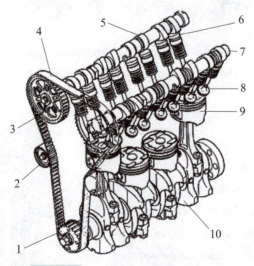

Fig.2-6-13   Double overhead camshaft

1—crankshaft timing pulley   2—tensioner pulley   3—camshaft timing pulley   4—timing belt
5—intake camshaft   6—valve lifter   7—exhaust camshaft   8—valve   9—piston   10—crankshaft

(2) Single Overhead Camshaft

This arrangement denotes an engine with a single camshaft per head. So if it is an inline-4 cylinder or inline-6 cylinder engine, it will have one camshaft; if it is a V6 engine or V8, it will have two camshafts (one for each head). See Fig. 2-6-14.

(3) Overhead Valve Engine

Like SOHC and DOHC engines, the valves in an overhead valve engine are located in the head, above the cylinder. The key difference is that the camshaft in an overhead valve engine is inside the engine block, rather than in the head. See Fig. 2-6-15.

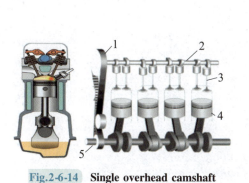
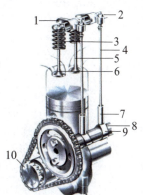

Fig.2-6-14 Single overhead camshaft
1—timing belt 2—camshaft 3—valve
4—piston 5—crankshaft

Fig.2-6-15 Overhead valve engine
1—rocker arm 2—rocker shaft 3—spring 4—push rod
5—exhaust valve 6—intake valve 7—tappet
8—camshaft 9—cam 10—camshaft sprocket

4 Types of Camshaft Drive Mechanism

In most engines, a belt or chain called the timing belt or timing chain (similar to a bicycle chain) connects the camshaft with the crankshaft. These belts and chains need to be replaced or adjusted at regular intervals. If a timing belt breaks, the cam stops spinning and the piston could hit the open valves. See Fig. 2-6-16.

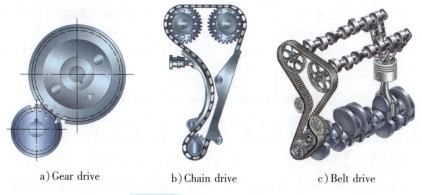

a) Gear drive   b) Chain drive   c) Belt drive

Fig.2-6-16 Camshaft drive ways

New Words and Expressions

camshaft	/ˈkæmʃɑːft/	n.	凸轮轴
push rod	/puʃ rɔd/	n.	推杆
lobe	/ləub/	n.	凸轮，凸耳
cam	/kæm/	n.	凸轮
nickel	/ˈnikl/	n.	镍
silicon	/ˈsilikən/	n.	硅
withstand	/wiðˈstænd/	vt.	抵挡，经受住
valve	/vælv/	n.	气门
spring	/spriŋ/	n.	弹簧
stud	/stʌd/	n.	螺栓，双头螺柱
pivot	/ˈpivət/	n.	枢轴
idler	/ˈaidlə/	n.	空转轮，惰轮
slack	/slæk/	n.	空隙，活动的间隙
		vt.	减速，松懈
elongation	/iːlɔŋˈgeiʃn/	n.	延长，延伸
hydraulic	/haiˈdrɔːlik/	adj.	液压的
clearance	/ˈkliər(ə)ns/	n.	间隙
valve train	配气机构，气门机构	valve spring	气门弹簧
rocker arm	摇臂	valve lifter	挺柱
steel alloy	合金钢	intake port	进气口
exhaust port	排气口，排出孔	valve face	气门锥面
valve seat	气门座	timing belt	正时带
timing chain	正时链		
double overhead camshaft（DOHC）		顶置双凸轮轴	
single overhead camshaft（SOHC）		顶置单凸轮轴	
overhead valve（OHV）		顶置气门	
push rod engine		推杆式发动机	

Notes to the Text

1. The engine valve is made up of the valve face, valve head and valve stem. Sometimes, the angle between its head and face is called margin or chamfer, which is 45° or 30°.
   气门由气门锥面、气门头部和气门杆组成。有时气门锥面和气门头部之间的夹角被称为锥角，通常是45°或30°。

2. These engines are sometimes named for the number of valves that they have, such as "24 Valves V6" which indicates a V6 engine with four valves per cylinder.
   有时，这些发动机会以其气门数量命名，就像"24气门V6发动机"，它代表一台V6发动机，每个气缸有4个气门。

3. The cam lobes are so positioned on the camshaft as to cause the valves to open and close in the cylinders at the proper time with respect to the actions taking place in the cylinder.
   凸轮轴上凸轮凸角的位置使气门在恰当的时候开关，以便与气缸的工作顺序相同。

4. These springs have to be very strong because at high engine speeds, the valves are pushed down very quickly, and it is the springs that keep the valves in contact with the rocker arms.
   弹簧必须坚固，因为在发动机高速运转时，快速向下推动气门，弹簧使气门与摇臂保持接触。

5. Some engines have two camshafts on each head, one for the intake valves and one for the exhaust valves.
   一些发动机每个缸盖上有两个凸轮轴，一个是进气门用的，一个是排气门用的。

6. In most engines, a belt or chain called the timing belt or timing chain (similar to a bicycle chain) connects the camshaft with the crankshaft.
   大多数发动机中，正时带或正时链条（类似于自行车链条）将凸轮轴与曲轴连接。

Exercises

Ⅰ. Answer the following questions according to the text.
   1. What is the function of the valve train?
   2. Please name the major parts that make up the valve train.
   3. Please name the major types of the valve train.
   4. Each cylinder has two valves, what are they?

Ⅱ. Choose the correct answer to fill in the blanks.
   1. In the four-cycle engine, every _____ revolutions of the crankshaft produce one revolution of the camshaft and one opening and closing.
      A. one   B. two   C. three   D. four
   2. The abbreviation of *single overhead camshaft* is _____.
      A. SOHV   B. OHV   C. SOHC   D. DOHC
   3. Some engines have two camshafts on each head, one for the intake valves and one for the exhaust valves. These engines are called _____ engines.
      A. SOHV   B. OHV   C. SOHC   D. DOHC
   4. _____ return the valves to their closed position after the rocker arms press down on the valves, opening them.
      A. Valve lifter   B. Push rod   C. Springs   D. Rocker arms
   5. What part of the cylinder makes cams press against to open valves?_____.
      A. Rocker arms   B. Springs   C. Valves   D. Push rods
   6. What are the key parts of the camshaft?_____.
      A. Pistons   B. Lobes   C. Cylinders   D. Valves
   7. What keeps the cams rotating in single and double overhead cam engines?_____.
      A. Crankshaft   B. Timing belt   C. Timing chain   D. Timing gear
   8. How many cams would a double overhead V-engine have? _____.
      A. 2   B. 3   C. 4   D. 5

Ⅲ. Read the following abbreviations and translate them into corresponding Chinese terms.

1. DOHC   double overhead camshaft   _____
2. SOHC   single overhead camshaft   _____
3. OHV   overhead valve   _____
4. ECU   electronic control unit   _____
5. VVL   variable valve lift   _____
6. SUV   sport utility vehicle   _____

Ⅳ. Write out the terms according to the pictures.

Picture 1 & Picture 2

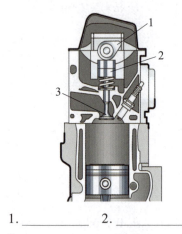
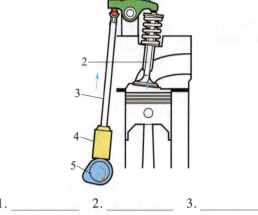

1. _____   2. _____   1. _____   2. _____   3. _____
3. _____   4. _____   5. _____

Picture 3: Material object map of valve assembly

1. _____   2. _____   3. _____   4. _____   5. _____
6. _____   7. _____   8. _____   9. _____   10. _____

Unit 7 Engine Ignition System

We have wondered why air-fuel mixture will be fired in the combustion chamber. The answer to it is ignition system which creates an electric spark with high voltage in order to ignite the air-fuel mixture.

The ignition system is part of the electric system of the automobile. It is used to ignite the air and fuel in the cylinder. In order to do this, a very high voltage is needed to force the electric current to jump across the spark plug gap and cause an electric spark. However, there is only a 12-volt battery within the automobile. The ignition system is designed to increase the voltage to the necessary amount at the right time for the spark to occur. In addition, the time of spark must be altered as speed and load increase or decrease.

The ignition system consists of three basic parts: the ignition distributor, the ignition coil, the spark plug, together with the connecting wires. See Fig.2-7-1.

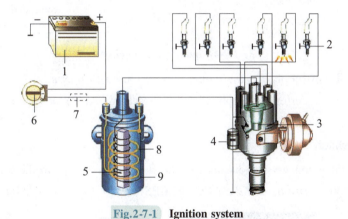

Fig.2-7-1 Ignition system
1—battery 2—spark plug 3—distributor 4—capacitor 5—ignition coil
6—ignition switch 7—resistor 8—primary winding 9—secondary winding

Actually, the ignition system is divided into two circuits: the primary and the secondary. The primary circuit is the low-voltage side of the system and controls the secondary circuit, which is the high-voltage side of the system. The primary circuit contains the battery, ignition switch, primary winding, breaker point and wiring. While, the secondary circuit contains the secondary winding, distributor cap, distributor rotor, spark plug and related wiring. See Fig. 2-7-2.

1 Components in the Ignition System

(1) Battery

The battery is used to provide the electrical energy needed to operate the system. The negative side is grounded to the frame, and the positive side is fed directly to the ignition switch. When

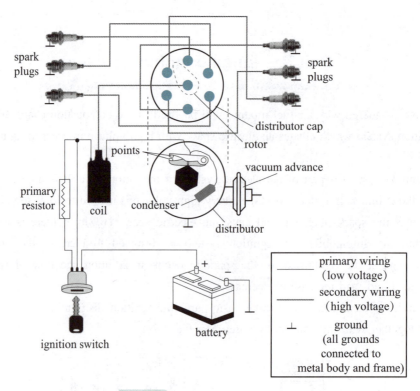

Fig.2-7-2　**Ignition system circuit**

starting the engine, it will supply the low voltage (12V) used to operate the primary circuit. After the engine is running, the current is supplied by the alternator (ALT) or by the combination of the alternator and battery.

(2) Ignition Switch

The ignition switch connects or disconnects the flow of electricity to the ignition system. The switch usually has four positions: LOCK, ACC(ACCESSORY), ON and START. See Fig.2-7-3.

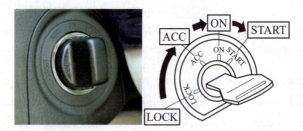

Fig.2-7-3　**Four positions of ignition switch**

(3) Igniter

The igniter temporarily interrupts the primary current with the ignition signal from the ECM and generates sparks at the spark plug.

(4) ECM

The ECM monitors the engine condition by signals from each sensor, calculates the ignition timing and sends an ignition signal to the igniter.

(5) Ignition Coil

The ignition coil allows the generation of a high voltage sufficient to cause a spark to jump across the spark plug gap.

(6) Distributor

The distributor distributes high voltage to the spark plug of each cylinder in the specified ignition order. Fig.2-7-4 shows the parts of the distributor.

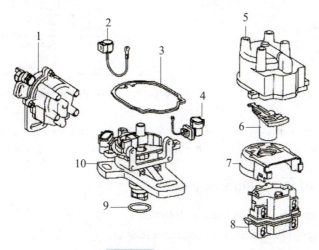

Fig.2-7-4 Distributor

1—distributor 2—condenser 3—dust proof packing 4—distributor break lead 5—distributor cap
6—rotor 7—dust proof cover 8—ignition coil 9—O-ring 10—distributor housing

(7) Distributor Rotor

The distributor rotor operates in conjunction with the distributor cap to distribute the high voltage from the ignition coil to the individual spark plug wires in the firing order.

(8) Distributor Cam

A cam in the center of the distributor pushes a lever connected to one of the points. Whenever the cam pushes the lever, it opens the points. This causes the coil to suddenly lose its ground, generating a high-voltage pulse.

(9) Spark Plug Wires

The spark plug wires are used to connect the high-voltage to each spark plug. The job of the spark plug wires is to get that enormous power to the spark plug without leaking out. Spark plug wires have to endure the heat of a running engine as well as the extreme changes in the weather.

(10) Spark Plug

The spark plugs provide a gap within the combustion chamber so that each time a high-voltage is delivered, a high-quality spark will occur. The electricity must be at a very high voltage in order to travel across the gap and create a good spark. The voltage at the spark plug can be anywhere from 40,000 to 100,000 volts, thus igniting the air-fuel mixture. See Fig.2-7-5.

Fig.2-7-6 shows the distributor ignition system circuit.

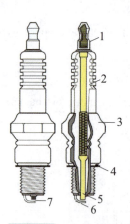

Fig.2-7-5 **Spark plug**

1—terminal 2—insulator 3—shell
4—gasket 5—centre electrode
6—earth electrode 7—spark plug gap

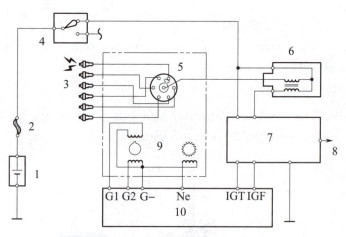

Fig.2-7-6 **Distributor ignition system circuit**

1—battery 2—fuse wire 3—spark plug
4—ignition switch 5—distributor 6—ignition coil 7—igniter
8—to tachometer 9—crankshaft position sensor 10—ECU

2 Classification of the Ignition System

The ignition system may be classified as follows:

1) Conventional ignition system with contact breaker.
2) Electronic ignition system using semiconductors or transistors.
3) Computer-controlled ignition system.

The computer-controlled ignition system is composed of the electronic control unit (ECU), various sensors, battery, ignition switch, igniter, ignition coil, distributor and spark plugs. Fig. 2-7-7 shows a distributor ignition system.

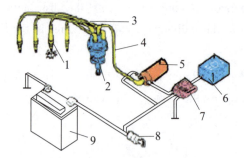

Fig.2-7-7 **Distributor ignition system**

1—spark plug 2—distributor 3—high-voltage wire 4—center high-voltage wire
5—ignition coil 6—ECU 7—igniter 8—ignition switch 9—battery

In the early 1990s, a new type of ignition system began to appear on many automobiles. It is called the distributorless ignition system, or direct ignition system. This system provides a high-voltage spark at the spark plug without many of the secondary system parts. The system can provide higher voltages and does so with fewer parts to wear out. According to the distributorless ignition system, the ignition system can be classified into single ignition system and double ignition system. See Fig. 2-7-8 and Fig. 2-7-9.

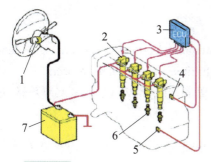

Fig.2-7-8 Single ignition system

1—ignition switch 2—ignition coil 3—ECU
4—camshaft position sensor
5—crankshaft position sensor
6—spark plug 7—battery

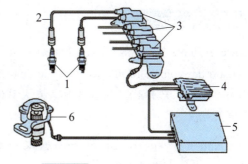

Fig.2-7-9 Double ignition system

1—spark plug 2—high voltage wire
3—three ignition coils (six cylinders)
4—ignition control module 5—ECU
6—camshaft position sensor

New Words and Expressions

voltage	/ˈvəultidŋ/	n.	电压,伏特
current	/ˈkʌrənt/	n.	电流,气流
		adj.	当前的
alter	/ˈɔːltə/	v.	改变
contact	/ˈkɔntækt/	n./vt.	接触;联系
breaker	/ˈbreikə/	n.	断电器,继电器
semiconductor	/ˌsemikənˈdʌktə/	n.	半导体
transistor	/trænˈzistə/	n.	晶体管
ground	/graund/	n./v.	接地,搭铁
positive	/ˈpɔzətiv/	adj.	阳的;肯定的;正的
temporarily	/ˈtemp(ə)rərili/	adj.	临时
interrupt	/ˌintəˈrʌpt/	vt.	打断;中断;妨碍
generation	/ˌdʒenəˈreiʃn/	n.	产生,发生
gap	/gæp/	n.	间隔,间隙
rotor	/ˈrəutə/	n	轮子,旋转器,转子,分火头
condenser	/kənˈdensə/	n.	电容器,冷凝器,[光]聚光器
distributor	/diˈstribjutə/	n.	分电器,配电器
accessory	/əkˈses(ə)ri/	n.	附件,配件,附属物
resistance	/riˈzist(ə)ns/	n.	电阻,热阻,阻力
insulated	/ˈinsəˌleitəd/	adj.	绝缘的,隔热的,保暖的
insulator	/ˈinsjuleitə/	n.	绝缘,绝缘体
terminal	/ˈtəːmin(ə)l/	n.	端子,接线头

ignition system	点火系统	centre electrode	中心电极
ignition switch	点火开关	earth electrode	搭铁
ignition coil	点火线圈	distributor rotor	分火头
ignition signal	点火信号	distributor cap	分电器盖
camshaft position sensor	凸轮轴位置传感器	breaker point	断电器触点
crankshaft position sensor	曲轴位置传感器	in conjunction with	连同,共同
primary winding	初级绕组		
secondary winding	次级绕组		

Notes to the Text

1. However, there is only a 12-volt battery within the automobile. The ignition system is designed to increase the voltage to the necessary amount at the right time for the spark to occur.
   然而，汽车上只有12V的蓄电池。点火系统用来在适当时刻将12V电压增大到足够高来产生电火花。

2. The ignition system consists of three basic parts: the ignition distributor, the ignition coil, the spark plug, together with the connecting wires.
   点火系统包括三个基本部分：点火分电器、点火线圈和火花塞，以及起连接作用的导线。

3. When starting the engine, it will supply the low voltage (12V) used to operate the primary circuit. After the engine is running, the current is supplied by the alternator (ALT) or by the combination of the alternator and battery.
   当发动机启动时，蓄电池向初级电路提供12V电压。发动机运转时，交流发电机或与蓄电池共同向系统提供电压。

4. The ignition coil allows the generation of a high voltage sufficient to cause a spark to jump across the spark plug gap.
   点火线圈产生足够高的电压以使电火花击穿火花塞间隙。

5. A cam in the center of the distributor pushes a lever connected to one of the points. Whenever the cam pushes the lever, it opens the points. This causes the coil to suddenly lose its ground, generating a high-voltage pulse.
   分电器中央的凸轮推动与断电器触点相连接的杆。一旦凸轮推动此杆，断电器的触点就会打开。点火线圈的接地端会突然断开，从而产生高压脉冲。

6. The job of the spark plug wires is to get that enormous power to the spark plug without leaking out. Spark plug wires have to endure the heat of a running engine as well as the extreme changes in the weather.
   火花塞导线必须确保绝缘，以保证高压电传输到火花塞。它应能承受发动机运行产生的大量的热并能适应外界温度的改变。

7. The electricity must be at a very high voltage in order to travel across the gap and create a good spark. The voltage at the spark plug can be anywhere from 40,000 to 100,000 volts, thus igniting the air-fuel mixture.
   此电必须是高压电以便在击穿火花塞间隙时，产生高品质的电火花。火花塞电压一般在40 000~100 000V，这样才能点燃可燃混合气。

8. The computer-controlled ignition system is composed of the electronic control unit (ECU), various sensors, battery, ignition switch, igniter, ignition coil, distributor and spark plugs.
   计算机控制的点火系统包括电子控制单元、各种传感器、蓄电池、点火开关、点火器、点火线圈、分电器和火花塞。

9. According to the distributorless ignition system, the ignition system can be classified into single ignition system and double ignition system.

根据无分电器点火系统，点火系统又可分为单缸独立点火系统和双缸同时点火系统。

Exercises

Ⅰ. Answer the following questions according to the text.

1. What's the function of the ignition system?
2. What kinds does the ignition system may be classified into?
3. Please name the major parts that make up the conventional ignition system.
4. What are the spark plug wires used to do?

Ⅱ. Choose the correct answer to fill in the blanks.

1. The _____ is designed to increase the voltage to the necessary amount at the right time for the spark to occur.
   A. ignition system   B. starting system   C. cooling system   D. braking system
2. The _____ connects or disconnects the flow of electricity to the ignition system.
   A. spark plug   B. battery   C. ignition switch   D. ignition coil
3. The _____ monitors the engine condition by signals from each sensor, calculates the ignition timing and sends an ignition signal to the igniter.
   A. ECU   B. EFI   C. OHV   D. ECM
4. The _____ allows the generation of a high voltage sufficient to cause a spark to jump across the spark plug gap.
   A. distributor   B. ignition coil   C. igniter   D. spark plug wires
5. The purpose of the battery is to supply additional current when the demand is _____ than the alternator can supply and to act as an electrical reservoir.
   A. higher   B. lower   C. fewer   D. high
6. For an engine to make the best use of the fuel, the spark should occur before the piston reaches the top of _____.
   A. the intake stroke   B. the compression stroke
   C. the exhaust stroke   D. the power stroke
7. The piston speed increases as the engine speed increases. This means that the faster the engine goes, the spark has to occur _____.
   A. earlier   B. later   C. no change is necessary
8. The primary role of the distributor is to distribute high voltage from the _____ to the correct cylinder.
   A. spark plug   B. piston   C. coil   D. camshaft

Ⅲ. Read the following abbreviations and translate them into corresponding Chinese terms.

1. CIS   conventional ignition system   _____
2. EIS   electronic ignition system   _____

3. ITDC   ignition top dead center   _____

4. DLI   distributorless ignition   _____

5. IT   ignition timing   _____

6. C3I   computer-controlled coil ignition   _____

7. ICM   ignition control module   _____

8. DFI   direct-fire ignition   _____

Ⅳ. Write out the terms according to the picture.

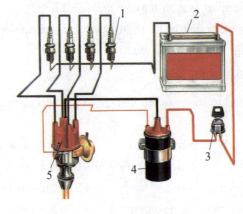

1. _____   2. _____   3. _____   4. _____   5. _____

Ⅴ. Look at the picture and label it correctly using the words and phrases given below.

battery	ignition key	distributor shaft	spark plug
time core	jump spark wire	distributor rotor	ignition module
pick-up coil	ignition switch	ignition coil	
primary connector		distributor cap	

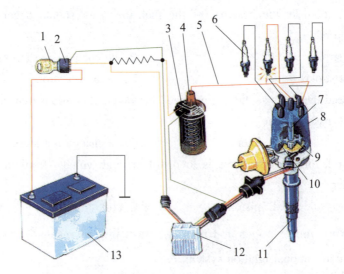

Unit 8　Engine Starting System

The starting system is the heart of the electrical system in the automobile. The starting system performs this function by changing electrical energy from the battery to mechanical energy in the starting motor. This motor then transfers the mechanical energy, through gears, to the flywheel on the engine's crankshaft. During cranking, the flywheel rotates and the air-fuel mixture is drawn into the cylinders, compressed, and ignited to start the engine. Most engines require a cranking speed of about 200r/min. The starting system includes the following components: battery, cable and wire, ignition switch, starter solenoid or relay, starting motor, starter drive and flywheel ring gear. Fig.2-8-1 shows the components in a simplified cranking system circuit.

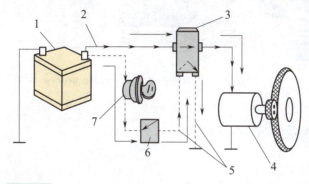

Fig.2-8-1　Components in a simplified cranking system circuit

1—battery　2—starting circuit　3—magnetic switch　4—starting motor
5—control circuit　6—starting safety switch　7—ignition switch

The starter is equipped on the transmission cap or the engine body, and a specific stand is equipped for fixing it. See Fig. 2-8-2. The function of the starting system is to crank the engine fast enough to allow the engine to start. The starting system and ignition system must work together for good engine starting.

Working Process

The starting system begins with the battery. The key is inserted into the ignition switch and then turned to the START position. A small amount of current then passes

Fig.2-8-2　Starter installation position

through the neutral safety switch to a starter relay which allows a high current to flow through the battery cables to the starting motor. The starting motor then cranks the engine so that the piston, moving downward, can create suction that will draw an air-fuel mixture into the cylinder, where a spark created by the ignition system will ignite this mixture. If the compression in the engine is high enough and all these happen at the right time, the engine will start. Starting system working process is shown in Fig.2-8-3.

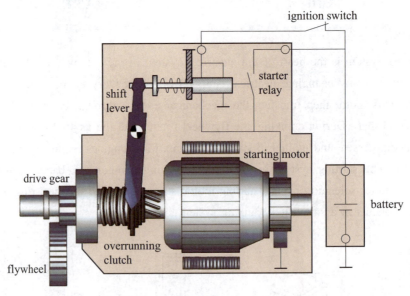

Fig.2-8-3 Starting system working process

Some Components of Starting System

1 Battery

The automotive battery serves as an energy "bank". It receives energy from the vehicle's charging system and stores it until needed. The battery converts electrical energy into chemical energy during charging. It then converts it back into electricity during discharging.

2 Ignition Switch

The key switch, or ignition switch, controls the ignition circuit. It also controls the starting system and the power for the instruments and vehicle accessories.

3 Starting Motor

The starting motor, or starter, is a compact but very powerful direct-current electric motor designed to crank the engine fast enough for it to start. It rotates a small gear called a pinion. A starter drive assembly connects the small pinion gear to the end of the starting motor. The pinion gear meshes with the ring gear on the engine's flywheel. When the driver turns the key switch, the starting motor drives the pinion gear, which drives the flywheel and cranks the engine. In a starting motor, field coils are used to produce the poles. Fig.2-8-4 and Fig.2-8-5 show the structure of the starter.

Chapter 2 Engine

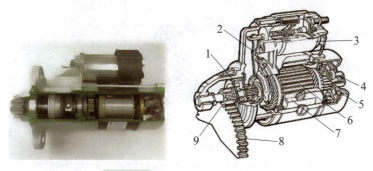

Fig.2-8-4 Structure of starter (a)

1—overrunning clutch 2—shift lever 3—solenoid 4—brush hold 5—commutator
6—motor armature 7—field coil 8—flywheel 9—pinion gear

Fig.2-8-5 Structure of starter (b)

1—overrunning clutch 2—drive end housing 3—solenoid/magnetic switch
4—armature 5—starter frame 6—brush end frame

4 Starter Clutch

The purpose of the starter clutch is to engage and disengage the pinion gear from the flywheel. When the starter is cranked, the pinion gear slides on the armature shaft and engages the flywheel. To avoid damaging the armature and the commutator, the starter drive assembly is designed to disengage the pinion gear from the ring gear as soon as the engine begins to operate.

5 Solenoid

The solenoid is a magnetic switch mounted on the top of the starting motor. It has two important functions: it controls the electrical circuit between the battery and starting motor and it shifts the pinion gear in and out of mesh with the ring gear. See Fig.2-8-6.

Fig.2-8-6 Solenoid

1—plunger 2—solenoid switch coil
3—contact plate 4—contact

6 Armature

Armature in a starting motor is a rotational part that has many loops of wire with a commutator. See Fig. 2-8-7.

Fig.2-8-7 Armature

1—shaft   2—armature winding   3—lamination   4—commutator

7 Brush

Brush is used to make electrical contact between the rotating armature and the stationary battery. See Fig. 2-8-8.

Fig.2-8-8 Brush and armature

1—brush and brush holder   2—armature

8 Drive Pinion

Drive pinion is also called pinion gear. As the starter solenoid works, it will shift the drive pinion to mesh with the flywheel ring gear.

9 Neutral Safety Switch

The neutral safety switch is installed at the automatic transmission (AT) (or at the clutch pedal). When the automatic transmission is not in "park" or "neutral" (or when the clutch pedal is not depressed), the neutral safety switch is open and the starter relay disconnects the starter control circuit. It prevents the starting system from opening when the automobile's transmission is in gear.

Notes to the Text

1. The starting system performs this function by changing electrical energy from the battery to mechanical energy in the starting motor. This motor then transfers the mechanical energy, through gears, to the flywheel on the engine's crankshaft.
   起动系的作用是将蓄电池的电能转变成起动机机械能。该起动机将机械能通过齿轮装置传递到发动机曲轴的飞轮上。

2. The starting motor then cranks the engine so that the piston, moving downward, can create suction that will draw an air-fuel mixture into the cylinder, where a spark created by the ignition system will ignite this mixture.

起动机随后带动发动机旋转。当活塞向下运动时，所产生的吸力会把可燃混合气吸入气缸内，此时点火系统产生电火花点燃混合气体。

3. The pinion gear meshes with the ring gear on the engine's flywheel. When the driver turns the key switch, the starting motor drives the pinion gear, which drives the flywheel and cranks the engine.
小齿轮与飞轮齿圈啮合。转动钥匙开关时，起动机驱动小齿轮，小齿轮起动飞轮来起动发动机。

4. To avoid damaging the armature and the commutator, the starter drive assembly is designed to disengage the pinion gear from the ring gear as soon as the engine begins to operate.
为了避免电枢和换向器的损坏，在发动机开始运转时起动机驱动装置就将小齿轮与齿圈脱离啮合。

5. Solenoid has two important functions: it controls the electrical circuit between the battery and starting motor and it shifts the pinion gear in and out of mesh with the ring gear.
电磁线圈有两个重要功能：控制蓄电池和起动机之间的电路，转换小齿轮和齿圈的啮合和分离。

6. Brush is used to make electrical contact between the rotating armature and the stationary battery.
电刷用于在旋转的电枢和静止的蓄电池之间导电。

7. When the automatic transmission is not in "park" or "neutral" (or when the clutch pedal is not depressed), the neutral safety switch is open and the starter relay disconnects the starter control circuit.
当自动变速器未挂入驻车档或空档（或未踩离合器）时，空档安全开关断开，起动继电器断开，起动电路断开。

New Words and Expressions

cable	/ˈkeibl/	n.	电缆
wire	/ˈwaiə/	n.	导线，金属线
cranking	/ˈkræŋkiŋ/	vt.	摇动；起动，开动
crank	/kræŋk/	vt.	起动
charging	/ˈtʃɑːdʒiŋ/	n.	充电，充气，进气
discharging	/disˈtʃɑːdʒiŋ/	n.	卸料，输出，放电的
instrument	/ˈinstrumənt/	n.	仪器，仪表，器具
solenoid	/ˈsəulinɔid/	n.	电磁线圈，螺线管线圈
relay	/ˈriːlei/	n.	继电器
motor	/ˈməutə/	n.	发动机；电动机
armature	/ˈɑːmətjuə/	n.	电枢（电极的部件）
commutator	/ˈkɔmjuteitə/	n.	换向器，转换器
field	/fiːld/	n.	场，电场；磁场
pole	/pəul/	n.	棒（柱，杆，极）；磁极；电极
disengage	/ˌdisinˈgeidŋ/	v.	脱离，解除，分离
brush	/brʌʃ/	n.	电刷
plunger	/ˈplʌn(d)ʒə/	n.	柱塞
insert	/inˈsəːt/	vt.	插入，嵌入
loop	/luːp/	n.	环状物，回路，循环

starting system	起动系	cranking system circuit	起动系电路
electrical energy	电能	gear reduction ratio	齿轮减速比
mechanical energy	机械能	overrunning clutch	单向离合器
cranking speed	(发动机)起动转速	pinion gear	驱动齿轮
starting motor	起动机	shunt coil	并联绕组
starter solenoid/drive	起动机电磁线圈/驱动机构	series coil	串联绕组
starter relay	起动继电器	clutch pedal	离合器踏板
lock-type switch	锁止开关	shift lever	拨叉
neutral safety switch	空档安全开关		

Exercises

Ⅰ. Answer the following questions according to the text.

1. What's the function of the starting system.
2. Please name the major parts that make up the conventional starting system.
3. Describe the work process of the starting motor.
4. What's the function of the solenoid?

Ⅱ. Choose the correct answer to fill in the blanks.

1. The battery converts _____ into chemical energy during charging. It then converts it back into electricity during discharging.
   A. electrical energy   B. chemical energy   C. mechanical energy   D. energy
2. A starter relay is installed in series between the battery and the _____.
   A. engine   B. alternator   C. key switch   D. starter
3. When the engine starts to spin faster than the starter, a device called an overrunning clutch automatically _____ the starter gear from the engine gear.
   A. installs   B. disengages   C. joins   D. links
4. The starter spins, but will not crank the engine. Which does cause that? _____.
   A. Ignition timing too far advanced   B. Starter mounting loose
   C. Internal starting motor problems   D. Broken starter drive gear
5. The _____ is a magnetic switch mounted on the top of the starting motor.
   A. solenoid   B. starting motor   C. starter clutch   D. starter relay
6. The _____ is a compact but very powerful direct-current electric motor designed to crank the engine fast enough for it to start.
   A. solenoid   B. starting motor   C. starter clutch   D. starter relay
7. The power to run a car's radio, CD player, headlights and windshield wipers comes from the _____.
   A. battery   B. motor   C. engine   D. condenser
8. In general, the starting motor includes the _____.
   A. control device, drive mechanism, armature
   B. control device, electromotor, drive mechanism

C. electromotor, drive pinion, armature

D. drive mechanism, armature, control device

9. Which component is to engage and disengage the pinion gear from the flywheel?_____.

   A. Clutch   B. Crankshaft   C. Armature   D. Commutator

10. Which component in the starting motor has many loops of wire with a commutator? _____.

   A. Field coil   B. Brush   C. Starter solenoid   D. Armature

Ⅲ. Translate the following phrases into Chinese or English.

1. cranking system circuit _____ 6. 空档安全开关 _____
2. starter relay _____ 7. 单向离合器 _____
3. gear reduction ratio _____ 8. 起动系 _____
4. cranking speed _____ 9. 驱动齿轮 _____
5. lock-type switch _____ 10. 拨叉 _____

Ⅳ. Write out the terms according to the pictures.

Picture 1

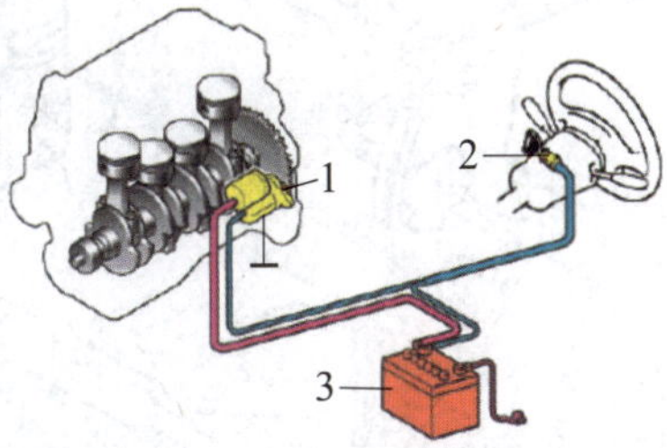

1. _____ 2. _____ 3. _____

Picture 2

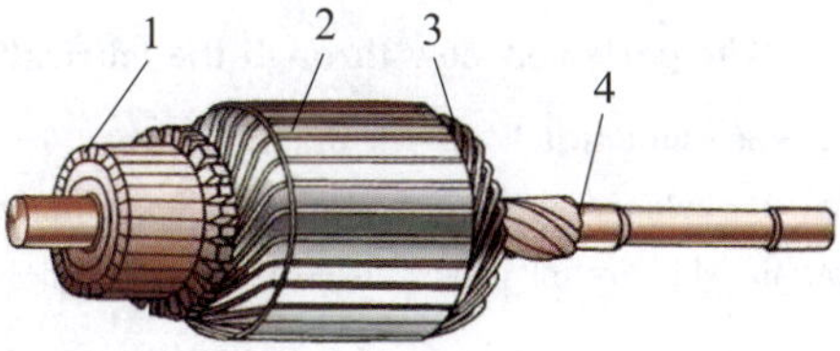

1. _____ 2. _____ 3. _____ 4. _____

Unit 9　Engine Lubrication System

Without the aid of friction, an automobile could not move itself. Excessive friction in the engine, however, would mean rapid destruction. We cannot eliminate internal friction, but we can reduce it to a controllable degree by the use of friction-reducing lubricants. There are three types: splash lubrication, pressure lubrication and grease lubrication. Oil is supplied to moving parts of the engine by pump pressure or splashing, or by a combination of both.

The purpose of the lubrication system is to circulate oil between moving engine parts. Oil between the parts prevents metal-to-metal contact which causes friction and wear. The circulating oil has other important jobs. It carries heat away from engine parts, cleans engine parts, and helps the piston rings seal in compression pressures. The several tasks of lubricating oil to perform as follows:

1) By lubrication, reduces friction between moving parts of engine.

2) By acting as a seal to prevent leakage between parts such as pistons, rings and cylinders.

3) By flowing between friction-generating parts to carry away heat.

4) By washing away abrasive metal worn from friction surfaces.

The parts and flow through the lubrication system are shown in Fig.2-9-1.

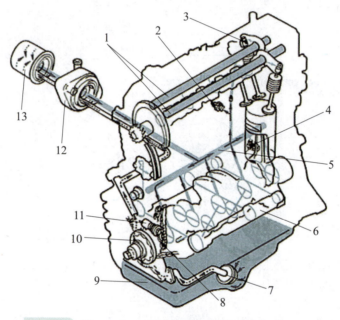

Fig.2-9-1   The parts and flow through the lubrication system

1—rocker shaft   2—pressure switch   3—hydraulic tappet   4—piston cooling jet
5—main oil gallery   6—balance shaft   7—strainer   8—timing chain   9—oil pan
10—oil pump   11—relief valve   12—oil cooler   13—oil filter

Some Components of Lubrication System

1 Oil Pan

The oil pan is located on the bottom of the engine and holds the excess oil during operation and no running conditions. The pan also collects oil that runs off engine parts after lubrication. The deep part of the oil pan houses an oil pump and pick-up screen. A plug in the bottom of the oil pan is used to drain the oil at required intervals. Engines usually have an oil pan that holds 4, 5 or 6 quarts (1 quart ≈ 0.946L). A pick-up screen in the oil pan is connected by a pipe to the inlet of the oil pump. See Fig.2-9-2.

a) Oil pan   b) Pick-up screen

Fig.2-9-2　Oil pan and pick-up screen

2 Oil Pump

The oil pump is located in the crankcase area so that oil can be drawn from the oil pan and sent into the engine. Oil pumps are mechanical devices used for distributing oil to the other moving parts of the engine of an automobile. More specifically, an oil pump is a pivotal part of an automobile lubrication system, which is used for dispensing pressurized oil through suction or by applying pressure. Typically, the types of oil pump are rotor oil pump, gear oil pump and internal gear oil pump. See Fig.2-9-3, Fig.2-9-4 and Fig.2-9-5.

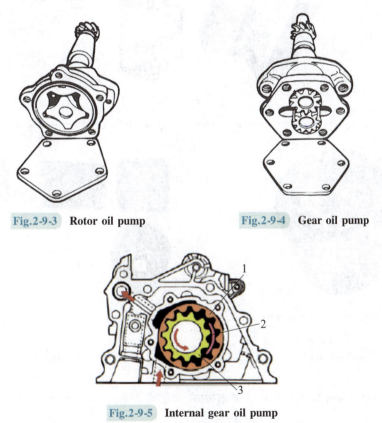

Fig.2-9-3　Rotor oil pump   Fig.2-9-4　Gear oil pump

Fig.2-9-5　Internal gear oil pump

1—driven gear(outer gear)　2—crescent　3—driving gear (inner gear)

3 Oil Pressure Relief Valve

Oil pressure relief valve is located in the oil pump housing. It is used to keep the pressure within the oil system at a constant maximum value.

4 Oil Coolers

Oil temperature for an engine should be in a certain range of degrees. Under normal conditions, oil is cooled by the right amount of oil in the oil pan. When excess temperatures occur, such as some heavy-duty gasoline engines and many diesel engines, oil coolers are used to keep the oil cool.

5 Oil Filter

Oil filter is adopted to clean the dirt particles out of the lubrication system. As the oil and dirt flow through the filter unit, contaminants are trapped inside the filter unit. It is changed when you change the engine oil. See Fig. 2-9-6, Fig. 2-9-7 and Fig. 2-9-8.

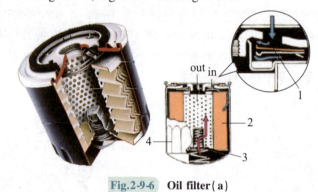

Fig.2-9-6　Oil filter(a)

1—check valve　2—element insert　3—relief valve　4—overflow valve

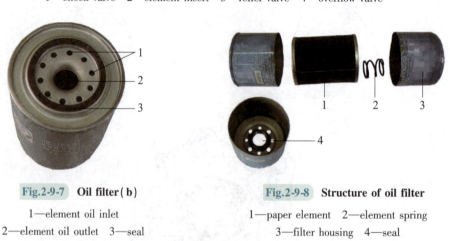

Fig.2-9-7　Oil filter(b)

1—element oil inlet
2—element oil outlet　3—seal

Fig.2-9-8　Structure of oil filter

1—paper element　2—element spring
3—filter housing　4—seal

6 Oil Pressure Sensors and Gauges

Oil pressure sensors are used to sense the oil pressure in the lubrication system. Oil pressure is usually sensed directly from the main oil gallery. The value is sent to the dashboard on the vehicle and the operator can read it. The systems commonly used are a pressure gauge and an oil indicator light. The pressure gauge reads the oil pressure within the system. The oil indicator light goes on when the oil pressure is lower than a certain value. See Fig.2-9-9.

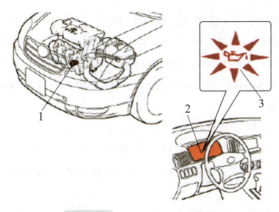

Fig.2-9-9　**Oil pressure indicator**

1—oil pressure switch　2—dashboard　3—oil indicator light

🛠 The Lubricating Oil Tube

Oil is circulated through the engine by an oil pump. Most oil pumps have two small gears that mesh with each other. A pressure-regulator valve in the pump is used to prevent the lubrication system from reaching a pressure that is too high. The oil pump pulls oil up from the oil pan through the pick-up screen. The screen collects any particles of dirt so that the oil entering the pump is fairly clean. The pump then directs the oil through an oil filter, which strains any remaining dirt out of the oil; the oil entering the engine lubrication passages should be clean. See Fig.2-9-10.

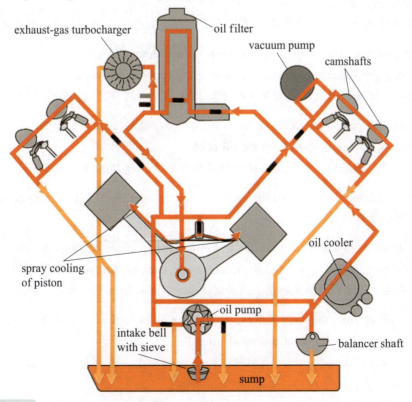

Fig.2-9-10　**Engine oil circulation for all relevant parts to provide lubrication and cooling**

The oil filter assembly is located on the outside of the cylinder block where it can be replaced easily. After the oil passes through the filter element, it reenters the engine block and then circulates into the lubrication passages. The oil filter is equipped with a bypass valve assembly. The bypass valve is used to protect the engine from a clogged filter. After the oil passes through the pump, it goes to the oil filter assembly.

When the oil leaves the filter assembly, it enters the passageways, or main galleries, running the length of the cylinder block. Oil flows down from the main galleries to the crankshaft main bearings. It lubricates them and then flows through the hollow crankshaft, lubricating each of the connecting rod bearings.

Oil also travels up from the main gallery, through the block to the camshaft bearing, to each of the cam lobe areas, and into each of the valve lifters. It is routed through the lifters and up the hollow push rods. Finally, it goes out of the top of the push rods, where it provides lubrication for the rocker arms and valve stems.

The rotating crankshaft throws off oil, which hits the cylinder wall. The piston and piston rings receive oil and distribute it over the cylinder wall for lubrication. This oil then runs back down into the oil pan to be used again.

Notes to the Text

1. We cannot eliminate internal friction, but we can reduce it to a controllable degree by the use of friction-reducing lubricants.
   我们不能消除内部摩擦，但是我们可以通过使用降低摩擦的润滑剂将其降低到可控程度。

2. More specifically, an oil pump is a pivotal part of an automobile lubrication system, which is used for dispensing pressurized oil through suction or by applying pressure.
   更具体地说，机油泵是汽车润滑系统的重要组成部分，用于通过抽吸或施压来供应高压油。

3. When excess temperatures occur, such as some heavy-duty gasoline engines and many diesel engines, oil coolers are used to keep the oil cool.
   当温度过高时，如某些大功率汽油机和许多柴油机上，使用机油冷却器来冷却机油。

4. The oil filter assembly is located on the outside of the cylinder block where it can be replaced easily.
   机油滤清器位于缸体外，以便更换。

5. Oil flows down from the main galleries to the crankshaft main bearings. It lubricates them and then flows through the hollow crankshaft, lubricating each of the connecting rod bearings.
   机油从主油道向下流到曲轴主轴承，润滑这些部件，然后经过空心曲轴，润滑每个连杆轴承。

6. Oil also travels up from the main gallery, through the block to the camshaft bearing, to each of the cam lobe areas, and into each of the valve lifters.
   机油还从主油道向上流动，通过气缸体流到凸轮轴轴承，流到每个凸轮区域，并进入每个气门挺杆。

7. The rotating crankshaft throws off oil, which hits the cylinder wall. The piston and piston rings receive oil and distribute it over the cylinder wall for lubrication.

旋转的曲轴抛甩机油，使其溅到气缸壁上。活塞和活塞环得到机油，并将其分布到整个气缸壁上来润滑。

New Words and Expressions

lubrication	/ˌluːbrɪˈkeɪʃn/	n.	润滑
lubricate	/ˈluːbrɪkeɪt/	vt.	润滑，加润滑油
circulate	/ˈsɜːkjuleɪt/	v.	循环
excessive	/ɪkˈsesɪv/	adj.	过多的，极度的；过分的
friction	/ˈfrɪkʃn/	n.	摩擦
screen	/skriːn/	n.	筛网，滤网
filter	/ˈfɪltə/	n.	过滤器，滤油器
passageway	/ˈpæsɪdʒweɪ/	n.	通道，出入口
gallery	/ˈɡæləri/	n.	通道，油道
relief	/rɪˈliːf/	n.	卸荷；减压；释放
particle	/ˈpɑːtɪkl/	n.	粒子，微粒
sense	/sens/	vt.	感到，感觉
dashboard	/ˈdæʃbɔːd/	n.	（汽车上的）仪表板
gauge	/ɡeɪdʒ/	n.	量规；仪表，量表
destruction	/dɪˈstrʌkʃn/	n.	破坏；毁灭，消灭
eliminate	/ɪˈlɪmɪneɪt/	vt.	除去，剔除，排除
controllable	/kənˈtrəʊləbl/	adj.	可管理的；可控制的；可操纵的
leakage	/ˈliːkɪdʒ/	n.	漏；漏损物；泄漏；漏损量
crescent	/ˈkresnt/	n.	月牙形
abrasive	/əˈbreɪsɪv/	n.	表面磨损，研磨剂
		adj.	磨平的

lubrication system	润滑系统	oil filter	机油滤清器
moving component	运动部件	lubrication passage	润滑油道
circulating oil	循环机油（润滑油）	bypass valve	旁通阀
compression pressure	压缩压力	relief valve	泄压阀
pick-up screen	集滤器	oil pressure switch	油压开关
splash lubrication	飞溅润滑	main oil gallery	主油道
pressure lubrication	压力润滑	oil indicator light	机油压力指示灯
grease lubrication	润滑脂润滑	pressure gauge	压力表
pressure-regulator valve	压力调节阀		

Exercises

I. Answer the following questions according to the text.

1. What's the function of the lubrication system?
2. Please name the major parts that make up the lubrication system.

3. What's the function of the oil filter?

4. Engines are lubricated in three ways, what are they?

Ⅱ. **Choose the correct answer to fill in the blanks.**

1. The job of the _____ is to distribute oil to the moving parts to reduce friction between surfaces that rub against each other.

   A. cooling system   B. ignition system

   C. starting system   D. lubrication system

2. _____ are used to sense the oil pressure in the lubrication system.

   A. Oil coolers   B. Oil filters

   C. Oil pressure relief valves   D. Oil pressure sensors

3. The _____ is located on the bottom of the engine and holds the excess oil during operation and no running conditions.

   A. oil filter   B. oil pump   C. oil pan   D. oil cooler

4. There is a (an) _____ near the oil pump that monitors pressure and sends this information to a warning light or a gauge on the dashboard.

   A. oil pressure sensor   B. oxygen sensor

   C. temperature sensor   D. speed sensor

5. As the piston moves inside the cylinder, the clearance is filled with _____ in order to move smoothly.

   A. acid   B. lime   C. oil   D. coolant

6. The _____ is the heart of the lubrication system, and is located in the oil pan on the bottom of the engine. And it pulls oil from the oil pan and makes the engine oil circulate through the engine.

   A. screened intake   B. oil filter   C. oil pump   D. oil pressure relief valve

7. Which component is the liver of the lubrication system? _____.

   A. Screened intake   B. Oil filter   C. Oil pump   D. Oil pressure relief valve

Ⅲ. **Fill in the blanks with the suitable terms according to the text.**

| oil pump | filter | fuel system | fuel pump | fuel tank | regulator |

1. The function of the _____ is to store and supply fuel to the cylinder chamber.

2. The fuel, which can be either gasoline or diesel, is stored in a _____.

3. A _____ draws the fuel from the tank through fuel lines and delivers it to either a carburetor or fuel injector, then the fuel is delivered to the cylinder chamber for combustion.

4. The _____ removes dirt or suspended particles in a liquid or in the air.

5. The _____ pulls oil up from the oil pan through the pick-up screen.

6. The _____ controls fluid flow, pressure, temperature, voltage, etc.

Ⅳ. **Translate the following sentences into Chinese.**

1. Engines are lubricated in three ways: splash lubrication, pressure lubrication and grease

lubrication.

2. The engine lubrication system supplies oil to all the friction surfaces between the engine moving parts.

3. The purpose of the lubrication system is to circulate oil between moving engine parts.

4. The engine lubrication system is designed to store, clean and circulate engine oil throughout the engine.

5. Finally, oil circulated on the cylinder walls seals the rings, improving the engine's compression.

V. Look at the picture and label it correctly using the words and phrases given below.

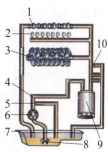

relief valve	hydraulic tappet
oil screen	oil pump
crankshaft	by pass valve
oil pan	camshaft
oil filter	main oil gallery/line

VI. Write out the terms according to the picture.

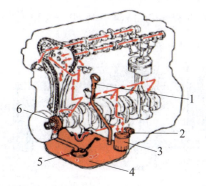

1. _____ 2. _____ 3. _____
4. _____ 5. _____ 6. _____

Unit 10 Engine Cooling System

Internal combustion engines must maintain a stable operating temperature, neither too hot nor too cold. A great deal of heat is produced in the engine by the burning of the air-fuel mixture. Some of this heat escapes from the engine through the exhaust gases (the hot gases left after the gasoline is burned), but enough remains in the engine. The engine can't work regularly if it can't cool itself properly. The cooling system takes care of this additional heat.

The purpose of the engine's cooling system is to remove excess heat from the engine, to keep the engine operating temperature at its most efficient level, and to get the engine up to the correct temperature as soon as possible after starting. A cooling system is also required to prevent the internal engine parts from melting from the heat of the burning fuel. See Fig. 2-10-1.

Fig.2-10-1 Cooling system

The cooling system is built into the engine. There are hollow spaces around each engine cylinder and combustion chamber. These hollow spaces are called water jackets, since they are filled with water. When the engine is running, the water takes heat from the engine, becoming hot in the process. A water pump pumps the hot water from the engine water jackets into the radiator. The radiator has two sets of passages. One set carries water, the other set carries air (pulled through by car motion and the engine fan). As the hot water passes through, it gives up its heat to the air passing through. The cooled water then reenters the engine, where it can pick up more heat. In operation, water continuously circulates between the engine and the radiator, carrying heat from the engine to the radiator. By this means, excess engine temperatures are prevented.

Sketch of simple circulating of cooling system is shown in Fig. 2-10-2.

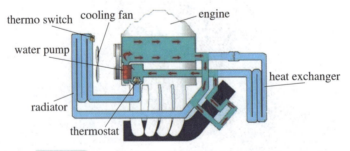

Fig.2-10-2 Sketch of simple circulating of cooling system

Generally speaking, there are two types of cooling systems: the liquid-cooling system and the air-cooling system. Fig. 2-10-3 shows the types of engine cooling systems. Nowadays, almost all kinds of engines are using the liquid-cooling system. The liquid-cooling system consists of the water pump, water jackets, engine fan, radiator, thermostat, hoses and other components.

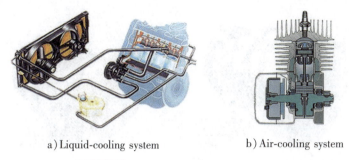

a) Liquid-cooling system   b) Air-cooling system

Fig.2-10-3   Types of engine cooling systems

1 Liquid Cooling Agent and Reserve Tank

Coolant or antifreeze is used as a cooling agent to circulate through the engine to absorb the heat and carry it to the radiator for disposal. The reserve tank is connected to the radiator so that it will reserve the overflowing coolant from the radiator. It can prevent the coolant from overflowing out. When the temperature of the coolant in the radiator rises, the coolant overflows into the reserve tank. When the radiator is cooled, it sips the coolant from the reserve tank. The position of the coolant should lie between "MAX" and "MIN". If the coolant level is below the "LOW", you should add the coolant. See Fig.2-10-4.

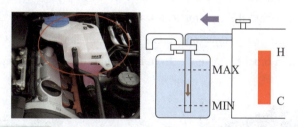

Fig.2-10-4   Liquid cooling agent and coolant recovery system

2 Water Pump

Water pump is used to circulate the coolant through the cooling system. It is mounted on the front of the cylinder block and driven by a timing belt. Coolant passages in the engine are connected to the pump. A drive belt from a crankshaft pulley is connected to the water pump. When the engine is running, the crankshaft turns the drive belt. The hot coolant is pumped out of the engine and through a heat exchanger, that is, a radiator. See Fig.2-10-5, Fig.2-10-6 and Fig.2-10-7.

Fig.2-10-5   Structure of water pump   Fig.2-10-6   Centrifugal pump

1—drain hole   2—water pump belt   3—water pump shaft   4—bearing   1—water pump shaft   2—pump impeller
  5—water pump body   6—pump impeller   7—water pump seal   3—inlet pipe   4—outlet pipe

Fig.2-10-7 Types of water pumps

3 Water Jacket

The water jacket is the open space within the cylinder block and cylinder head through which coolant passes. See Fig.2-10-8.

Fig.2-10-8 Water jacket

4 Radiator and Fan

The radiator performs the function of cooling the coolant which has passed through the water jacket and become hot, and it is mounted in the front of the vehicle. A fan is mounted behind the radiator to assist the flow of air through the radiator. The radiator consists of the radiator core, lower tank and upper tank. The fan operates when the engine coolant temperature becomes high in order to prevent it from becoming too high. See Fig.2-10-9 and Fig.2-10-10.

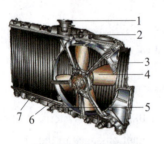

Fig.2-10-9 Radiator

1—radiator cap 2—upper tank 3—radiator core
4—fan 5—coolant drain plug
6—cooling airduct 7—lower tank

Fig.2-10-10 Structure of cooling fan

1—cooling fan 2—cooling airduct
3—electric motor

5 Radiator Cap

A relief valve (pressure valve) and a vacuum valve (negative pressure valve) are built into the radiator cap. It is used to maintain the correct and constant pressure on the cooling system. The pressure valve gives the coolant pressure. When the temperature of the coolant exceeds 100℃, there is a great difference in temperature so that it can cool the engine more efficiently.

With the pressure rising, the pressure valve opens and sends the coolant back to the reserve tank.

With the pressure dropping, the vacuum valve opens and the coolant flows out. See Fig.2-10-11.

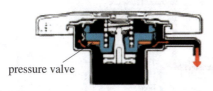
pressure valve

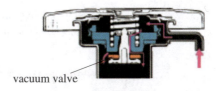
vacuum valve

a) With the pressure rising, the temperature is going up b) With the pressure dropping, the temperature is declining

Fig.2-10-11 Radiator cap

6 Thermostat

The thermostat is one of the most important parts of the cooling system. The thermostat controls the moving direction of coolant and is used to keep the engine coolant at the most efficient temperature. If the coolant remains cold, it will be closed. In this case, a large amount of coolant goes to the bypass tube without being cooled. The remaining coolant passes through the radiator to be cooled. If the coolant temperature rises to the opening point, the thermostat opens slightly. As the temperature increases further, the thermostat opens more. When the engine is under full load, the thermostat will be fully open. The maximum amount of coolant will be sent to the radiator for cooling, and a small amount will continue to flow through the bypass tube. See Fig. 2-10-12 and Fig.2-10-13.

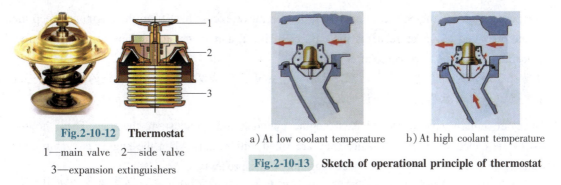

Fig.2-10-12 Thermostat
1—main valve 2—side valve
3—expansion extinguishers

a) At low coolant temperature b) At high coolant temperature

Fig.2-10-13 Sketch of operational principle of thermostat

Under the thermostat's control, there are two flowing routes in the cooling system: large circle and small circle. In the small circle condition, the temperature of the coolant is low, the thermostat prevents the coolant from going through the radiator. In the large circle condition, the temperature of the coolant is too high, the thermostat makes the coolant go through the radiator to cool it.

Fig.2-10-14 shows the coolant circulating routes, Fig.2-10-15 shows the cooling cycle to ensure that the engine keeps the best temperature.

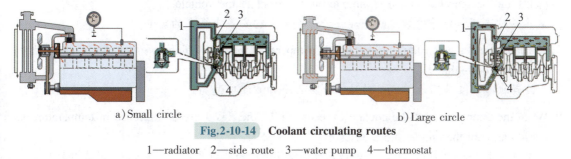

a) Small circle   b) Large circle

Fig.2-10-14 Coolant circulating routes
1—radiator 2—side route 3—water pump 4—thermostat

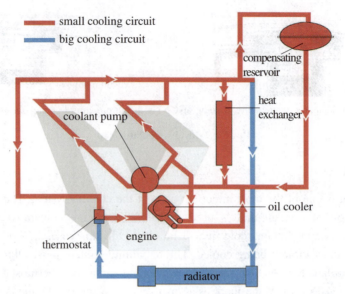

Fig.2-10-15 Cooling cycle to ensure that the engine keeps the best temperature

Notes to the Text

1. The purpose of the engine's cooling system is to remove excess heat from the engine, to keep the engine operating temperature at its most efficient level, and to get the engine up to the correct temperature as soon as possible after starting.
   发动机冷却系的用途是消除发动机产生的多余热量；保持发动机工作在最佳的温度水平上；使发动机在起动后尽快达到合适的温度。

2. There are hollow spaces around each engine cylinder and combustion chamber. These hollow spaces are called water jackets, since they are filled with water. When the engine is running, the water takes heat from the engine, becoming hot in the process.
   在每个气缸体和燃烧室周围都有空腔，这些空腔装满了水，因此称之为水套。在发动机运行过程中水被加热，并以水循环方式把热量从发动机中带走。

3. Coolant or antifreeze is used as a cooling agent to circulate through the engine to absorb the heat and carry it to the radiator for disposal.
   冷却液或防冻液作为冷却介质在发动机内循环，吸收热量并由散热器消除热量。

4. The radiator performs the function of cooling the coolant which has passed through the water jacket and become hot, and it is mounted in the front of the vehicle.
   散热器对流经水套并被加热的冷却液进行冷却，它安装在汽车的前部。

5. The fan operates when the engine coolant temperature becomes high in order to prevent it from becoming too high.
   当发动机冷却液升温后，风扇转动，以防止冷却液温度过高。

6. When the temperature of the coolant exceeds 100℃, there is a great difference in temperature so that it can cool the engine more efficiently.
   冷却液温度升至100℃以上时，冷却液温度和空气温度的差别更大，这样可以改善冷却效果。

7. In the small circle condition, the temperature of the coolant is low, the thermostat prevents the coolant from going through the radiator. In the large circle condition, the temperature of the coolant is too high, the thermostat makes the coolant go through the radiator to cool it.

小循环时，冷却液温度较低，节温器阻止冷却液通过散热器；大循环时，冷却液温度过高，节温器使冷却液通过散热器冷却。

New Words and Expressions

coolant	/ˈkuːlənt/	n.	冷却液，冷却剂
cooler	/ˈkuːlə/	n.	冷却器
removal	/riˈmuːvəl/	n.	移动，消除
excess	/ikˈses/	adj.	过度的，过剩的，过量的
fin	/fin/	n.	（散热器冷却）片
fan	/fæn/	n.	风扇
thermostat	/ˈθɜːməstæt/	n.	节温器，恒温器
jacket	/ˈdʒækit/	n.	（水、护）套，（保护）罩
radiator	/ˈreidieitə/	n.	散热器，水箱
hose	/həuz/	n.	软管
load	/ləud/	n.	负荷；装载量；负载，加载
		v.	装载

operating temperature	工作温度	radiator hose	散热器软管
liquid-cooling	液冷式，液体冷却式	radiator cap	散热器盖
air-cooling	风冷式，空气冷却式	coolant recovery system	冷却液回收系统
circulating fluid	循环流体	coolant passage	冷却液通路
heat exchanger	热交换器	center core	（散热器）芯
water pump	水泵，冷却液泵		

Exercises

Ⅰ. **Answer the following questions according to the text.**

1. What's the function of the cooling system?
2. Please name the major components that make up the liquid-cooling system.
3. What's the function of the radiator?
4. What does a liquid-cooling system mean?
5. How to define the full circulation?

Ⅱ. **Choose the correct answer to fill in the blanks.**

1. The cooling system controls temperature through _____.
   A. heat transfer B. airflow C. sensor D. ECU
2. The cooling system transfers heat from the engine to the _____.
   A. coolant B. circulating coolant
   C. circulation D. coolant circulating

3. The basic components of a _____ are radiator, radiator cooling fans, pressure cap and reserve tank, water pump and thermostat.

  A. cooling system   B. ignition system

  C. starting system   D. lubrication system

4. What is the cooling agent in the liquid cooling system? _____.

  A. Coolant   B. Air   C. Lubrication   D. Gasoline

5. Which component is not included in the cooling system? _____.

  A. Water pump   B. Thermostat   C. Radiator   D. Sump

6. Which component is driven by the engine through one of the fans or the timing belts? _____.

  A. Water pump   B. Thermostat

  C. Water temperature sensor   D. Bypass valve

7. To avoid loss of antifreeze due to expansion, the cooling system _____.

  A. must not be completely filled   B. must install a bypass valve

  C. must install a pressure control valve D. must be sealed

8. The engine coolant level is checked when the engine is _____ only.

  A. hot   B. warm   C. cold   D. cool

Ⅲ. Translate the following phrases into Chinese or English.

1. coolant recovery system   _____
2. operating temperature   _____
3. liquid-cooling   _____
4. heat exchanger   _____
5. radiator hose   _____
6. center core   _____
7. 冷却液通路   _____
8. 风冷式,空气冷却式   _____
9. 循环流体   _____
10. 水泵,冷却液泵   _____
11. 散热器盖   _____

Ⅳ. Translate the following passage into Chinese.

  As fuel is burning in the engine, about one-third of the energy in the fuel is converted into power. Another third goes out through the exhaust pipe unused, and the remaining third must be handled by the cooling system. This means that the engine can work effectively only when the heat energy is equally handled so as to keep the engine temperature in balance.

_____

_____

_____

_____

Chapter 2 Engine

V. Read the following abbreviations and translate them into corresponding Chinese terms.

1. LO   lubricating oil   _____
2. CC   coolant control   _____
3. LLC   long life coolant   _____
4. OLB   oil-lubricated bearing _____
5. ODI   oil drain intervals   _____

VI. Look at the pictures and label them correctly using the words and phrases given below.

Picture 1

| fluid reservoir | radiator | radiator cap | lower hose | fan |
| thermostat | water pump | upper hose | coolant | |

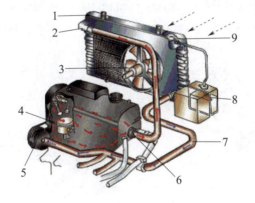

Picture 2

| transmission oil cooler | coolant flow | top tank |
| bottom tank | cooling tubes | radiator cap |

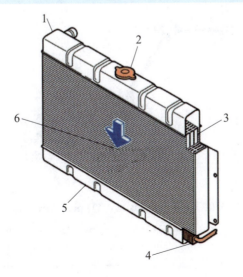

083

Chapter 3

Chassis

Unit 1 Power Train System

The power train serves two functions: it transmits power from the engine to the drive wheels, and it varies the amount of torque. The power train system can be classified into FF, FR, MR, four-wheel drive (4WD) and so on. FF and FR are widely used on vehicles. MR is mainly used on racers. 4WD is mainly used in cross-country vehicles and luxury sedans. See Fig. 3-1-1, Fig. 3-1-2 and Fig. 3-1-3.

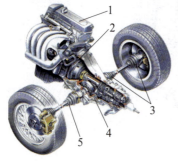

Fig.3-1-1 Components of FF power train system

1—engine 2—clutch 3—drive shaft cover
4—transaxle 5—drive shaft

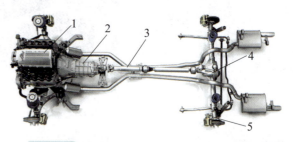

Fig.3-1-2 Components of FR power train system

1—engine 2—transmission 3—drive shaft
4—rear axle 5—half shaft

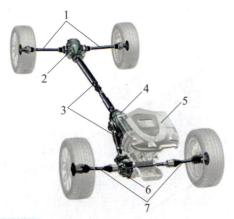

Fig.3-1-3 Components of 4WD power train system

1—rear half shaft 2—rear axle 3—drive shaft 4—transmission
5—engine 6—front differential 7—front half shaft

The automobile transmission system mainly consists of the following components:

1) Engine: that produces power.
2) Transmission: either manual or automatic.
3) Clutch: used only on manual transmission, or torque converter used only on automatic transmission.
4) Drive shaft: that transmits the power from the transmission to the differential.
5) Differential: that carries the power to the two wheel axles. See Fig.3-1-4.

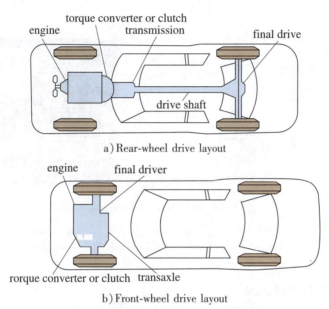

a) Rear-wheel drive layout

b) Front-wheel drive layout

Fig.3-1-4　Power train arrangement

1 Manual Transmission

Although modern automatic transmissions used on automotive vehicles vary in detail, they all operate in a similar manner.

The function of a manual transmission, shown in Fig.3-1-5, is to transfer engine power to the drive shaft and rear wheels. The transmission provides different gear ratios between the engine and wheels. This is necessary with the gasoline engine, since the engine produces little power at low speed. Thus, for accelerating the car from a standing start, considerable power is required; the engine should be running at a fairly high speed. The driver, therefore, shifts the transmission gears into first; this gear position permits the engine to run at a fairly high speed. A typical first-gear ratio would be that the engine shaft turns 12 times to turn the rear wheel once. Thus, the engine develops high power, and the car moves away from the curb and accelerates quickly. In second, the car accelerates to a higher speed and the typical ratio would be 8∶1. Finally, the driver shifts to third. In this gear position, there is a direct drive through the transmission; the propeller shaft turns at the

Fig.3-1-5　Position of the transmission (FF)
1—engine　2—transmission　3—drive shaft

same speed as the engine crankshaft. In third, a typical ratio would be 1∶1. There is another gear position, reverse. In this position, the propeller shaft is made to rotate in a reverse direction so that the car goes backward.

Manual transmissions usually have four or five speeds, and often have "overdrive", which means that the output shaft can turn faster than the input shaft for fuel economy on the highway. When you use it, it will reduce the engine speed by one-third, while maintaining the same road speed. See Fig. 3-1-6.

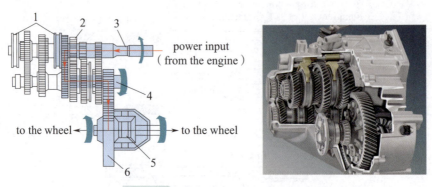

Fig.3-1-6　Structure of the transmission

1—synchronizer　2—speed-change gear　3—input shaft
4—out put shaft　5—differential assembly　6—final gear

2 Automatic Transmission

Both an automatic transmission and a manual transmission accomplish exactly the same thing. In automatic transmissions, the varying ratios between the engine crankshaft and the wheels are achieved by automatic means. That is, the driver does not need to shift gears because the automatic controls on the automatic transmission supply the proper ratio to suit the driving condition.

Automatic transmissions are used in many rear-wheel drive and four-wheel drive vehicles. Automatic transaxles are used in most front-wheel drive vehicles. The major components of a transaxle are the same as those in a transmission, except the transaxle assembly includes the final drive and differential gears, in addition to the transmission.

An automatic transmission receives engine power through a torque converter, which is driven by the engine's crankshaft. Hydraulic pressure in the converter allows power to flow from the torque converter to the transmission's input shaft. The input shaft drives a planetary gear set that provides the different forward gears, a neutral position, and one reverse gear. Power flow through the gears is controlled by multi-disk clutches, one-way clutches and friction bands.

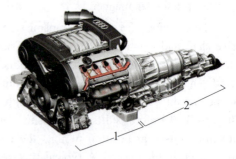

Fig.3-1-7　Position of the automatic transmission (FR vehicle type)

1—engine　2—automatic transmission

See Fig.3-1-7, Fig.3-1-8 and Fig.3-1-9.

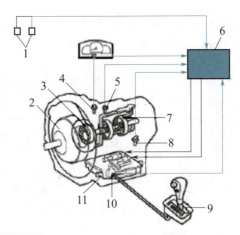

Fig.3-1-8 Components of the automatic transmission

1—sensor   2—torque converter   3—oil pump   4—speed sensor   5—counter gear speed sensor (output)
6—ECU   7—planetary gear   8—turbine speed sensor (input)   9—change lever
10—hydraulic control unit   11—magnet valve

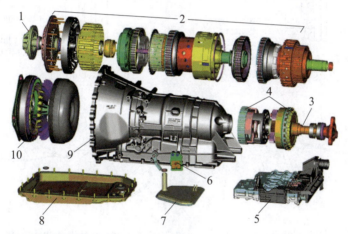

Fig.3-1-9 Internal structure of the automatic transmission

1—oil pump   2—clutch and arrester parts   3—output shaft   4—planetary gear   5—main valve body
6—shift position console switch   7—oil filter   8—oil pan   9—transmission housing   10—torque converter

3 Clutch

The clutch is located in the power train between the engine and the transmission. The function of the clutch when used in an automotive application is to connect or disconnect the power from the engine's crankshaft with or from the gearbox and transmission.

Driving a car with a manual transmission, you depress the clutch, select a gear, and release the clutch while applying power to get the car to move. The clutch allows engine power to be applied gradually when a vehicle is starting out, and interrupts power to avoid gear crunching when shifting. Engaging the clutch allows power to transfer from the engine to the transmission and drive wheels. Disengaging the clutch stops the power transfer and allows the engine to continue turning without force to the drive wheels.

The major components of the clutch include the flywheel, clutch disk, cover assembly, pressure plate, release bearing and clutch linkage. See Fig.3-1-10, Fig.3-1-11 and Fig.3-1-12.

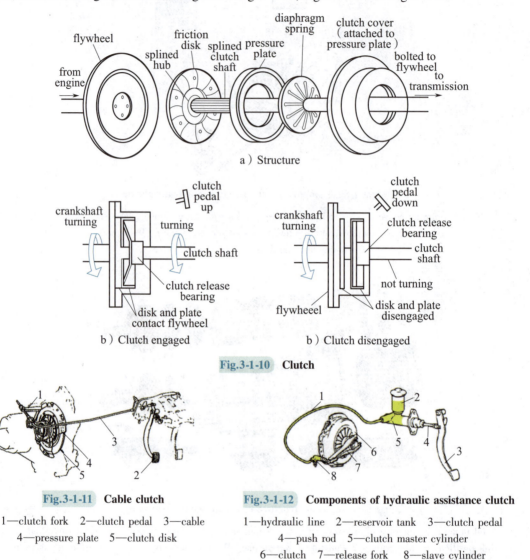

Fig.3-1-10 Clutch

Fig.3-1-11 Cable clutch
1—clutch fork 2—clutch pedal 3—cable
4—pressure plate 5—clutch disk

Fig.3-1-12 Components of hydraulic assistance clutch
1—hydraulic line 2—reservoir tank 3—clutch pedal
4—push rod 5—clutch master cylinder
6—clutch 7—release fork 8—slave cylinder

The flywheel is bolted to the crankshaft of the engine. Its main function is to transfer engine torque from the engine to the transmission.

The clutch disk is basically a steel plate, covered with a frictional material that goes between the flywheel and the pressure plate.

A pressure plate is bolted to the flywheel. It includes a sheet metal cover, heavy release springs, a metal pressure ring that provides a friction surface for the clutch disk.

The release bearing is the heart of the clutch operation. When the clutch pedal is depressed, the throw-out bearing moves toward the flywheel, pushing in the pressure plate's release fingers and moving the pressure plate fingers or levers against the pressure plate spring force.

The clutch cover assembly contains the pressure plate, springs and other parts according to the design of the clutch. The cover is bolted to the flywheel and rotates with it at crankshaft speed.

The linkage transmits and multiplies the driver's leg force to the fork of the clutch pressure plate.

4 Torque Converter

The key to the modern automatic transmission is the torque converter. It takes the place of a clutch in a manual transmission to send the power from the engine to the transmission input shaft. The torque converter offers the advantage of multiplying the turning power provided by the engine.

It has three parts that help multiply the power: an impeller (or pump) connected to the engine's crankshaft, a turbine to turn the turbine shaft which is connected to the gears, and a stator (or guide wheel) between the two. See Fig. 3-1-13.

The torque converter is filled with transmission fluid that is moved by the impeller blades. The stator's vanes catch the oil thrown off from the impeller, and use it to move the turbine's blades. When the impeller spins above a certain speed, the turbine spins, driven by the impeller.

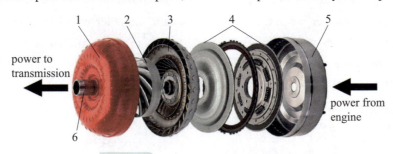

Fig.3-1-13   Structure of torque converter

1—impeller   2—stator   3—turbine   4—lock-up clutch   5—case   6—drive interface

5 Planetary Gearing

Planetary gears provide for the different gear ratios needed to move a vehicle in the desired direction at the correct speed. A planetary gear set consists of a sun gear, planet gears and an internal ring. See Fig.3-1-14.

In the center of the planetary gear set is the sun gear. Planet gears surround the sun gear, just like the earth and other planets in our solar system. These gears are mounted and supported by the planet carrier and each gear spins on its own separate shaft. The planet gears are in constant mesh with the sun and ring gears.

The planetary gear set can provide a gear reduction or overdrive, direct drive or reverse, or a neutral position.

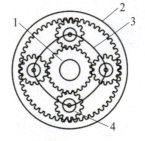

Fig.3-1-14   Planetary gear set

1—sun gear   2—ring gear
3—planetary gear carrier   4—planetary gear

6 Differential

On FWD cars, the differential unit is normally part of the transaxle assembly. On RWD cars, it is part of the rear axle assembly. Located inside the differential case are the differential pinion shafts and gears and the differential side gears. See Fig.3-1-15.

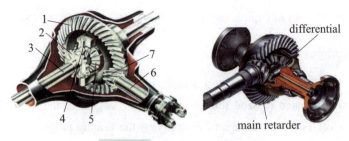

Fig.3-1-15 Ordinary differential

1—driven gear 2—left half shaft gear 3—output shaft 4—pinion gear
5—right half shaft gear 6—transmission shaft 7—driving gear

The differential assembly revolves with the ring gear. Axle side gears are splined to the rear axle or front axle drive shafts, which include the differential, rear axles, wheels and bearings.

If the car were to be driven in a straight line without having to make turns, then no differential would be necessary. However, when the car rounds a turn, the outer wheel must travel farther than the inner wheel. The differential permits the two rear wheels to rotate different amounts when the car goes around a turn, while still delivering power to both rear wheels.

See Fig.3-1-16 and Fig. 3-1-17.

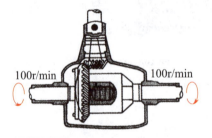

Fig.3-1-16 A car is moving straight

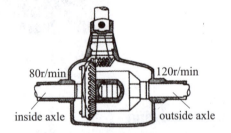

Fig.3-1-17 A car turns a sharp corner

New Words and Expressions

vary	/ˈvɛəri/	vt.	改变，变更
manual	/ˈmænjuəl/	adj.	手的，手动的
automatic	/ˌɔːtəˈmætik/	adj.	自动的
		n.	自动装置
clutch	/klʌtʃ/	n.	离合器
converter	/kənˈvəːtə/	n.	变换器
differential	/ˌdifəˈrenʃəl/	n.	差速器
axle	/ˈæksl/	n.	轮轴，车轴
transfer	/trænsˈfəː/	vt.	传递，传导
gear	/giə/	n.	齿轮，传动装置
transaxle	/trænsˈæksl/	n.	驱动桥（与变速器连成一体，用于前轮驱动的汽车）
depress	/diˈpres/	vt.	压下
interrupt	/ˌintəˈrʌpt/	vt.	中断
engage	/inˈgeidŋ/	vt.	接合，啮合
disengage	/ˌdisinˈgeidŋ/	v.	脱离啮合

linkage	/ˈlinkidŋ/	n.	联接
frictional	/ˈfrikʃnəl/	adj.	摩擦的，摩擦力的
bolt	/bəult/	v.	用螺栓固定
accomplish	/əˈkɔmpliʃ/	vt.	完成，达到，实现
achieve	/əˈtʒiːv/	vt.	完成，获得
planetary	/ˈplænitri/	adj.	行星的
component	/kəmˈpəunənt/	n.	部件，零件
shift	/ʃift/	vt.	变速，变档
gearshift	/ˈgiəʃift/	n.	变速杆
reverse	/riˈvəːs/	n.	倒档
neutral	/ˈnjuːtrəl/	n.	空档
park	/pɑːk/	n.	驻车档
deceleration	/ˌdiːseləˈreiʃn/	n.	减速

power train	传动系	one-way clutch	单向离合器
drive wheel	驱动轮	clutch pedal	离合器踏板
manual transmission	手动变速器	release bearing	分离轴承
torque converter	液力变矩器	impeller blade	泵轮叶片
automatic transmission	自动变速器	sun gear	太阳齿轮，中心齿轮
manual transaxle	手动变速驱动桥	planetary gear	行星齿轮
front-wheel drive（FWD）	前轮驱动	ring gear	齿圈
rear-wheel drive（RWD）	后轮驱动	gear reduction ratio	齿轮减速比
four-wheel drive（4WD）	四轮驱动	transaxle assembly	驱动桥总成
planetary gear set	行星齿轮组	rear axle assembly	后桥总成
final drive	主减速器	rear axle drive shaft	后桥驱动轴
differential gear	差速器	front axle drive shaft	前桥驱动轴
multi-disk clutches	多盘式离合器	drive shaft	驱动轴

Notes to the Text

1. Manual transmissions usually have four or five speeds, and often have "overdrive", which means that the output shaft can turn faster than the input shaft for fuel economy on the highway.
   手动变速器通常有四个或五个档位。还有"超速档"，就是说输出轴比输入轴转速快，以求行驶燃油经济性。

2. The clutch allows engine power to be applied gradually when a vehicle is starting out, and interrupts power to avoid gear crunching when shifting.
   离合器使发动机动力在起动汽车时逐步产生。在换档时，切断动力，以免齿轮打齿。

3. When the clutch pedal is depressed, the throw-out bearing moves toward the flywheel, pushing in the pressure plate's release fingers and moving the pressure plate fingers or levers against the pressure plate spring force.
   踩离合器踏板时，分离轴承朝飞轮方向移动，挤入压盘的分离指中，使压盘分离指或杆抵住压盘弹簧力。

4. The torque converter is filled with transmission fluid that is moved by the impeller blades.
   液力变矩器里面充满了变速器油，靠泵轮叶片流动。

5. Planetary gears provide for the different gear ratios needed to move a vehicle in the desired direction at the correct speed.
   行星齿轮提供所需的不同速比，使汽车以正确的车速朝着预想的方向行驶。

6. If the car were to be driven in a straight line without having to make turns, then no differential would be necessary.
   如果汽车按直线行驶，就不需要差速器了。

7. The differential permits the two rear wheels to rotate different amounts when the car goes around a turn, while still delivering power to both rear wheels.
   差速器可在汽车转弯时，使两个后轮以不同的转速转动，同时还向两个后轮提供动力。

Exercises

Ⅰ. Answer the following questions according to the text.

1. What's the function of the power train? What does the power train consist of?
2. What's the function of a manual transmission?
3. What are the three elements of a planetary gear set?
4. What's the character of the typical automatic transmission?
5. How does the differential work when the car begins to round a curve?
6. Please describe the principle of the torque converter.

Ⅱ. Choose the correct answer to fill in the blanks.

1. The major parts of the _____ include the transmission case, input shaft, output shaft, countershaft, driving gear, transmission fork, etc.
   A. transmission   B. clutch   C. torque converter   D. fuel filter

2. The basic _____ consists of a sun gear, a ring gear and two or more planet gears, all remaining in constant mesh.
   A. clutch   B. automatic transmission
   C. engine   D. planetary gear set

3. The _____ is connected to the planet carrier which is also connected to a "multi-disk" clutch pack.
   A. input shaft   B. countershaft
   C. output shaft   D. planet gear

4. The transmission is used to change the ratio between _____ speed and driving wheels speed.
   A. transmission   B. clutch   C. engine   D. torque converter

5. The _____ acts like a clutch to allow the vehicle to come to a stop in gear while the engine is still running.
   A. one-way clutch   B. fuel pressure regulator
   C. hydrodynamic torque converter   D. air cleaner

III. Translate the following phrases into English or Chinese.

1. planetary gear set　　　　＿＿＿＿＿＿＿＿＿＿＿＿＿＿＿＿
2. final drive　　　　　　　　＿＿＿＿＿＿＿＿＿＿＿＿＿＿＿＿
3. differential gear　　　　　＿＿＿＿＿＿＿＿＿＿＿＿＿＿＿＿
4. manual transmission　　　＿＿＿＿＿＿＿＿＿＿＿＿＿＿＿＿
5. gear reduction ratio　　　＿＿＿＿＿＿＿＿＿＿＿＿＿＿＿＿
6. 液力变矩器　　　　　　　　＿＿＿＿＿＿＿＿＿＿＿＿＿＿＿＿
7. 行星齿轮　　　　　　　　　＿＿＿＿＿＿＿＿＿＿＿＿＿＿＿＿
8. 自动变速器　　　　　　　　＿＿＿＿＿＿＿＿＿＿＿＿＿＿＿＿
9. 驱动桥总成　　　　　　　　＿＿＿＿＿＿＿＿＿＿＿＿＿＿＿＿
10. 单向离合器　　　　　　　　＿＿＿＿＿＿＿＿＿＿＿＿＿＿＿＿

IV. Read the following abbreviations and translate them into corresponding Chinese terms.

1. AT　　　　automatic transmission　　　　＿＿＿＿＿＿＿＿＿＿
2. MT　　　　manual transmission　　　　　＿＿＿＿＿＿＿＿＿＿
3. ATF　　　 automatic transmission fluid　　＿＿＿＿＿＿＿＿＿＿
4. PO　　　　power output　　　　　　　　 ＿＿＿＿＿＿＿＿＿＿
5. PCM　　　power train control module　　＿＿＿＿＿＿＿＿＿＿
6. PTU　　　power transfer unit　　　　　　＿＿＿＿＿＿＿＿＿＿
7. FWD　　　front-wheel drive　　　　　　　＿＿＿＿＿＿＿＿＿＿
8. RWD　　　rear-wheel drive　　　　　　　 ＿＿＿＿＿＿＿＿＿＿

V. The following picture shows the internal structure of the automatic transmission. Look at the picture and label it correctly using the words and phrases given below.

clutch and arrester parts	transmission housing	output shaft	
shift position console switch	planetary gear	oil filter	
main valve body	torque converter	oil pump	oil pan

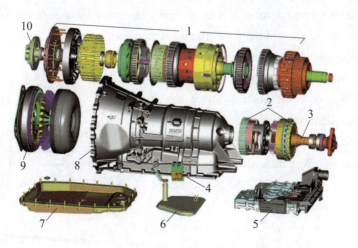

Ⅵ. **The following picture shows the components of the FR power train system. Write out the terms according to the picture.**

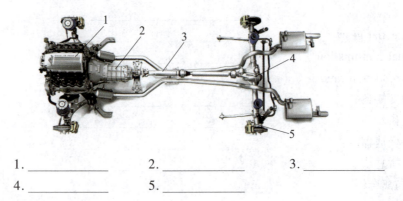

1. _____ 2. _____ 3. _____
4. _____ 5. _____

Unit 2　Braking System

1 Introduction of Braking System

Stopping of the vehicle is as necessary as its starting. Once the vehicle is started, it must be stopped somewhere. Brakes are applied on the wheels to stop the vehicle. The braking system is the most important system for the vehicle. The function of the braking system is to slow down or bring to rest a moving vehicle in the shortest possible distance, or to hold the vehicle stationary if already halted. If the brakes don't work properly, the result can be disastrous. So good brakes are essential for safety.

There are two kinds of braking systems: service brake system and parking brake system. A service brake system can slow down or even stop the car that is running at a high speed and guarantee the safety of passengers. It is foot-operated by the driver depressing and releasing the brake pedal. The primary purpose of the parking brake is to hold the vehicle stationary while it is unattended. The parking brake system is mechanically operated by a separate parking brake foot pedal or hand lever. It can prevent the auto slipping away from its parking place, even if it is parked on a steep slope. It is also called the hand brake.

Basically, all car brakes are friction brakes. When the driver applies the brake, the control device forces brake shoes, or pads, against the rotating brake drums or disks at the wheels. Friction between the shoes or pads and the drums or disks then slows or stops the wheels so that the car is braked. The principle of braking is shown in Fig. 3-2-1.

The braking system assemblies are actuated by mechanical, hydraulic or pneumatic devices. The me-

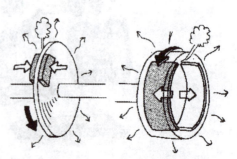

Fig.3-2-1　**Principle of braking**

chanical leverage is used in the parking brakes fitted in all automobiles. When the brake pedal is depressed, the rod pushes the piston of the brake master cylinder which presses the fluid. The fluid flows through the pipelines to the power brake unit and then to the wheel cylinder. The fluid pressure expands the cylinder piston thus pressing the shoes to the drum or disk. If the pedal is released, the piston returns to the initial position, the pull-back springs retract the shoes, the fluid is forced back to the master cylinder and braking ceases.

2 Disk Brake

The disk brake is the best brake we have found so far. In recent years, brakes have changed greatly in design. Disk brakes, used for years for front wheel applications, are fast replacing drum brakes on the rear wheels of modern cars. This is generally due to their simpler design, lighter weight and better braking performance. The greatest advantage of disk brakes is that they provide significantly better resistance to "brake fade" compared to drum-type braking systems.

The disk brake has a metal disk instead of a drum. A flat shoe, or disk-brake pad, is located on each side of the disk. The shoes squeeze the rotating disk to stop the car. Fluid from the master cylinder forces the pistons to move in, toward the disk. This action pushes the friction pads tightly against the disk. The friction between the shoes and the disk slows and stops it. This provides the braking action. Pistons are made of either plastic or metal.

The main components of a disk brake are: brake pads, caliper (which contains a piston) and disk or rotor (which is mounted to the hub). See Fig. 3-2-2.

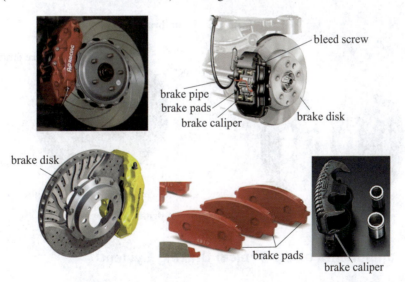

Fig.3-2-2　Erection diagram and components of disk brake

There are three general types of disk brakes. They are the floating-caliper type, the fixed-caliper type and the sliding-caliper type. Floating-caliper and sliding-caliper disk brakes use a single piston. Fixed-caliper disk brakes have either two or four pistons.

If disk brakes are so great, how come we still have cars with drum brakes? The reason is costs.

While all vehicles produced for many years have disk brakes on the front, drum brakes are cheaper to produce for the rear wheels. The main reason is the parking brake system.

3 Drum Brake

The drum brake consists of the brake drum, an expander, pull-back springs, a stationary back plate, two shoes with friction linings and anchor pins. See Fig.3-2-3 and Fig.3-2-4. The stationary back plate is secured to the flange of the axle housing or to the steering knuckle. The brake drum is mounted on the wheel hub. There is a clearance between the inner surface of the drum and the shoe lining. To apply brakes, the driver pushes the pedal, and the expander expands the shoes and presses them to the drum. Friction between the brake drum and the friction linings brakes the wheels and the vehicle stops. To release the brakes, the driver releases the pedal, the pull-back spring retracts the shoes thus permitting free rotation of the wheels.

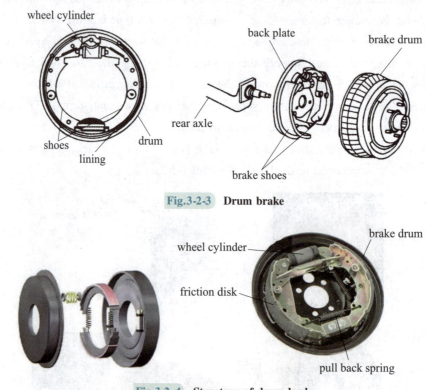

Fig.3-2-3 Drum brake

Fig.3-2-4 Structure of drum brake

4 Basic Components of the Typical Braking System

（1）Master Cylinder

Master cylinder is located under the hood, and is directly connected to the brake pedal, converting your foot's mechanical pressure into hydraulic pressure.

In the modern braking system, the master cylinder is power-assisted by the engine. The master cylinder is located in the engine compartment on the firewall, directly in front of the driver's seat. A typical master cylinder has actually two completely separate master cylinders in one housing, each handling two wheels. That is to say, if one side fails, you will still be able to stop the car. The brake warning light on the dash will light if either side fails, alerting you to the problem. Master cylinders have become very reliable and rarely malfunction; however, the most common problem that they experience is an internal leak. This will cause the brake pedal to slowly sink to the floor when your foot applies steady pressure. Letting go of the pedal and immediately stepping on it again brings the pedal back to normal height.

Rear-wheel drive vehicles use a dual split master cylinder. Dual split master cylinders use two separate pressure-building sections. One section operates the front brakes and the other section operates the rear brakes on vehicles equipped with a front or rear split system. See Fig. 3-2-5.

Front-wheel drive vehicles use a diagonal split master cylinder. In this design, one section of the master cylinder operates the right front and the left rear brakes and the other section operates the left front and right rear. In the event of a failure in one section, at least one front brake will still function. See Fig. 3-2-6.

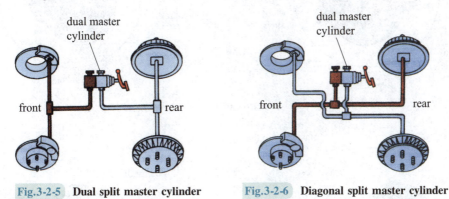

Fig.3-2-5　Dual split master cylinder　　Fig.3-2-6　Diagonal split master cylinder

（2）Brake Lines and Brake Hoses

Brake lines and brake hoses connect the master cylinder to the wheel cylinders located at each wheel. The brake fluid travels from the master cylinder to the wheels through a series of steel tubes and reinforced rubber hoses. Rubber hoses are only used in places that require flexibility, such as at the front wheels, which move up and down as well as steer.

（3）Brake Fluid

Brake fluid is specially designed to work in extreme conditions and fills the system.

Brake fluid is special oil that has specific properties. It is designed to withstand cold temperatures without thickening as well as very high temperatures without boiling. If the brake fluid boils, it will cause you to have a spongy pedal and the car will be hard to stop.

（4）Shoes and Pads

Shoes and pads are pushed by the wheel cylinders to contact the drums or disks thus causing braking force, which makes cars slow down or stops the moving car.

Fig. 3-2-7 shows a typical braking system with all typical components. These are known as service brakes, base brakes, or foundation brakes. Fig. 3-2-8 shows the typical braking system components with disk brakes on the front and drum brakes on the rear.

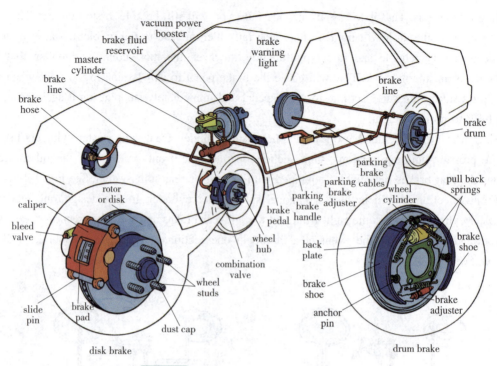

Fig.3-2-7 Structure of typical braking system

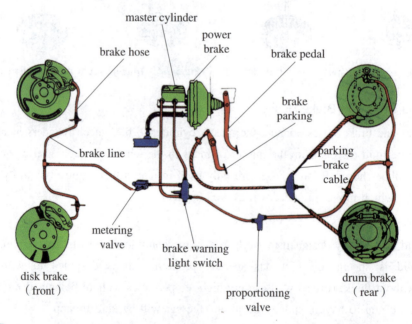

Fig.3-2-8 Typical braking system components with disk brakes on the front and drum brakes on the rear

Notes to the Text

1. The function of the braking system is to slow down or bring to rest a moving vehicle in the shortest possible distance, or to hold the vehicle stationary if already halted.
制动系统的功能是使汽车减速或在尽可能短的距离内停车，或保持已停止的车辆处于静止状态。

2. The parking brake system is mechanically operated by a separate parking brake foot pedal or hand lever. It can prevent the auto slipping away from its parking place, even if it is parked on a steep slope.
   驻车制动系是机械装置，它设置成独立的驻车制动踏板或手动杆件。它的用途是在汽车无人看管时，使汽车保持静止状态，防止汽车在不平场地溜车。

3. If the pedal is released, the piston returns to the initial position, the pull-back springs retract the shoes, the fluid is forced back to the master cylinder and braking ceases.
   如果松开制动踏板，活塞回位，回位弹簧拉回制动蹄，制动液被压回制动主缸，便解除制动。

4. There are three general types of disk brakes. They are the floating-caliper type, the fixed-caliper type and the sliding-caliper type.
   通常有三种类型的盘式制动器，即浮钳式、固定卡钳式和移动卡钳式。

5. The drum brake consists of the brake drum, an expander, pull-back springs, a stationary back plate, two shoes with friction linings and anchor pins.
   鼓式制动系统由制动鼓、伸张器、回位弹簧、制动底板、带两个摩擦衬片的制动蹄和定位销组成。

6. Front-wheel drive vehicles use a diagonal split master cylinder. In this design, one section of the master cylinder operates the right front and the left rear brakes and the other section operates the left front and right rear.
   前轮驱动汽车使用对角分配制动缸。在这种设计中，制动缸的一部分操控右前轮和左后轮的制动，而另一部分则操控左前轮和右后轮的制动。

7. Rubber hoses are only used in places that require flexibility, such as at the front wheels, which move up and down as well as steer.
   橡胶软管只用在需要柔性的地方，如可以上下运动以及转向的前轮。

8. Shoes and pads are pushed by the wheel cylinders to contact the drums or disks thus causing braking force, which makes cars slow down or stops the moving car.
   制动蹄和制动摩擦块由轮缸推动使其与制动鼓或制动盘接触，从而产生制动力，使汽车减速或停止。

New Words and Expressions

brake	/breik/	n.	制动器
		v.	制动
pedal	/ˈpedl/	n.	踏板
		v.	踩……的踏板
stationary	/ˈsteiʃənəri/	adj.	静止的，固定的
unleveled	/ʌnˈlev(ə)ld/	adj.	不平坦的，有坡度的
friction	/ˈfrikʃn/	n.	摩擦，摩擦力
pad	/pæd/	n.	(摩擦)衬块
drum	/drʌm/	n.	(制动)鼓
disk	/disk/	n.	圆板，圆盘，(制动)盘
resistance	/riˈzistəns/	n.	阻力
caliper	/ˈkælipə/	n.	卡钳

hydraulic	/haiˈdrɔːlik/	adj.	液力的，液压的
lining	/ˈlainiŋ/	n.	衬片
compartment	/kəmˈpɑːtmənt/	n.	室，舱
firewall	/ˈfaiəwɔːl/	n.	防火墙
alert	/əˈləːt/	v.	警报
dash	/dæʃ/	n.	仪表板
malfunction	/mælˈfʌŋkʃn/	n.	故障
reinforce	/ˌriːinˈfɔːs/	vt.	加强，补充
anchor	/ˈæŋkə/	vt.	抛锚；使固定
knuckle	/ˈnʌk(ə)l/	n.	关节；指节；转向节；转向节臂
pneumatic	/njuːˈmætik/	n.	气胎
		adj.	气动的；充气的；有气胎的
initial	/iˈniʃəl/	n.	词首大写字母
		adj.	最初的；字首的
retract	/riˈtrækt/	vt./vi.	缩回；缩进；取消
expander	/ikˈspændə/	n.	扩展器；膨胀器

service brake	行车制动系	hydraulic pressure	液压
parking brake	驻车制动系	brake line	制动管路
brake pedal	制动踏板	brake hose	制动软管
hand brake	手制动器	engine compartment	发动机舱
brake shoe	制动蹄	brake warning light	制动警告灯
disk brake	盘式制动器	power brake booster	制动助力器
drum brake	鼓式制动器	pull back spring	回位弹簧
brake lining	制动衬片	anchor pins	定位销
brake fluid	制动液	floating-caliper type	浮钳式
disk rotor	盘形转子，制动盘	fixed-caliper type	固定卡钳式
brake pad	制动块	sliding-caliper type	移动卡钳式
wheel/brake cylinder	车轮(液压)制动分缸，轮缸		

Exercises

Ⅰ. Answer the following questions according to the text.

1. What is the function of the brake?
2. How is the service brake operated?
3. When is the parking brake used?
4. What does the typical hydraulic brake system consist of?
5. What is the function of the master cylinder?

Ⅱ. Translate the following phrases into Chinese or English.

1. parking brake　　　＿＿＿＿＿＿＿　　　7. 回位弹簧　　　＿＿＿＿＿＿＿
2. hand brake　　　　＿＿＿＿＿＿＿　　　8. 制动蹄　　　　＿＿＿＿＿＿＿
3. disk brake　　　　＿＿＿＿＿＿＿　　　9. 制动助力器　　＿＿＿＿＿＿＿
4. fixed-caliper type　＿＿＿＿＿＿＿　　　10. 鼓式制动器　　＿＿＿＿＿＿＿
5. wheel/brake cylinder　＿＿＿＿＿＿＿　　11. 制动液　　　　＿＿＿＿＿＿＿
6. brake line　　　　＿＿＿＿＿＿＿

Chapter 3　Chassis

Ⅲ. Read the following abbreviations and translate them into corresponding Chinese terms.

1. BP　　　　　brake power　　　　　　　　　　_____
2. BPMV　　　brake power modulator valve　　_____
3. BC　　　　　brake cylinder　　　　　　　　　 _____
4. BHP　　　　brake horsepower　　　　　　　　_____
5. BMEP　　　brake mean effective pressure　　_____
6. BMC　　　　brake master cylinder　　　　　　_____

Ⅳ. Choose the correct word form to complete each sentence.

| release | act | mount | push | (be) made of |

1. The service brake _____ to slow, stop, or hold the vehicle during normal driving.
2. The fluid _____ shoes, or pads, against revolving drums or disks.
3. The brake drum _____ on the wheel hub.
4. Pistons _____ either plastic or metal.
5. If the pedal _____, the piston returns to the initial position.

Ⅴ. Write out the terms according to the picture.

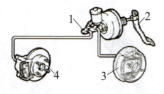

1. _____　　2. _____　　3. _____　　4. _____

Ⅵ. Look at the pictures and label them correctly using the words and phrases given below.

Picture 1: Drum brake system decomposition diagram

| location pin spring | pull back spring | brake lining | brake drum |
| brake adjuster | wheel cylinder | brake shoe | anchor pin |

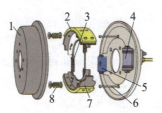

Picture 2: Disk type brake

brake caliper piston	brake pad
brake caliper	brake caliper mounting bracket
friction plate	brake disk

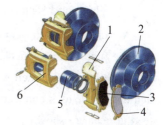

Unit 3　Steering System

During the traveling of the car, steering movement is the most basic movement. We manipulate and control the vehicle's running direction by using the steering wheel in order to realize our intentions. The function of the steering system is to achieve changes of the running directions and to keep a stable running route. See Fig. 3-3-1. Automobile steering systems can be divided into the manual steering system and power steering system by different energy of steering. Manual steering system relies on the driver's steering power to steer the wheel. Under the control of the driver, power steering system can steer the wheel through the use of liquid pressure produced by engine or motor driving force.

Electronic control power steering system (EPS) could make steering wheel convenient and flexible at low speed; steering at high speed, EPS also promises to provide optimal power magnification and stability to handle, thus enhancing the stability of the control during high-speed traveling. So it has been commonly used in car manufacturing in every country.

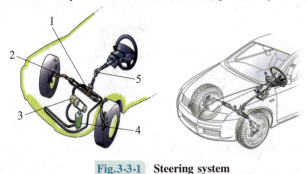

Fig.3-3-1　Steering system

1—rack and pinion configuration　2—universal joint　3—fluid reservoir
4—steering power pump　5—front tie rod

1 Manual Steering System

There are a couple of different types of steering gears. The most common ones are rack and pinion and recirculating-ball steering gears. Rack and pinion steering is quickly becoming the most common type of steering on compact cars, small trucks and SUVs in which the engine compartment space is limited. It is actually a pretty simple mechanism.

（1）Rack and Pinion Steering

A rack and pinion gear set is enclosed in a metal tube, with each end of the rack protruding from the tube. A rod, called a tie rod, connects to each end of the rack. The pinion gear is attached to the steering shaft. When we turn the steering wheel, the gear spins, moving the rack. The tie rod at each end of the rack connects to the steering arm on the spindle. The basic parts of a rack and pinion steering gear are shown in Fig.3-3-2 and Fig.3-3-3.

The rack and pinion gear set does two things:

1) It converts the rotational motion of the steering wheel into the linear motion needed to turn the wheels.

2) It provides a gear reduction, making it easier to turn the wheels.

On most cars, it takes three to four complete revolutions of the steering wheel to make the wheels turn from lock to lock (from far left to far right).

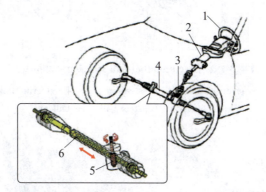

Fig.3-3-2 **Rack and pinion steering system (a)**
1—steering wheel 2—steering column 3—steering gear 4—gear housing 5—gear 6—steering rack

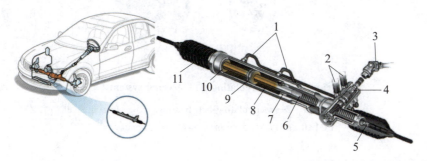

Fig.3-3-3 **Rack and pinion steering system (b)**
1—fluid lines 2—power steering hoses 3—steering shaft 4—pinion 5—inner tie rod
6—steering rack 7,10—end seal 8—power steering fluid 9—hydraulic piston 11—steering rack boot

(2) Recirculating-Ball Steering

Recirculating-ball steering is used on many trucks and SUVs today. The linkage that turns the wheels is slightly different than that on a rack and pinion system. The larger and heavier the car, the more difficult it is to steer. Most large cars are equipped with a recirculating-ball steering gear. This type of steering gear is very low in friction and provides a good mechanical advantage for a heavy vehicle.

The recirculating-ball steering gear consists of several parts contained in a steering gear housing. The steering gear shaft is connected to the steering wheel either directly or through some types of flexible joint. The basic parts of a recirculating-ball steering gear are shown in Fig. 3-3-4 and Fig. 3-3-5.

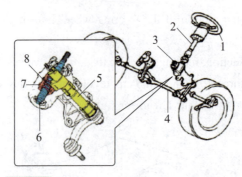

Fig.3-3-4　Recirculating-ball steering system（a）

1—steering wheel　2—steering column　3—steering gear　4—steering link　5—sector shaft
6—screw arbor　7—steel ball　8—ball nut

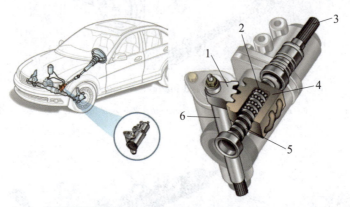

Fig.3-3-5　Recirculating-ball steering system（b）

1—sector gear　2—recirculating-ball bearings　3—steering shaft
4—ball nut rack　5—worm gear　6—pitman shaft

2　Power Steering System

Power steering system is designed to reduce the effort required by the driver to turn the steering wheel. Actually, automobile power steering is "power-assisted steering". In a power steering system, power-assisted units use either hydraulic or air-assist setups to make steering effort easier. Nowadays, electric power-aided steering is also adopted on some small cars. Here, we just discuss the hydraulic type, which is widely used on various kinds of vehicles.

Power steering system adds a hydraulic pump, fluid reservoir, hoses, lines, and a power assist unit either mounted on, or integral with a steering wheel gear assembly. In addition, a control valve is incorporated somewhere in the hydraulic circuit. See Fig. 3-3-6.

The power steering pump, which is driven by a belt from the crankshaft pulley, sends fluid under pressure into the steering gear. This high-pressure fluid does about 80 percent of the work of steering. In operation, the pump produces a high pressure on the power-steering fluid, which is a kind of special oil.

Under normal conditions, only the minor part of the energy used for turning is supplied by the driver, while the major part is supplied by the engine via the steering gear. When the power steering gear fails to work, the driver has to supply all the turning power.

According to the source of the power and the way of control, the modern power steering system can be classified into the hydraulic power steering system, the electronic power steering system and the electric hydraulic power steering system. See Fig. 3-3-7, Fig. 3-3-8 and Fig. 3-3-9.

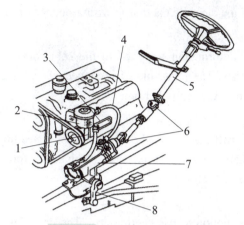
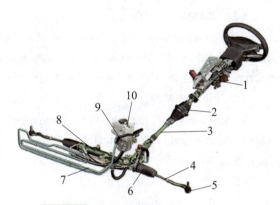

Fig.3-3-6 Power steering system
1—power cylinder pump 2—fluid reservoir
3—pressure hose 4—return hose 5—steering column
6—universal joints 7—steering gear 8—pitman arm

Fig.3-3-7 Hydraulic power steering system
1—steering column 2—boot 3—steering drive shaft
4—tie rod 5—ball joint 6—boot 7—return line
8—power cylinder 9—steering pump 10—fluid reservoir

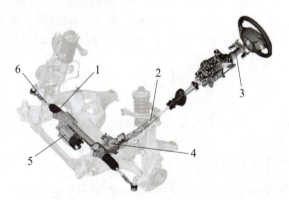
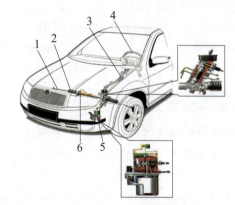

Fig.3-3-8 Electronic power steering system
1—boot 2—steering drive shaft 3—steering column
4—steering gear 5—power-assisted motor
6—steering tie rod

Fig.3-3-9 Electric hydraulic power steering system
1—steering tie rod 2—steering tie rod boot seal
3—steering column 4—steering wheel
5—pump electric motor 6—steering gear box

3 Some Main Components of Steering Mechanism

The steering mechanism is comprised of a steering wheel, a steering column, a steering box, a pitman, a drag link, etc.

（1）Steering Wheel

Steering wheels are commonly referred to as the driving wheels. This device is an integral part of the automotive steering system that is controlled and operated by the driver of the vehicle. Steering wheels are round-shaped wheels that are connected to the steering column with the help of one or more spokes.

（2）Steering Column

The steering column consists of mechanical devices, which are used for steering an automobile. In the steering column assembly, the steering column shaft is usually attached to two needle bearings fastened in rubber mountings. Another important part of the steering column is wiring connectors.

（3）Universal Joints

The universal joints of the steering shaft diminish deformation imparted to the cab from the frame and reduce the dimensions of the steering mechanism. The joint yokes are connected with the steering shaft on the top and with the steering gear drive shaft on the bottom.

（4）Pitman Arms

Pitman arms are attached to the steering box sector shaft that assists the movement of a steering wheel. Pitman arms are basically a type of lever that converts torque into mechanical force facilitating the smooth movement of the steering linkage.

（5）Drag Link

Drag link's function is to transmit the pitman arm's motion to the steering arm. The drag link, steering arm and pitman arm's relative motion is space motion, for it does not have the movement interference, and the pin ball is used to connect the three parts.

（6）Damper

Along with the vehicle speed enhancement, the modern steering wheel will sometimes have the oscillation. Not only will this affect automobile's stability, but also affect automobile's comfortableness, and aggravate the front wheel tires' attrition. Installing a damper can overcome the steering wheel oscillation very effectively.

Notes to the Text

1. Automobile steering systems can be divided into the manual steering system and power steering system by different energy of steering.
   汽车转向系统可按转向的能源不同分为手动转向系统和动力转向系统两类。

2. Rack and pinion steering is quickly becoming the most common type of steering on compact cars, small trucks and SUVs in which the engine compartment space is limited.
   齿轮齿条转向机构很快成为紧凑型汽车、小型货车和运动型多功能汽车上最普遍的转向机构类型，这些车辆上发动机舱空间有限。

3. Most large cars are equipped with a recirculating-ball steering gear. This type of steering gear is very low in friction and provides a good mechanical advantage for a heavy vehicle.
   大多数大型汽车采用循环球转向机构。这类转向机构对于重型车辆来说，摩擦低、提供机械效益好。

4. In a power steering system, power-assisted units use either hydraulic or air-assist setups to make steering effort easier.
   在动力转向系统中，既可以使用液压助力转向也可以使用空气助力转向机构来使得转向更省力。

5. The power steering pump, which is driven by a belt from the crankshaft pulley, sends fluid under pressure into the steering gear.
   由曲轴带轮通过带驱动的动力转向泵把压力油液送到转向器中。

6. The steering mechanism is comprised of a steering wheel, a steering column, a steering box, a pitman, a drag link, etc.
   转向机械机构包括转向盘、转向柱、转向器、转向摇臂、转向直拉杆等。

7. The universal joints of the steering shaft diminish deformation imparted to the cab from the frame and reduce the dimensions of the steering mechanism.
   转向万向节简化了驾驶室的结构设计，同时也可以减小转向操纵机构的尺寸。

8. Pitman arms are basically a type of lever that converts torque into mechanical force facilitating the smooth movement of the steering linkage.
   转向摇臂实际上就是一种杠杆，它能够将转动力矩转化为使转向连接部件运动更加平稳的机械力。

New Words and Expressions

manipulate	/məˈnipjuleit/	vt.	(熟练地)操作，使用(机器等)
handle	/ˈhændl/	vt.	触摸，运用，买卖，处理，操作
hydraulic	/haiˈdrɔːlik/	adj.	液压的，水压的
magnification	/ˌmæɡnifiˈkeiʃn/	n.	扩大，放大倍率
pinion	/ˈpinjən/	n.	小齿轮
integral	/ˈintəɡrəl/	adj.	构成整体所需的，完整的
incorporate	/inˈkɔːpəreit/	v.	把……合并，列入，包含
pulley	/ˈpuli/	n.	滑轮，带轮
linear	/ˈliniə/	adj.	线性的，直的
compact	/ˈkɔmpækt/	adj.	紧凑的，紧密的
rack	/ræk/	n.	齿条
protruding	/prəˈtruːdiŋ/	adj.	突出的；伸出的
spindle	/ˈspind(ə)l/	n.	主轴
mounting	/ˈmauntiŋ/	n.	配件，装置件
diminish	/diˈminiʃ/	vt.	使减少；使变小
deformation	/ˌdiːfɔːˈmeiʃn/	n.	变形，畸形
enhancement	/inˈhaːnsmənt/	n.	增加；放大
oscillation	/ˌɔsiˈleiʃn/	n.	振动，摇摆
aggravate	/ˈæɡrəveit/	vt.	使恶化，使更严重
attrition	/əˈtriʃn/	n.	摩擦，磨损
steering wheel			转向盘
steering column			转向柱
steering shaft			转向轴
steering arm/pitman arm			转向摇臂
pulley-driven pump			带轮驱动泵
steering gear			转向器，转向装置，转向齿轮机构
rack and pinion steering gear			齿轮齿条转向器
recirculating-ball steering gear			循环球式转向器
air assist setups			空气助力机构
crankshaft pulley			曲轴带轮
rotary valve			旋转阀

pinion gear	小齿轮，主动齿轮
steering linkage	转向传动机构
lock to lock	（转向盘）总回转圈数
electronic control power steering system（EPS）	电子控制动力转向系统
universal joints	万向节
drag link	转向直拉杆

Exercises

Ⅰ. Answer the following questions according to the text.

1. What's the function of the steering system?
2. Please list the main components of the steering system.
3. When are the two types of the steering gears widely used?
4. What are the advantages of the electronic control power steering system（EPS）?
5. According to the source of the power and the way of control, the modern power steering system can be classified into three types, what are they?

Ⅱ. Choose the correct answer to fill in the blanks.

1. What kind of vehicle is more likely to use a recirculating-ball steering system?_____.
   A. A sedan   B. A truck or SUV   C. A station wagon   D. A sports car
2. Of the two common types, which is becoming more common? _____.
   A. Recirculating-ball steering system   B. Rack and pinion steering system
3. The _____ converts the rotation motion of the steering wheel into the straight-line motion.
   A. steering gear   B. steering knuckle   C. drag link   D. tie rod
4. What are the two main types of steering systems that cars use?_____.
   A. Recirculating-ball and power assisted   B. Rack and pinion and power assisted
   C. Power assisted and active steering   D. Recirculating-ball and rack and pinion
5. Rather than a rack and pinion gear set, the recirculating-ball steering system use _____.
   A. linear gears   B. a recirculating ball   C. clockwork gears   D. the ball bearing

Ⅲ. Translate the following phrases into Chinese or English.

1. steering column   _____
2. steering shaft   _____
3. pulley-driven pump   _____
4. rack and pinion steering gear   _____
5. steering linkage   _____
6. 万向节   _____
7. 转向盘   _____
8. 转向直拉杆   _____
9. 循环球式转向器   _____
10. 转向器，转向装置，转向齿轮机构   _____

Chapter 3　Chassis

IV. Read the following abbreviations and translate them into corresponding Chinese terms.

1. VSC　　　　vehicle stability control　　　　_____
2. ABS　　　　anti-lock braking system　　　　_____
3. ABSCM　　　ABS control module　　　　　　_____
4. PSCU　　　　power steering control unit　　　_____
5. PS　　　　　 power steering　　　　　　　　　_____
6. EPS　　　　 electronic control power steering system　_____

V. Choose the correct word form to complete each sentence.

| keep | convert | call | equalize | swing |

1. The pressure _____ on both sides of the piston.
2. Friction _____ low by using balls between the major moving parts.
3. The steering gear _____ a worm-and-roller steering gear.
4. The sector-gear movement causes the pitman arm _____ one way or the other.
5. The steering gear _____ the rotary motion of the steering wheel into straight-line motion.

VI. Look at the pictures and label them correctly using the words and phrases given below.

Picture 1: Common hydraulic power steering system

steering column boot seal	steering knuckle	steering gearbox
steering tie rod boot seal	steering shaft	steering tie rod
steering wheel	vane pump	oil cooler　　oil tank

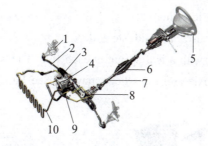

Picture 2: Electronic power steering system

| steering column adjusting hand wheel | steering shaft |
| steering wheel | servo motor |

Unit 4　Suspension System

The suspension is a device to make the vehicle body float with the aid of springs and other elastic components. See Fig.3-4-1. The suspension should improve the ride comfort and ensure the ride stability as well. The functions of a suspension system are as follows:

1) To prevent the road shocks from being transmitted to the vehicle frame.
2) To preserve the stability of the vehicle in pitching or rolling, while in motion.
3) To safeguard the occupants from road shocks.
4) To provide good road holding while driving, cornering and braking.
5) To maintain proper steering geometry.

1　Types of Suspension Systems

The suspension system supports the weight of the engine, transmission, car body, and whatever the car body is carrying. There are two basic suspension systems in use today. One is the solid axle and leaf spring composed of non-independent suspension; the other is the independent suspension using long and short swinging arms. There are various adaptations of these systems, but all use the same basic principle.

Fig.3-4-1　Suspension structure

The solid axle suspension uses a solid steel dead axle (does not turn with wheels) with a leaf spring at each side. The wheels swivel on each end via a pivot arrangement between the axle and the wheel spindle. See Fig. 3-4-2.

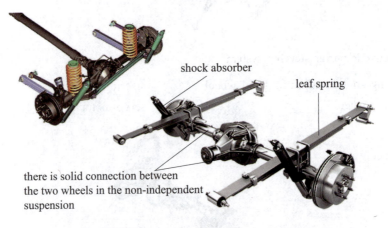

Fig.3-4-2　Non-independent suspension

With an independent suspension, each front wheel is free to move up and down with a minimum effect on the other wheel. In an independent suspension system, there is also far less twisting motion imposed on the frame than in a system with a solid axle. See Fig.3-4-3.

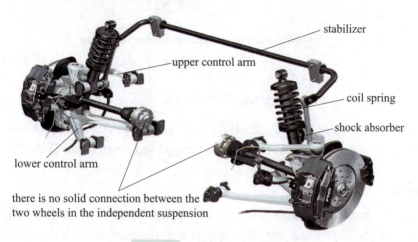

Fig.3-4-3 Independent suspension

Almost all modern front suspension systems are independent. A few off-road, four-wheel drive vehicles and large trucks continue to use a solid axle front suspension. Types of front suspension systems include the conventional front suspension, coil spring front suspension, torsion bar front suspension, MacPherson strut front suspension and solid axle front suspension. See Fig.3-4-4 and Fig. 3-4-5.

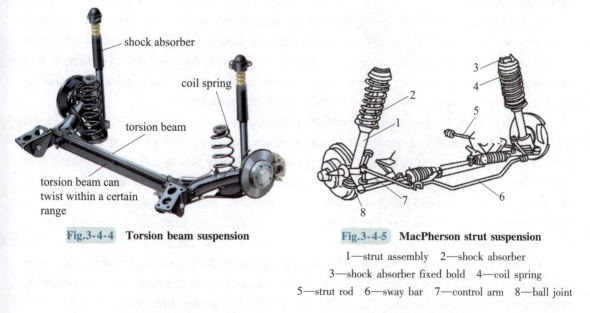

Fig.3-4-4 Torsion beam suspension

Fig.3-4-5 MacPherson strut suspension

1—strut assembly 2—shock absorber
3—shock absorber fixed bold 4—coil spring
5—strut rod 6—sway bar 7—control arm 8—ball joint

The rear suspension may be of the solid axle or independent design. Many cars have solid axle rear suspension. Either design may have different kinds of springs. However, the coil spring and leaf spring types are the most popular. See Fig. 3-4-6.

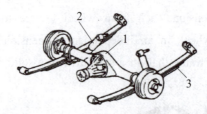

Fig.3-4-6　**Leaf type of non-independent suspension**
1—rear-axle case　2—shock absorber　3—leaf spring

2 Automotive Springs and Shock Absorbers

Most suspension systems have the same basic parts, i.e. springs and shock absorbers and operate basically in the same way. They differ, however, in the type and arrangement of the linkages used to connect these parts to the frame and wheels.

(1) Springs

In a suspension system, the major component is springs. Springs are vital to vehicles because they support the weight of your car and allow it to remain stable even in rough driving conditions. They have the ability to expand when you hit dips on the road and compress when you encounter bumps or cut into hard corners.

The springs used on today's vehicles are engineered in a wide variety of types, shapes, sizes, rates and capacities for each kind of automobile and truck depending on your vehicle's suspension design. There are four basic types of spring used in suspensions: leaf spring, coil springs, torsion bar spring and air spring.

1) Coil springs. The coil spring is made from a special spring steel wire. This spring is generally circular in cross section and of suitable diameter to have the desired stiffness. The wire is wound in the shape of a coil. The spring is formed at a high temperature, and cooled and proper heat treatment is given to it in order to have the characteristics of elasticity. Coil springs are generally used in independent suspension systems and other light-duty vehicles.

2) Leaf springs. Leaf springs are made from flat strips of spring steel. Each strip is called a leaf. Several strips are placed one on the other. They are joined together by clamps and a central bolt. The length of each leaf decreases so that the spring assembly acts as a flexible beam and is of uniform strength. The longest strip is called the main leaf spring or master leaf spring. The ends of the master spring are formed into loops called spring eyes. One end of the spring is attached to the frame through a spring bolt passing through the spring eye. The other end is secured through shackles. The shackles help in accommodating the change in the length of the spring.

3) Torsion bar springs. A torsion bar is a long, alloy-steel bar, fixed rigidly to the chassis or sub-frame, at one end, and to the suspension control arm at the other. Spring rate depends on the length of the bar, and its diameter. The shorter and thicker the bar, the stiffer its spring rate.

4) Air springs. Air springs, which consist of a cylindrical chamber of air positioned between the wheel and the car's body, use the compressive qualities of air to absorb wheel vibrations.

See Fig. 3-4-7 and Fig. 3-4-8.

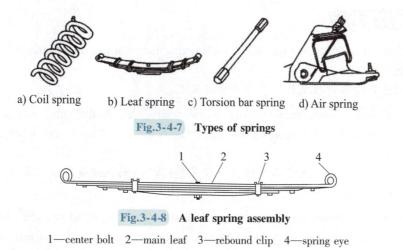

a) Coil spring   b) Leaf spring   c) Torsion bar spring   d) Air spring

Fig.3-4-7   Types of springs

Fig.3-4-8   A leaf spring assembly

1—center bolt   2—main leaf   3—rebound clip   4—spring eye

(2) Shock Absorbers

Springs alone will not give a satisfactory ride; shock absorbers must be used with them. On a car without shock absorbers, the repeated up-and-down movement of the springs and wheels would produce a very rough ride. Further, the driver would have great difficulty in controlling the car, particularly on curves.

To eliminate the excessive up-and-down movement of the springs and wheels, a shock absorber is placed at each wheel. Shock absorbers are filled with fluid. In operation, wheel movement causes the shock absorber to force this fluid through small openings (orifices). Since fluid can pass through restricted openings rather slowly, this puts a restraint on wheels and spring movement. The restraint imposed prevents excessive wheel movement. It also damps out the spring oscillations quickly after the hole or bump is passed. See Fig. 3-4-9 and Fig. 3-4-10.

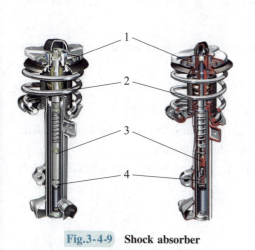

Fig.3-4-9   Shock absorber

1—oil seal   2—coil spring
3—piston bar   4—piston

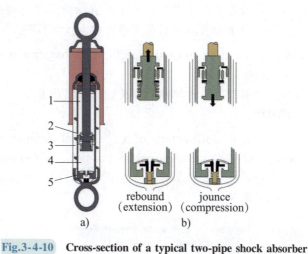

Fig.3-4-10   Cross-section of a typical two-pipe shock absorber

1—rebound chamber   2—rebound intake valve
3—reserve chamber   4—compression chamber
5—compression intake valve

Notes to the Text

1. The suspension is a device to make the vehicle body float with the aid of springs and other elastic components.
   悬架是借助于弹簧等弹性元件使车身浮动的装置。

2. There are two basic suspension systems in use today. One is the solid axle and leaf spring composed of non-in dependent suspension; the other is the independent suspension using long and short swinging arms.
   目前使用的悬架系统基本上分为两种,一种是整体桥与钢板弹簧组成的非独立悬架,另一种是使用长短摆臂的独立悬架。

3. Types of front suspension systems include the conventional front suspension, coil spring front suspension, torsion bar front suspension, MacPherson strut front suspension and solid axle front suspension.
   前悬架系统的类型包括传统的悬架系统、螺旋弹簧前悬架、扭杆弹簧前悬架、麦弗逊滑柱式前悬架和非独立式前悬架。

4. There are four basic types of spring used in suspensions: leaf spring, coil springs, torsion bar spring and air spring.
   通常悬架所用弹簧有四种类型:螺旋弹簧、钢板弹簧、扭杆弹簧和空气弹簧。

5. The spring is formed at a high temperature, and cooled and proper heat treatment is given to it in order to have the characteristics of elasticity.
   弹簧是在高温下加工而成的,冷却后进行适当的热处理使其具有弹性。

6. The length of each leaf decreases so that the spring assembly acts as a flexible beam and is of uniform strength. The longest strip is called the main leaf spring or master leaf spring. The ends of the master spring are formed into loops called spring eyes.
   簧片的长度逐片递减,形成了具有相同强度反弹性的梁。最长的簧片被叫做主钢板弹簧。主钢板弹簧的两端被制成环形结构,叫作卷耳。

7. Spring rate depends on the length of the bar, and its diameter. The shorter and thicker the bar, the stiffer its spring rate.
   弹簧的刚度取决于扭杆的长度,以及它的直径。扭杆的长度越短、直径越大,那么弹簧也就越硬。

8. Air springs, which consist of a cylindrical chamber of air positioned between the wheel and the car's body, use the compressive qualities of air to absorb wheel vibrations.
   空气弹簧,由安装在车轮与车架之间的圆柱形气室组成,利用气体的可压缩性来吸收车轮的振动能量。

New Words and Expressions

geometry	/dʒiˈɔmitri/	n.	几何学,几何结构
pitch	/pitʃ/	v.	前后颠簸,纵倾[区别于侧倾(roll)]
adaptation	/ˌædæpˈteiʃn/	n.	改造(物)
frame	/freim/	n.	车架
swivel	/ˈswivl/	v.	使旋转

twist	/twist/	v.	扭转，扭曲
strut	/strʌt/	n.	滑柱，支柱
beam	/biːm/	n.	梁，横梁
cylindrical	/siˈlindrikəl/	adj.	圆柱形的；圆柱体的
elasticity	/elæˈstisiti/	n.	弹性；弹力；灵活性
sway	/swei/	n./v.	摇摆，摇动
lateral	/ˈlætərəl/	adj.	侧面的，横向的
transverse	/ˈtrænzvəːs/	adj.	横向的
rebound	/riˈbaund/	v./n.	回弹
stiffness	/ˈstifnis/	n.	刚度
traction	/ˈtrækʃn/	n.	牵引，牵引力
vertical	/ˈvəːtikəl/	adj.	垂直的
oscillate	/ˈɔsileit/	v.	振荡，摆动，振动
uncontrollable	/ʌnkənˈtrəuləb(ə)l/	adj.	无法控制的，难以控制的
bounce	/bauns/	v.	（使）反跳，弹起，跳振，跳动
spindle	/ˈspindl/	n.	轴
stabilizer	/ˈsteibilaizə/	n.	稳定器

suspension system	悬架系	double-wishbone suspension	双横臂式悬架， 双 V 形式悬架
shock absorber	减振器		
coil spring	螺旋弹簧	multi-link suspension	多连杆式悬架
leaf spring	钢板弹簧	torsion beam	扭力梁
torsion bar spring	扭杆弹簧	spring rate	弹簧刚度， 弹簧刚度系数
air spring	空气弹簧		
front suspension system	前悬架系	live axle	活动轴，活轴
rear suspension system	后悬架系	dead axle	不动车轴，不回转的车轴，定轴
traction bar	牵引杆		
leaf pack	钢板弹簧组件	non-independent suspension	非独立悬架
spring oscillation	弹簧的往复振动	solid axle suspension	整体桥悬架
front axle	前桥	independent suspension	独立悬架
rear axle	后桥	MacPherson strut	麦弗逊滑柱
rigid axle	刚性整体车桥	MacPherson strut front suspension	麦弗逊滑柱式前悬架
lower control arm	下控制臂		
sway bar	横向稳定杆	electronic controlled suspension system	电控悬架系统
strut rod	支撑杆		
stabilizer bar	横向稳定杆		

Exercises

Ⅰ. Answer the following questions according to the text.

1. What's the function of the suspension system?

2. There are two basic suspension systems in use today, what are they?

3. What are the key components that make up the suspension system?

4. Please list three types of spring in general use today.

5. What's the function of the shock absorber?

II. Choose the correct answer to fill in the blanks.

1. _____ are made from flat strips of spring steel. Each strip is called a leaf.
   A. Coil springs   B. Leaf springs   C. Torsion bar springs   D. Air springs

2. One of the main purposes of a car suspension is to maximize the friction between _____.
   A. the shocks and the springs   B. the tires and the road surface
   C. the driver and the passengers   D. the spring and the absorbers

3. What is the most common type of spring used in modern car suspensions? _____.
   A. Leaf springs   B. Coil springs   C. Torsion bar springs   D. Air springs

4. What term describes the ability of a vehicle to travel a curved path? _____.
   A. Cornering   B. Road holding   C. Road isolation

5. What are the two different cycles of shock absorbers? _____.
   A. Velocity cycle and momentum cycle   B. Depression cycle and expansion cycle
   C. Compression cycle and extension cycle

III. Translate the following phrases into Chinese or English.

1. non-independent suspension   _____
2. MacPherson strut front suspension   _____
3. leaf spring   _____
4. torsion bar spring   _____
5. double-wishbone suspension   _____
6. 横向稳定杆   _____
7. 多连杆式悬架   _____
8. 独立悬架   _____
9. 螺旋弹簧   _____
10. 空气弹簧   _____

IV. Read the following abbreviations and translate them into corresponding Chinese terms.

1. SUS   suspension   _____
2. FA   front axle   _____
3. RA   rear axle   _____
4. LS   leaf spring   _____
5. TB   torsion bar   _____
6. IS   independent suspension _____

V. Choose the correct word form to complete each sentence.

| include | do | refer | use | bend |

1. A rear-suspension system _____ coil springs.
2. The suspension also _____ shocks or struts and sway bars.
3. A lot of the system's work _____ by the spring.

4. Suspension, when discussing cars, _____ to the use of the front and rear springs to suspend a vehicle's "sprung" weight.
5. Because the leaf spring includes a series of thin leaves, one on the top of another, it does not break when it _____.

VI. Write out the terms according to the pictures.

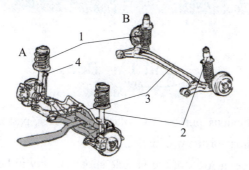

A. _____   B. _____
1. _____   2. _____
3. _____   4. _____

_____   _____   _____

Chapter 4

Body and Electrical System

Unit 1 Body

The body serves the obvious purpose of holding the driver, passengers and goods, providing shelter, comfort and protection for the occupants.

The body provides three-quarters of the vehicle's total rigidity in bending and in torsion. In the case of collision, it is intended to resist and minimize intrusions into the occupant space. In addition, it provides a cushioning effect through the use of padded interiors, a compliant windshield, and an energy-absorbing steering column and dash, all of which help ameliorate the impact of an unrestrained occupant against the interior of the passenger compartment. The body, therefore, is a relatively rigid structure with a compliant interior. Limited exterior structural compliance, however, is desirable to reduce the acceleration of collision experienced by the body.

The body panels are stamped from sheet metal at fabrication plants and transmitted to the assembly plant in special containers or racks. Structurally, it is made of large and thin panels with a typical gage thickness of 0.76 to 1.02 mm. See Fig.4-1-1.

Fig.4-1-1 Body

The body is generally divided into four sections: the front, the rear, the top and the underbody. These sections can be further divided into a lot of assemblies and parts, such as the hood, the fenders, the roof panels, the door, the instrument panel, the bumpers and the luggage compartment. The body assembly map is shown in Fig.4-1-2.

For assembly, the parts are placed in jigs which travel along the assembly line and maintain alignment while welding takes place. The assemblies of the whole body are combined by spot welding and bolting.

When the main body structure has sufficient stiffness to stand along, the jigs are removed and the remaining structure parts are attached. Finally, doors, windows, truck lids, trim items and so on are added to complete the assembly. The designers have begun to pay attention to the body construction and hope to get it more luxurious and more comfortable.

Chapter 4 Body and Electrical System

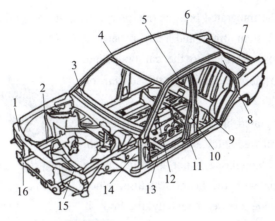

Fig.4-1-2 Body assembly map

1—front end panel 2—front side member 3—cross member under windshield
4—front roof bow 5—roof rail 6—rear roof bow 7—rear end panel 8—rear pillar
9—side member 10—center pillar 11—cross member under seat 12—center pillar
13—side member 14—wheel well 15—engine-support cross member 16—front cross member

The common body types of modern automobiles include separate frame construction and integrated body. See Fig. 4-1-3.

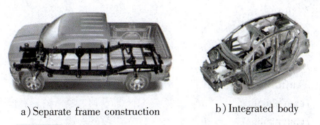

a) Separate frame construction b) Integrated body

Fig.4-1-3 Separate frame construction and integrated body

In the separate frame construction, the engine, transmission system and body assembly are fixed to a rigid frame that is connected to the wheels by front and rear suspension devices.

The separate frame construction is composed of a beam through the whole body structure, providing high chassis strength and good anti-jolting performance. Even if the four wheels are stressed unevenly, they are also borne by the frame and will not be transferred to the body. The body is not easy to distort and deform, so the separate frame construction is often used for trucks, buses or off-road vehicles. See Fig. 4-1-4.

Fig.4-1-4 Structure of separate frame construction

1—front side member 2—rear side member 3—rear cross member
4—middle cross member 5—side member

The whole body of the integrated body is one piece, there are no girders throughout the whole, the engine, transmission system, front and rear suspension and other components are assembled to the car body, and the body load is passed to the wheel through the suspension device. See Fig.4-1-5.

The car with the integrated body has the advantages of smooth driving, low natural frequency, small noise and light weight, but the strength of the chassis is not as strong as the separate frame construction with the beam structure. When the four wheels of the car are stressed unevenly, the body is prone to deformation.

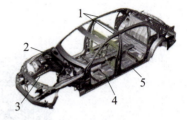

Fig.4-1-5 Structure of integrated body
1—roof rail 2—engine baffle plate
3—engine mounting frame
4—bottom reinforced beam 5—side member

Compared to older techniques, in which a body is bolted to a frame, integrated body cars are less expensive, lighter, more rigid and can be more protective of occupants in a crush when appropriately designed. This kind of body is widely used in cars.

New Words and Expressions

obvious	/ˈɔbviəs/	adj.	明显的
shelter	/ˈʃeltə/	n.	保护，庇护
protection	/prəˈtekʃn/	n.	保护
occupant	/ˈɔkjupənt/	n.	乘员
intrusion	/inˈtruːʒn/	n.	打扰，侵入
cushion	/ˈkuʃn/	v.	对(某事物)起缓冲作用
compliant	/kəmˈplaiənt/	adj.	柔顺的，顺从的，百依百顺的
compliance	/kəmˈplaiəns/	n.	柔顺性，配合性
ameliorate	/əˈmiːliəreit/	v.	改进，改善
unrestrained	/ˌʌnriˈstreid/	adj.	无节制的，放肆的
stamp	/stæmp/	v.	冲压
structurally	/ˈstrʌktʃərli/	adv.	结构上地
gage	/geidŋ/	n.	计量，标准
thickness	/ˈθiknis/	n.	厚度
underbody	/ʌndəˈbɔdi/	n.	底板
hood	/hud/	n.	发动机罩
fender	/ˈfendə/	n.	挡泥板
roof	/ruːf/	n.	车身顶板
bumper	/ˈbʌmpə/	n.	汽车保险杠
luggage	/ˈlʌgeidŋ/	n.	行李
jig	/dʒig/	n.	夹具
stiffness	/ˈstifnis/	n.	坚硬
lid	/lid/	n.	盖，罩
trim	/trim/	n.	装饰，(汽车内部)装潢
item	/ˈaitəm/	n.	一件物品
luxurious	/lʌgˈʒuəriəs/	adj.	豪华的
comfortable	/ˈkʌmfətəbl/	adj.	舒服的

three-quarters	四分之三	energy-absorbing steering column	能量吸收式转向柱
padded interiors	内部加垫装修	separate frame construction	非承载式车身
occupant space	承载空间	integrated body	承载式车身，无大梁车身

Notes to the Text

1. The body provides three-quarters of the vehicle's total rigidity in bending and in torsion.
   在产生弯曲和扭矩时，汽车的整体坚固性的四分之三由车身承担。

2. In addition, it provides a cushioning effect through the use of padded interiors, a compliant windshield, and an energy-absorbing steering column and dash, all of which help ameliorate the impact of an unrestrained occupant against the interior of the passenger compartment.
   此外，为了缓解冲撞，进行内部加垫装修，采用平顺的风窗玻璃，装有能量吸收式转向柱和缓冲器，所有这些措施可减小车内未系安全带的乘员所受的振动。

3. The body is generally divided into four sections: the front, the rear, the top and the underbody.
   车身一般分为四个部分：车前部，车后部，车顶部和车下部。

4. For assembly, the parts are placed in jigs which travel along the assembly line and which maintain alignment while welding takes place.
   为了便于装配，部件放在沿装配线运行的夹具中，焊接时夹具保持定位。

5. When the main body structure has sufficient stiffness to stand along, the jigs are removed and the remaining structure parts are attached.
   当车身的主结构基本定型，就可以移走夹具，把余下的结构件安装上去。

6. In the separate frame construction, the engine, transmission system and body assembly are fixed to a rigid frame that is connected to the wheels by front and rear suspension devices.
   非承载式车身中，发动机、传动系统、车身的总成部分固定在一个刚性车架上，车架通过前后悬架装置与车轮相连。

7. The whole body of the integrated body is one piece, there are no girders throughout the whole, the engine, transmission system, front and rear suspension and other components are assembled to the car body, and the body load is passed to the wheel through the suspension device.
   承载式车身汽车的整个车身是一体的，没有贯穿整体的大梁，发动机、传动系统、前后悬架等部件都装配到车身上，车身负载通过悬架装置传给车轮。

Exercises

Ⅰ. **Answer the following questions according to the text.**

1. What's the main function of the body structure?
2. The body is generally divided into four sections, what are they?
3. What is the body of a typical car made of?
4. List the components of the integrated body construction.

Ⅱ. Choose the correct answer to fill in the blanks.

1. The car with the integrated body has the advantages of smooth driving, _____.
   A. low natural frequency   B. small noise   C. light weight   D. all of the above
2. The body provides _____ of the vehicle's total rigidity in bending and in torsion.
   A. 1/2   B. 1/3   C. 3/4   D. 1/5
3. The separate frame construction is often used for _____.
   A. trucks   B. buses   C. off-road vehicles   D. all of the above
4. In the _____, the engine, transmission system and body assembly are fixed to a rigid frame that is connected to the wheels by front and rear suspension devices.
   A. separate frame construction   B. integrated body
   C. self-supporting body   D. unit-construction body
5. _____ is widely used in cars.
   A. Separate frame construction   B. Integrated body

Ⅲ. Translate the following phrases into Chinese or English.

1. front end panel   _____
2. engine-support cross member   _____
3. cross member under windshield   _____
4. front cross member   _____
5. separate frame construction   _____
6. 能量吸收式转向柱   _____
7. 后座下横梁   _____
8. 前柱   _____
9. 前纵梁   _____
10. 承载式车身,无大梁车身   _____

Ⅳ. The following are some expressions for the famous brands. Match the following brands in Column A with their Chinese equivalents in Column B.

Column A

1. _____   2. _____   3. _____   4. _____   5. _____

6. _____   7. _____   8. _____   9. _____   10. _____

Chapter 4　Body and Electrical System

Column B

A. Mercedes-Benz	梅赛德斯-奔驰		B. Alfa Romeo	阿尔法·罗密欧
C. Volkswagen	大众		D. Renault	雷诺
E. Maybach	迈巴赫		F. Buick	别克
G. BMW	宝马		H. Cadillac	凯迪拉克
I. Lamborghini	兰博基尼		J. Ferrari	法拉利

Ⅴ. **The following picture shows an automobile body. Look at the picture and label it correctly using the words and phrases given below.**

door handle	head lamp	mirror	door	guard
radiator support	bumper	bar absorber	bonnet	grill

Ⅵ. **The following picture shows the components of an automobile body. Write out the terms according to the picture.**

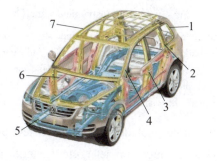

1. _____　　2. _____　　3. _____　　4. _____
5. _____　　6. _____　　7. _____

Unit 2　Instrument Panel

Vehicle information displaying system is one of the important systems of the automobile. The driver can know whether the cars, especially the various operating parameters of the engine are normal or not in order to take timely measures to prevent the occurrence of physical and mechanical accidents.

Traditional instruments widely use the combination of analog displaying instruments, and various measuring instruments are fixed on the dashboard in front of the driver's seat. The instrumentations in different vehicle instrument panels are not the same. As is shown in Fig.4-2-1 and Fig.4-2-2, it is a typical combination car instrument panel.

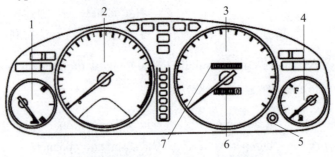

Fig.4-2-1 Car instrument panel(a)

1—temperature gauge   2—tachometer   3—speedometer   4—fuel gauge
5—trip meter reset button   6—odometer   7—trip meter

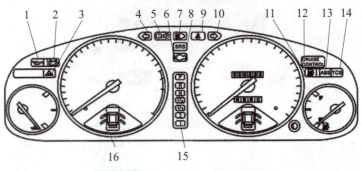

Fig.4-2-2 Car instrument panel(b)

1—low oil pressure indicator   2—charging system indicator   3—hazard warning indicator
4—left turn signal light   5—parking brake and braking system indicator   6—check engine indicator
7—high beam indicator   8—SRS indicator   9—seat belt indicator   10—right turn signal light
11—low fuel indicator   12—cruise control indicator   13—ABS indicator
14—TCS indicator   15—shift lever position indicator   16—door monitor

The instruments commonly used include the speedometer, engine tachometer, oil pressure gauge, water temperature gauge, fuel gauge, ammeter, etc. Changes in the monitored object's status are directly shown in most instruments through the sensors.

With the development of automotive electronic technology, the multifunctional and high-precision instrument with intuitive readings, which is shown by electronic digital and image, has been used in vehicles continuously.

1 Indicators

(1) Low Oil Pressure Indicator (Shown in Fig. 4-2-3)

It is an engine oil pressure warning light. The light should come on every time when your ignition key is turned to ON or START, and should go off when the engine starts. If the light stays on or comes on while the engine is running, you have lost oil pressure and continued operation will cause severe engine damage. Stop and check.

(2) Charging System Indicator (Shown in Fig. 4-2-4)

This light comes on every time when you turn your ignition key to ON or START. The light should go off when the engine starts and the alternator begins to charge. If the light stays on or comes on when the engine is running, have the charging system checked as soon as possible.

(3) Parking Brake and Braking System Indicator (Shown in Fig. 4-2-5)

This light has two functions:

1) It lights as a reminder that you have set the parking brake. On some types, the light goes on briefly when the ignition switch is turned to START with the parking brake released. Driving with the parking brake set can damage the brakes and tires, and cause the ABS to turn off.

2) It can indicate the brake fluid level is low if it remains light after you release the parking brake or comes on while driving. This is normally due to worn brake pads. Have your dealer check the braking system for worn pads or fluid leaks.

(4) Seat Belt Indicator and Buzzer (Shown in Fig. 4-2-6)

This indicator lights when you turn the ignition ON. It is a reminder to you and your passengers to protect yourselves by fastening the seat belts. A beeper also sounds if you have not fastened your seat belt and it will stop after a few seconds. But the light stays on until you do. Both the light and the beeper stay off if you fasten your seat belt before turning on the ignition.

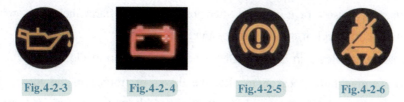

Fig.4-2-3   Fig.4-2-4   Fig.4-2-5   Fig.4-2-6

(5) Check Engine Indicator (Shown in Fig.4-2-7)

This light comes on when the engine electronic control system is not working properly. Take the vehicle to the dealer immediately.

(6) Anti-Lock Braking System (ABS) Indicator (Shown in Fig.4-2-8)

This light normally comes on when you turn the ignition switch to ON and goes off after the engine starts. If it comes on at other time, there is a problem in the ABS. If this happens, take the car to your dealer to have it checked. With the light on, your car still has normal braking ability but no anti-lock.

(7) Door and Brake Lamp Monitor (Shown in Fig.4-2-9)

The appropriate light comes on in this display if the boot or any door is not closed tightly. If a brake light does not work, the BRAKE LAMP indicator comes on when you push down the brake pedal with the ignition switch ON. A burned-out brake light is a hazard when drivers behind you can not be told that you are braking. Have your brake light repaired right away. All the lights in the monitor display come on for a few seconds when you turn the ignition switch to ON.

(8) Low Washer Fluid Indicator (Shown in Fig.4-2-10)

This light illuminates when there is less than a quarter of the container of washer fluid left. Add washer fluid.

Fig.4-2-7   Fig.4-2-8   Fig.4-2-9   Fig.4-2-10

(9) Low Fuel Indicator (Shown in Fig. 4-2-11)

This light comes on when your fuel gauge indicates approximately 1/8 fuel of tank. Fill up the tank with fuel.

(10) Cruise Control Indicator (Shown in Fig. 4-2-12)

This light comes on when you set the cruise control. When you tap the brake or clutch pedal, or press the SET and RESUME buttons at the same time, the CRUISE CONTROL light on the instrument panel will go out and the car will begin to slow down. You can use the accelerator pedal in the normal way.

(11) Traction Control System (TCS) Indicator (Shown in Fig.4-2-13)

The TCS light normally comes on when you turn the ignition switch to ON and goes off after the engine starts. If it doesn't, or it stays on after possible engine starts, there is a problem with the traction control system. Check it as soon as possible.

(12) Supplemental Restrain System (SRS) Indicator (Shown in Fig. 4-2-14)

The airbag warning light goes on to alert the driver of trouble in the SRS system when a malfunction is detected in the center airbag sensor assembly self-diagnosis. In normal operating conditions when the ignition switch is turned to the ON position, the light goes on for about 6 seconds and then goes off.

Fig.4-2-11   Fig.4-2-12   Fig.4-2-13   Fig.4-2-14

(13) Brake Friction Plate Indicator (Shown in Fig.4-2-15)

The light is used to show the condition of the brake friction plate. It comes on when the brake friction plate has problems or wears too much. It turns off after changing the brake.

(14) Brake Pedal Indicator (Shown in Fig.4-2-16)

The light is used on vehicles that are equipped with automatic transmissions. It prompts you can shift P gear or N gear to the other gears when you step on the brake pedal.

(15) Electronic Stability Program Control System Indicator (ESP Indicator) (Shown in Fig.4-2-17)

The light is used to show the working condition of the electronic stability program control system and its problems. The light comes on for a few seconds when your ignition key is turned to ON, and the vehicle carries on self-checking. And the light turns off after a few seconds. The light stays on if the electronic stability program control system has problems. The light stays flashing if the system is working when you are driving.

(16) Engine Coolant Temperature Indicator (Shown in Fig.4-2-18)

The light should come on for a few seconds when your ignition key is turned to ON, and then it will go out. If the light stays on or flashing, it shows that the temperature of the fluid is too high or the coolant level is too low. So you should turn off the engine to check the coolant level. Follow the instructions in the maintenance book and add coolant if necessary.

Fig.4-2-15

Fig.4-2-16

Fig.4-2-17

Fig.4-2-18

2 Gauges

(1) Temperature Gauge

It shows the temperature of the coolant of the engine. During normal operation, the pointer should rise from C (Cold) to the NORMAL band. When you are driving in heavy traffic or uphill in hot weather, the pointer may reach the top of the NORMAL band. If it reaches the H (Hot) band, the engine is over heating and may cause engine damage. Stop and check.

(2) Fuel Gauge

It shows how much fuel you have in the fuel tank. For the fuel gauge's proper operation, the ignition switch must be in the OFF position before you add fuel to the fuel tank. It is accurate when the car is on level ground. It may vary slightly while the vehicle is in motion.

(3) Speedometer

It shows your speed in kilometers per hour (km/h). On some types, when the speed is over approximately 120 km/h, a buzzer sounds.

(4) Tachometer

It shows the engine speed in revolutions per minute (r/min). To protect the engine from damage, never drive with the tachometer needle in the red zone.

(5) Odometer

This meter shows the total number of kilometers your car has been driven. The trip odometer shows the number of kilometers or miles driven since you last reset it. To reset it, press the reset button to return the trip odometer to zero.

New Words and Expressions

various	/ˈvɛəriəs/	adj.	不同的，各种各样的，多方面的
parameter	/pəˈræmitə/	n.	参数，参量
occurrence	/əˈkʌrəns/	n.	发生
speedometer	/spiˈdɔmitə/	n.	速度表
tachometer	/tæˈkɔmitə/	n.	转速表
ammeter	/ˈæmitə/	n.	电流表
intuitive	/inˈtju(ː)itiv/	adj.	直觉的
continuously	/kənˈtinjuəsli/	adv.	不断地，连续地
instrument	/ˈinstrumənt/	n.	器具，仪器
panel	/ˈpænl/	n.	仪表板，仪表盘
hazard	/ˈhæzəd/	n.	危险
warning	/ˈwɔːniŋ/	n.	警告
indicator	/ˈindikeitə/	n.	指示器，指示表
pressure	/ˈpreʃə/	n.	压力
charging	/ˈtʃɑːdʒiŋ/	n.	充电
signal	/ˈsignl/	n.	信号
check	/tʃek/	v.	检查，检测
odometer	/əˈdɔmitə/	n.	里程表
cruise	/kruːz/	v. /n.	（汽车）以快而平稳的车速长距离行驶，常称为"巡航"
gauge	/geidŋ/	n.	仪表，计量计
monitor	/ˈmɔnitə/	n.	监视器
severe	/siˈviə/	adj.	严重的；剧烈的
damage	/ˈdæmidŋ/	n. /v.	损坏，故障
alternator	/ˈɔːltəneitə/	n.	发电机
reminder	/riˈmaində/	n.	提醒物；提示
worn	/wɔːn/	adj.	损坏的，破旧的
dealer	/ˈdiːlə/	n.	销售商；特约维修店
buzzer	/ˈbʌzə/	n.	蜂鸣器
fasten	/ˈfɑːsn/	v.	系牢，扣住
beeper	/ˈbiːpə/	n.	喇叭
electronic	/iˌlekˈtrɔnik/	adj.	电子的
appropriate	/əˈprəupreit/	adj.	恰当的
boot	/ˈbuːt/	n.	（汽车后部的）行李舱
illuminate	/iˈluːmineit/	v.	照明，照亮
tap	/tæp/	v.	（用脚）踩，踏
resume	/riˈzjuːm/	v. /n.	重新开始
supplemental	/sʌpliˈmentl/	adj.	辅助的
restrain	/riˈstrein/	v.	约束，制止
airbag	/ˈɛəbæg/	n.	气囊
alert	/əˈləːt/	v.	警示
self-diagnosis	/ˌselfˈdaiəgnəusis/	n.	自我诊断

combination car instrument panel	汽车组合仪表板
oil pressure gauge	机油压力表
water temperature gauge	水温表
fuel gauge	燃油表
hazard warning indicator	危险警告灯
charging system	充电系统
left turn signal light	左转向信号灯
parking brake and braking system	驻车制动及踏板制动系统
high beam	远光灯
seat belt	座椅安全带
cruise control indicator	巡航控制指示灯
shift lever	变速杆
washer fluid	洗涤液
brake lamp monitor	制动灯监视器
burn out	熄灭
traction control system (TCS)	牵引力控制系统
supplemental restrain system (SRS)	辅助约束保护系统
heavy traffic	交通繁忙

Notes to the Text

1. The instruments commonly used include the speedometer, engine tachometer, oil pressure gauge, water temperature gauge, fuel gauge, ammeter, etc.
   常用的仪表有车速表、发动机转速表、机油压力表、水温表、燃油表、电流表等。

2. If the light stays on or comes on while the engine is running, you have lost oil pressure and continued operation will cause severe engine damage.
   如果发动机正常运转时,指示灯仍然亮,则机油压力过低,继续工作将会导致发动机损坏。

3. A beeper also sounds if you have not fastened your seat belt and it will stop after a few seconds.
   如果您没有系好安全带,蜂鸣器会响,几秒钟后停下。

4. If a brake light does not work, the BRAKE LAMP indicator comes on when you push down the brake pedal with the ignition switch ON.
   如果制动灯不工作,当您踩制动踏板,同时把点火开关拨至"ON"位置时,制动灯的监视器"BRAKE LAMP"会亮。

5. The airbag warning light goes on to alert the driver of trouble in the SRS system when a malfunction is detected in the center airbag sensor assembly self-diagnosis.
   当中央气囊传感器总成自诊系统检测出故障时,安全气囊警告灯亮,提示驾驶人SRS有故障。

Exercises

I. Choose the correct answer to fill in the blanks.

1. If the engine electronic control system is not working properly, which light comes on? _____.
   A. Brake system indicator   B. Charging system indicator
   C. Low oil pressure indicator   D. Check engine indicator

2. The airbag warning light goes on to alert the driver of trouble in the _____ system when a malfunction is detected in the center airbag sensor assembly self-diagnosis.
   A. TCS   B. SRS   C. CCS   D. ASR

3. It is the control panel of a car. It contains gauges used to measure speed, distance traveled, etc. It is generally located in front of the driver. What is it?_____.
   A. Cigarette lighter   B. Dashboard   C. Steering wheel   D. Engine compartment

4. Which meter on the dashboard measures the instantaneous speed of an auto?_____.
   A. Speedometer   B. Odometer   C. Tachometer

5. Which symbol is the high beam indicator?_____.

   A.   B.   C.   D.

6. What does the symbol mean?_____.
   A. Brake lamp monitor
   B. ABS indicator
   C. Hazard warning lamp

7. Which gauge shows the engine speed?_____.
   A. Speedometer   B. Odometer   C. Tachometer

II. Translate the following passages into Chinese.

  The instruments commonly used include the speedometer, engine tachometer, oil pressure gauge, water temperature gauge, fuel gauge, ammeter, etc. Changes in the monitored object's status are directly shown in most instruments through the sensors.

  With the development of automotive electronic technology, the multifunctional and high-precision instrument with intuitive readings, which is shown by electronic digital and image, has been used in vehicles continuously.

_____
_____
_____
_____
_____
_____

III. Translate the following phrases into Chinese or English.

1. low oil pressure indicator   _____

Chapter 4　Body and Electrical System

2. parking brake and braking system indicator　_____
3. check engine indicator　_____
4. door and brake lamp monitor　_____
5. combination car instrument panel　_____
6. left turn signal light　_____
7. supplemental restrain system (SRS)　_____
8. traction control system (TCS)　_____

Ⅳ. Write out the terms according to the pictures.

Picture 1

1. _____　2. _____　3. _____　4. _____　5. _____

6. _____　7. _____　8. _____　9. _____　10. _____

Picture 2: Automobile instrument panel

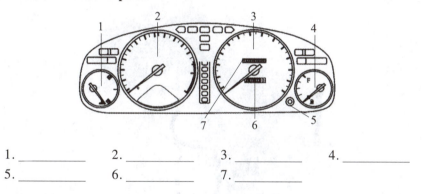

1. _____　2. _____　3. _____　4. _____
5. _____　6. _____　7. _____

Ⅴ. The following picture shows symbols of meter and indicator. Look at the picture and label it correctly using the words and phrases given below.

fuel level indicator	cruise control indicator	tachometer
maintenance required indicator	speedometer	temperature gauge
trip meter reset button	trip meter	odometer

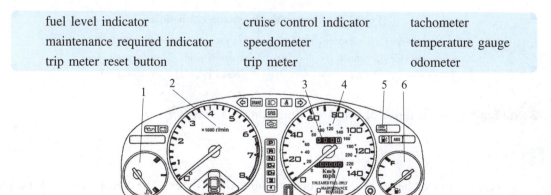

Unit 3 Air Conditioning System

When the weather gets hot outside, there is nothing more important than making sure it stays cool and comfortable inside your car. Automobile air conditioning is a system that cools and dehumidifies air entering the passenger compartment. Automobile air conditioning ushered a revolution in the automobile sector, redefining the benchmark of luxury cars. Introduced in the 1940s, automobile air conditioning has gained so much popularity.

Air conditioning system has such functions as follows:

1) Keep us cool in hot days.
2) Get us warm in cold days.
3) Make the interior air of the car clean and dehumidify.
4) Let outside air enter the car at the desired speed.

Vehicles have primarily three different types of air conditioning systems. While each of the three types differs, the concept and design are very similar to one another. The most common components that make up these automotive systems are the following: compressor, condenser, evaporator, expansion valve, receiver-drier, etc. See Fig.4-3-1.

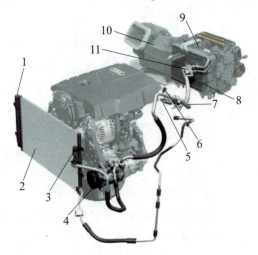

Fig.4-3-1 Air conditioning system composition

1—receiver-drier 2—condenser 3—refrigerant pressure and temperature sensor
4—compressor 5—quick coupling 6—maintenance joint 7—refrigerant pipe
8—evaporator 9—air-conditioner 10—air intake box 11—expansion valve

Some Main Components of the Air Conditioning System

1 Compressor

Referred to as the "heart" of the air conditioning (A/C) system. The compressor is what takes the refrigerant (the gas) and pressurizes it so it will cool the air. It's run by an engine belt. The compressor also has an electrically operated clutch that turns the compressor on and off as we demand more cool air. The purpose of the clutch on the compressor is to transmit power from the engine to the compressor and provide a means of engaging and disengaging the system from engine operation. And it is driven by power from the engine crankshaft. Compressor has two sides, which serve the function of suction and pump. The suction takes in gas from the evaporator, while the pump sends it to the condenser. Condenser is where the gas is dissipated. Hot gas is cooled in the condenser. See Fig. 4-3-2 and Fig. 4-3-3.

Fig.4-3-2　**Compressor**

a) Rotary vane type　　　b) Scroll type　　　c) Axial piston type　　　d) Reciprocating piston type

Fig.4-3-3　**Types of compressor**

2 Condenser

Designed like a car radiator, a condenser does not perform a function obverse to the former. It is usually mounted at the front of the car right next to the big radiator. Sometimes the condenser will have its own electric cooling fan, too. The purpose of the condenser is to condense or liquefy the high-pressure hot vapor coming from the compressor. See Fig. 4-3-4.

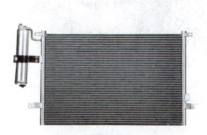 

Fig.4-3-4　**Shape diagram of condenser**

3 Evaporator

Located inside the vehicle, the evaporator is another little radiator that does just the opposite task as the condenser. The evaporator serves as the heat absorption component. The evaporator provides several functions. Its primary duty is to remove heat from the inside of the vehicle. A secondary benefit is dehumidification.

Evaporator functions as the site where heat is absorbed from the vehicle. The optimum temperature for the evaporator is 0℃. See Fig. 4-3-5.

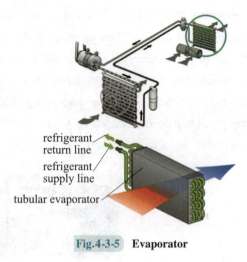

Fig.4-3-5　Evaporator

4 Thermal Expansion Valve

Another common refrigerant regulator is the thermal expansion valve (TXV). This type of valve can sense both temperature and pressure, and is very efficient at regulating refrigerant flow to the evaporator in the cycling clutch thermostatic expansion valve (CCTXV) system.

5 Receiver-Drier

The receiver-drier is used on the high side of the cycling clutch thermostatic expansion valve system that uses a thermal expansion valve. This type of metering valve requires liquid refrigerant. To ensure that the valve gets liquid refrigerant, a receiver is used. The primary function of the receiver-drier is to separate gas and liquid. The secondary purpose is to remove moisture and filter out dirt. The receiver-drier usually has a sight glass in the top. This sight glass is often used to charge the system. Under normal operating conditions, vapor bubbles should not be visible in the sight glass. See Fig. 4-3-6.

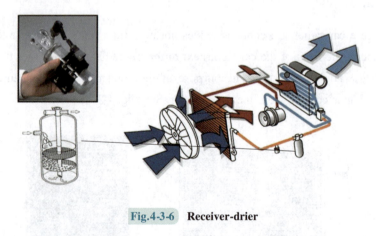

Fig.4-3-6　Receiver-drier

6 Pressure Regulating Device

There are different types of pressure regulating devices, mostly tubes that help to regulate the flow of refrigerant air into and out of the compressor.

Fig. 4-3-7 shows the cooling process of the air condition.

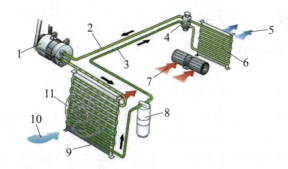

Fig.4-3-7　Cooling process of the air condition

1—compressor　2—low-pressure side　3—high-pressure side
4—expansion valve　5—cooled fresh air　6—evaporator　7—warm fresh air
8—receiver-drier　9—condenser　10—cooling air　11—electric fan

  In recent years, R-134a is widely used as refrigerant instead of R-12 in air conditioning systems. It has more advantages than R-12. It does not deplete the ozone layer which helps to protect us from the ultraviolet rays from the sun, and its evaporation temperature is much higher than that of R-12.

New Words and Expressions

dehumidify	/ˌdiːhjuːˈmidifai/	v.	除湿,使干燥
interior	/inˈtiəriə/	adj.	车身内部的,室内的,里面的;内部(侧);驾驶室
desired	/diˈzaiəd/	adj.	期望的,预期的
differ	/ˈdifə/	v.	不一致,不同
evaporator	/iˈvæpəˌreitə/	n.	蒸发器
benchmark	/ˈbentʃˌmɑːk/	n.	基准
accumulator	/əˈkjuːmjuleitə/	n.	储能器
Freon	/ˈfriːɔn/	n.	氟,氟里昂
drier	/ˈdraiə/	n.	干燥器
compressor	/kəmˈpresə/	n.	压缩机
orifice	/ˈɔːrəfis/	n.	孔,口
liquefy	/ˈlikwifai/	vt.	液化;溶解
dissipate	/ˈdisipeit/	v.	散去,驱除
refrigerant	/riˈfridʒərənt/	adj.	制冷的
		n.	制冷剂
condense	/kənˈdens/	v.	冷凝,压缩
condenser	/kənˈdensə/	n.	冷凝器
suction	/ˈsʌkʃn/	n.	吸入
evaporate	/iˈvæpəreit/	v.	蒸发
radiator	/ˈreidieitə/	n.	散热器
dehumidification	/ˌdiːhjuːˌmidifiˈkeiʃn/	n.	除去湿气
air conditioning（A/C）		空气调节装置	
expansion valve		膨胀阀,溢流阀,蒸发阀	
orifice tube		节流孔管	
air flow volume		空气流量	
air passage sensor		风道传感器	
air conditioning amplifier		空调放大器	
receiver-drier		储液干燥器	

Notes to the Text

1. Automobile air conditioning is a system that cools and dehumidifies air entering the passenger compartment.
   汽车空调是一个对进入座舱的空气进行冷却、除湿的系统。

2. The purpose of the clutch on the compressor is to transmit power from the engine to the compressor and provide a means of engaging and disengaging the system from engine operation.
   离合器的作用是把发动机的动力传递给压缩机，并能让压缩机与发动机结合或分离。

3. The purpose of the condenser is to condense or liquefy the high-pressure hot vapor coming from the compressor.
   冷凝器的作用是冷凝或液化来自压缩机的高压热蒸汽。

4. The primary function of the receiver-drier is to separate gas and liquid. The secondary purpose is to remove moisture and filter out dirt.
   储液干燥器的主要功能是使气液分离。其另一功能是除去湿气和滤除杂质。

Exercises

Ⅰ. Answer the following questions according to the text.

1. What's the function of the air conditioning system?
2. Please name the major parts that make up the air conditioning system.
3. What's the function of the compressor?
4. Please describe the cooling process of the air conditioning.

Ⅱ. Translate the following phrases into Chinese.

1. evaporator pressure regulator　　　　_____
2. air conditioner control assembly　　　_____
3. air conditioning amplifier　　　　　　_____
4. ambient temperature sensor　　　　　 _____
5. high-pressure side　　　　　　　　　 _____
6. expansion valve　　　　　　　　　　 _____
7. air passage sensor　　　　　　　　　 _____
8. air conditioning（A/C）　　　　　　　_____

Ⅲ. Choose the best answer from the following choices.

1. Which system is really to remove the heat that makes us uncomfortable, and return the air to the car's interior in an un-hearted condition? _____.

   A. Water-cooled system　　　　　　B. Air-cooled system
   C. Lubrication system　　　　　　　D. Air conditioning system

2. Which one is located inside the liquid line between the condenser and the evaporator? _____.

   A. Accumulator　　B. Receiver-drier　　C. Orifice tube　　D. Evaporator

3. Which part contains a desiccant that is a chemical that attracts moisture?_____.
   A. Expansion valve
   B. Pressure regulating device
   C. Receiver-drier
   D. Condenser
4. Which device is used to regulate the flow of liquid refrigerant into the evaporator?_____.
   A. Receiver
   B. Metering device
   C. Compressor
   D. Condenser
5. Which component in the heart of the air conditioning system?_____.
   A. Receiver
   B. Compressor
   C. Condenser
   D. Evaporator
6. Which component in the A/C system is to liquefy the high-pressure hot vapor coming from the compressor?_____.
   A. Receiver
   B. Accumulator
   C. Condenser
   D. Metering device
7. This is a device that is like a condenser, but much smaller than a condenser. It is located in the air handling case along with the blower. What is it?_____.
   A. Accumulator
   B. Evaporator
   C. Receiver-drier
   D. Radiator

IV. Translate the following passage into Chinese.

Vehicles have primarily three different types of air conditioning systems. While each of the three types differs, the concept and design are very similar to one another. The most common components that make up these automotive systems are the following: compressor, condenser, evaporator, expansion valve, receiver-drier, etc.

_____
_____
_____
_____
_____
_____

V. The following is an automotive air-conditioning refrigeration system. Write out the terms according to the picture.

1. _____ 2. _____ 3. _____
4. _____ 5. _____ 6. _____

Unit 4　Automobile Sensors

Why is sensor technology important to automobiles? Sensors are the technology piece that enables both the driver and the passenger to play an interactive role with the automobile in the driving experience. Sensor inputs are used in the decision-making process to give the driver more comfort, performance, safety and control. There are over 110 sensors in the average vehicle today. The majority of those sensors are pressure and acceleration sensors. The performance of any control system is, first of all, related to the accuracy with which information about the operating variables or parameters is relayed to the controlling process. Common measures in automobiles are temperature, pressure, flow, position, speed, knock and oxygen concentration.

1 Temperature Sensor

The ECM needs to adjust a variety of systems based on temperatures. It is critical for proper operation of these systems that the engine reaches operating temperature and the temperature is accurately sent to the ECM. Temperature sensor measures engine coolant temperature (ECT), in take air temperature (IAT), exhaust gas recirculation (EGR) temperature, etc.

2 Engine Coolant Temperature (ECT) Sensor

The ECT sensor responds to changes in engine coolant temperature. By measuring engine coolant temperature, the ECM knows the average temperature of the engine. The ECT sensor is usually located in the coolant passage just before the thermostat.

3 Intake Air Temperature (IAT) Sensor

The IAT sensor detects the temperature of the incoming air stream. On vehicles equipped with a manifold absolute pressure (MAP) sensor, the IAT sensor is part of the mass air flow (MAF) sensor. The IAT sensor is used for detecting ambient temperature during a cold start and intake air temperature as the engine heats up the incoming air.

4 Exhaust Gas Recirculation (EGR) Temperature Sensor

The EGR temperature sensor is located in the EGR passage and measures the temperature of the exhaust gases.

5 Pressure Sensor

Pressure sensors are used to measure intake manifold pressure, atmospheric pressure, vapor pressure in the fuel tank, etc.

Chapter 4 Body and Electrical System

6 Manifold Absolute Pressure (MAP) Sensor

In the manifold absolute pressure sensor, there is a silicon chip inside a reference chamber. On one side of the chip is a reference pressure. On the other side is the pressure to be measured. When the silicon chip flexes with the change in pressure, the electrical resistance of the chip changes. This change in resistance alters the voltage signal. The ECM interprets the voltage signal to pressure and any change in voltage means there was a change in pressure. Intake manifold pressure is directly related to engine load. The ECM needs to know the intake manifold pressure to calculate how much fuel to inject, when to ignite the cylinder, and perform other functions.

7 Barometric Pressure Sensor

The barometric pressure sensor, sometimes called a high altitude compensator (HAC), operates the same as the MAP sensor except that it measures the atmospheric pressure. It is located inside the ECM. If it is defective, the entire ECM must be replaced.

8 Vapor Pressure Sensor

The vapor pressure sensor (VPS) measures the vapor pressure in the evaporative emission control system, the vapor pressure sensor may be located on the fuel tank, near the charcoal canister assembly. This sensor operates the same as the MAP sensor except that it measures the vapor pressure in the evaporative emission control system.

9 Mass Air Flow (MAF) Sensors

Air flow sensor includes three types of sensors: MAF sensor, hot wire type MAF sensor and vane air flow meter.

The mass air flow sensors convert the amount of air drawn into the engine into a voltage signal. The ECM needs to know the intake volume to calculate engine load. This is necessary to determine how much fuel to inject, when to ignite the cylinder, and when to shift the transmission. The air flow sensor is located directly in the intake air stream, between the air cleaner and throttle body where it can measure incoming air.

The vane air flow meter provides the ECM with an accurate measure ment of the load placed on the engine. The ECM uses it to calculate basic injection duration and basic ignition advance angle.

10 Position Sensor

In many applications, the ECM needs to know the position of mechanical components. The throttle position sensor (TPS) indicates the position of the throttle valve. Accelerator pedal position (APP) sensor indicates the position of the accelerator pedal. Exhaust gas recirculation (EGR) valve position sensor indicates the position of the EGR valve. Electrically, these sensors operate the same way.

11 Throttle Position Sensor

The TPS is mounted on the throttle body and converts the throttle valve angle into an electrical signal. As the throttle opens, the signal voltage increases.

The ECM uses throttle valve position information to:

1) Know engine mode: idle, pare throttle, wide open throttle (WOT).
2) Switch off A/C and emission controls at wide open throttle.
3) Correct air-fuel ratio.
4) Cut fuel.

12 Accelerator Pedal Position (APP) Sensor

The APP sensor is mounted on the throttle body. The APP sensor converts the accelerator pedal movement and position into two electrical signals. Electrically, the APP sensor is identical in operation to the TPS.

13 EGR Valve Position Sensor

The EGR valve position sensor is mounted on the EGR valve and detects the height of the EGR valve. The ECM uses this signal to control EGR valve height. The EGR valve position sensor converts the movement and position of the EGR valve into an electrical signal. Operation is identical to the TPS except that the signal arm is moved by the EGR valve.

14 Position/Speed Sensors

Position/speed sensors provide information to the ECM about the position of a component, the speed of a component and the change in speed of a component. The following sensors provide this data:

1) Camshaft position sensor (also called G sensor).
2) Crankshaft position sensor (also called NE sensor).
3) Vehicle speed sensor.

The camshaft position sensor, crankshaft position sensor and one type of vehicle speed sensor are of the pick-up coil type sensor.

15 Camshaft Position Sensor (G Sensor)

This sensor is located near one of the camshafts. An alternating current signal is generated that is directly proportional to camshaft speed. That is, as the camshaft revolves faster, the frequency increases. By knowing the position of the camshaft, the ECM determines when cylinder No. 1 is on the compression stroke.

16 Crankshaft Position Sensor (NE Sensor)

The ECM uses crankshaft position signal to determine engine speed, crankshaft position and engine misfire. This signal is referred to as the NE signal. The NE signal, combined with the G signal, indicates the cylinder that is on compression and the ECM can determine from its programming the engine firing order.

17 Vehicle Speed Sensor (VSS)

The VSS signal originates from a sensor measuring transmission/transaxle output speed or wheel speed. Different types of sensors have been used depending on models and applications.

18 Knock Sensors

The knock sensor detects engine knock and sends a voltage signal to the ECM. The ECM uses the knock sensor signal to control timing. The knock sensor, located in the engine block, cylinder head or intake manifold is tuned to detect that frequency. Inside the knock sensor is a piezoelectric element. Piezoelectric elements generate a voltage when pressure or vibration is applied to them. The piezoelectric element in the knock sensor is tuned to the engine knock frequency. The vibrations from engine knocking vibrate the piezoelectric element generating a voltage. The voltage output from the knock sensor is highest at this time.

19 Oxygen/Air Fuel Sensors

The ECM uses an oxygen sensor to ensure the air/fuel ratio is correct for the catalytic converter. Based on the oxygen sensor signal, the ECM will adjust the amount of fuel injected into the intake air stream. There are different types of oxygen sensors, but two of the more common types are:

1) Narrow-range oxygen sensor: the oldest style, simply called the oxygen sensor.
2) Wide-range oxygen sensor: the newest style, called the air/fuel ratio (A/F) sensor.

20 Oxygen Sensor

This style of oxygen sensor has been in service for the longest time. The oxygen sensor generates a voltage signal based on the amount of oxygen in the exhaust compared to the atmospheric oxygen.

21 Air/Fuel Ratio Sensor

The air/fuel ratio (A/F) sensor is similar to the narrow-range oxygen sensor. The advantage of using the A/F sensor is that the ECM can more accurately meter the fuel reducing emissions. To accomplish this, the A/F sensor:

1) Operates at approximately 650℃, much hotter than the oxygen sensor (400℃).
2) Changes its current (amperage) output in relation to the amount of oxygen in the exhaust stream.

New Words and Expressions

performance	/pəˈfɔːməns/	n.	性能，本事，表演，表现；履行，执行
parameter	/pəˈræmitə/	n.	参数，参量
recirculation	/riːˌsɜːkjəˈleiʃn/	n.	再循环，回流，信息重记，信息重复循环
detect	/diˈtekt/	vt.	察觉，发觉，侦查，探测
ambient	/ˈæmbiənt/	adj.	周围的，周遭的；环绕的

absolute	/ˈæbsəluːt/	adj.	绝对的，完全的
		n.	绝对
interpret	/inˈtəːprit/	v.	解释，说明，口译，通译
barometric	/ˌbærəuˈmetrik/	adj.	气压的，气压计的
compensator	/ˈkɔmpənseitə/	n.	补偿器，补助器，补偿（或赔偿）者；补偿（或赔偿），[电]自耦变压器，调相
evaporative	/iˈvæpəreitiv/	adj.	成为蒸气的；蒸发的
vane	/vein/	n.	叶片，刀片，瓣，轮叶，风向标
duration	/djuˈreiʃn/	n.	（时间的）持续，持久
revolve	/riˈvɔlv/	vt.	使旋（绕）转；使周转，细想，盘算
piezoelectric	/piːˌeizəuiˈlektrik/	adj.	[物]压电的，压电式
relay	/ˈriːlei/	n.	继电器，继动器
		vt.	中断；转播；接力
accuracy	/ˈækjurəsɪ/	n.	准确(性)，精确度，正确(性)
signal	/ˈsign(ə)l/	n.	信号，标志
		v.	发信号；标志着
		adj.	显著的
concentration	/ˌkɔnsnˈtreiʃn/	n.	浓度，浓缩，集中，集合，专心
calculate	/ˈkælkjuleit/	vt.	计算，核算，估计，推测，计划，打算
identical	/aiˈdentik(ə)l/	adj.	(to, with)相同(等)的；同样的
defective	/diˈfektiv/	adj.	有缺陷的；有瑕疵的

temperature sensor	温度传感器
engine coolant temperature（ECT）sensor	发动机冷却液温度传感器
intake air temperature（IAT）sensor	进气温度传感器
pressure sensor	压力传感器
manifold absolute pressure（MAP）sensor	进气歧管绝对压力传感器
silicon chip	硅片
barometric pressure sensor	大气压力传感器
high altitude compensator（HAC）	海拔补偿器
vapor pressure sensor（VPS）	蒸发压力传感器
charcoal canister assembly	活性炭罐总成
mass air flow（MAF）sensor	空气质量流量传感器
throttle position sensor（TPS）	节气门位置传感器
accelerator pedal position（APP）sensor	加速踏板位置传感器
EGR valve position sensor	废气再循环阀位置传感器
pick-up coil	耦合线圈，线圈，传感线圈，感应线圈
primary winding	一次线圈，初级线圈
secondary winding	二次线圈，次级线圈
pull-in solenoid	吸拉线圈
hold-on solenoid	保位线圈
alternating current（AC）	交流电
direct current（DC）	直流电
revolutions per minute（RPM）	转/分
vehicle speed sensor（VSS）	车速传感器
knock sensor（KS）	爆燃传感器
piezoelectric element	压电元件
oxygen sensor	氧传感器

Notes to the Text

1. The performance of any control system is, first of all, related to the accuracy with which information about the operating variables or parameters is relayed to the controlling process.
任何控制系统的性能,首先与反馈到控制过程中的操作变量或参数的信息精确度相关。

2. It is critical for proper operation of these systems that the engine reaches operating temperature and the temperature is accurately sent to the ECM.
发动机的温度达到运行温度,并将温度信号准确地传送到ECM,这对各系统的正常运行是非常重要的。

3. The EGR temperature sensor is located in the EGR passage and measures the temperature of the exhaust gases.
废气再循环温度传感器安装在废气再循环装置的通道上,用于测量废气的温度。

4. The ECM needs to know the intake manifold pressure to calculate how much fuel to inject, when to ignite the cylinder, and perform other functions.
ECM需要知道进气歧管的压力,以便于计算燃油喷射量、点火时间和执行其他的功能。

5. The TPS is mounted on the throttle body and converts the throttle valve angle into an electrical signal.
TPS被安装在节气门体上,并且将节气门的开度角转换成电信号。

6. The vibrations from engine knocking vibrate the piezoelectric element generating a voltage.
发动机爆燃产生的振动振击压电元件,致使压电元件产生电压。

7. The advantage of using the A/F sensor is that the ECM can more accurately meter the fuel reducing emissions.
使用空燃比传感器的优点是,ECM能够更精确地计算出燃油量,减少排放污染。

Exercises

Ⅰ. Answer the following questions according to the text.

1. Why do we have to use sensors in automobiles?
2. Can you list the sensors we have studied in the text?
3. What are the sensors used for?
4. What is the function of the MAP sensor?
5. What does the position sensor consist of?

Ⅱ. Choose the best answer from the following choices according to the text.

1. An alternating current signal is generated that is directly _____ to camshaft speed.
   A. proportional   B. proposition   C. identical   D. same
2. Crankshaft position signal is _____ to as the NE signal.
   A. named   B. know   C. refer   D. referred

3. Performance of any control system is related to the accuracy with which information about the operating variables or _____ is relayed to the controlling process.
   A. parameters   B. temperature   C. pressure   D. position
4. By measuring engine coolant temperature, the ECM knows the _____ temperature of the engine.
   A. effective   B. average   C. highest   D. lowest
5. The mass air flow sensors convert the amount of air drawn into the engine into _____ signals.
   A. frequency   B. electrical   C. voltage   D. position
6. The APP sensor converts the accelerator pedal movement and position into _____ electrical signals.
   A. one   B. two   C. three   D. four
7. Engine knock occurs within a specific _____ range.
   A. voltage   B. resistance   C. frequency   D. temperature
8. The ECM needs to adjust a _____ of systems based on temperatures.
   A. great   B. various   C. variety   D. vary

Ⅲ. Translate the following phrases into Chinese.

1. manifold absolute pressure   _____
2. oxygen concentration   _____
3. piezoelectric element   _____
4. vehicle speed sensor   _____
5. barometric pressure   _____
6. pick-up coil   _____
7. camshaft position sensor   _____
8. alternating current   _____
9. silicon chip   _____

Ⅳ. Choose the best answer from the following choices.

| A. TPS | B. MAP | C. MAF | D. IAT | E. CKPS |
| F. IAC | G. KS | H. O_2 | I. EGR | J. VSS |

1. 空气流量传感器 _____   2. 怠速控制阀 _____
3. 爆燃传感器 _____   4. 进气压力传感器 _____
5. 氧传感器 _____   6. 进气温度传感器 _____
7. 废气再循环 _____   8. 车速传感器 _____
9. 节气门位置传感器 _____   10. 曲轴位置传感器 _____

Chapter 4　Body and Electrical System

Unit 5　Anti-Lock Braking System

1 Introduction

An anti-lock braking system (ABS) is a computer-controlled braking system that helps prevent wheel lockup during braking. When the wheel locks, it stops rotating and the tire skids or slides over the road surface, thus, the vehicle requires a greater distance to stop than if the tires were not skidding. In addition to a greater distance, the driver loses directional control of the vehicle when it skids. Therefore, to stop the vehicle in the shortest possible distance and in as straight a line as possible, the wheels must be prevented from locking, the ABS system can maintain control of the vehicle. It works by limiting the pressure to any wheel, which decelerates too rapidly. This allows maximum stopping force to be applied without brake lockup. In operation, the wheel speed sensors at each wheel send electronic pulse signals to the control unit. If wheel lockup is detected during brake application, the computer signals the modulator valve controls to limit the hydraulic pressure to the wheel cylinder. See Fig. 4-5-1.

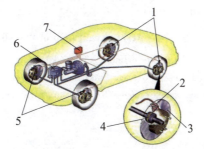

Fig.4-5-1　Schematic diagram of ABS system structure
1—rear wheel speed sensor　2—sensor　3—brake disk　4—pulse generator
5—front wheel speed sensor　6—ABS controller　7—ABS control unit

The function of an anti-lock, or anti-skid, braking system is to prevent the wheels from locking under hard braking. Maximum braking force is obtained just before the wheels lock and skid. Such anti-skid systems are useful on slippery surfaces, such as ice and snow, where the wheels may lock easily.

The ABS consists of components such as the wheel-speed sensors, hydraulic unit in hydraulic brake booster(HBB), ECU and pressure regulator, as shown in Fig. 4-5-2.

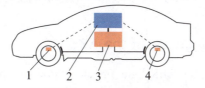

Fig.4-5-2　Components of ABS
1—wheel-speed sensor (front wheel)　2—ECU　3—pressure regulator
4—wheel-speed sensor (rear wheel)

145

The system uses a sensor that knows when one wheel (or a pair of wheels) is skidding. The sensor sends a signal to a computer, which signals a modulator valve. The modulator connects to the hydraulic system and can momentarily release the brake pressure and prevent the wheels from locking. (The pressure release is so fast that a driver is seldom aware of it.) Pressure is then reapplied until the sensor again senses that the wheel is about to lock up. Thus, this system keeps the wheels as close to lock up as possible, without actually allowing the wheels to lock up and skid. This is called incipient lock up. Maximum braking occurs at that point. See Fig. 4-5-3 and Fig. 4-5-4.

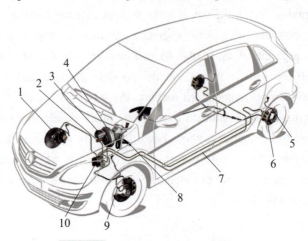

Fig.4-5-3　Arrangement map of the ABS

1—front brake　2—brake master cylinder　3—brake reservoir　4—brake booster
5—rear wheel-speed sensor　6—rear brake　7—brake pipe　8—brake pedal
9—front wheel-speed sensor　10—pressure regulator and ECU

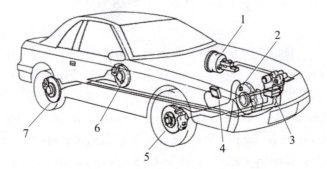

Fig.4-5-4　Anti-lock braking system

1—vacuum booster and master cylinder　2—front wheel-speed sensor　3—modulation assembly
4—electronic control unit　5—front disk brake　6—rear wheel-speed sensor　7—rear disk brake

2　Some Occasional Things about the ABS

When starting the vehicle, an ABS light on the instrument panel will illuminate for a few seconds; this is normal. But if the ABS light stays on, the ABS is not working; if the ABS light and brake warning light both stay on, the brakes do not exist.

When the ABS is active, various ABSs sound or feel differently and this is normal. Some of the effects, for example, are:

1) A groaning noise.

2) A rapid pulsing of the brake pedal.

3) A periodic dropping of the brake pedal.

4) A hard brake pedal.

5) A light that turns on to say "low" traction.

If the brakes squeal under normal braking, this may mean the brake pads are worn and need replacing. A pulsing brake pedal applied every time may mean warped brake rotors and/or seized brake calipers that require servicing.

The ABS works by comparing the speed of the wheels. When replacing tires, use the same size originally supplied with the car. Tire size and construction can affect wheel speed and may cause the system to work inconsistently.

A car with an ABS may require a longer distance to stop on loose or uneven surfaces than an equivalent car without anti-lock. Sometimes the ABS cannot make up for bad road conditions or judgment. It is still your responsibility to drive at reasonable speeds for weather and traffic conditions, and to leave a margin of safety.

3 The Advantages of ABS

Developed to improve the running performance of vehicles, ABS is designed on the principle that makes good use of the coefficient of wheel and ground. When the ABS senses a wheel lock-up, it modulates the brake hydraulic pressure; the proper brake force will be applied to the wheel.

The advantages of ABS:

1) It can decrease the distance of brake on even surfaces.

2) It enhances the stability of moving vehicles. The accident proportion will decrease by about 8 percent for the vehicles equipped with ABS.

3) It improves the wear properties of tires.

4) It can be used easily and can work steadily.

Fig. 4-5-5 shows the ABS braking diagram.

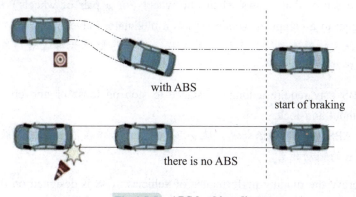

Fig.4-5-5　ABS braking diagram

New Words and Expressions

booster	/ˈbuːstə/	n.	助力器
modulator	/ˈmɔdjuleitə/	n.	调节器
momentarily	/ˈməuməntərili/	adv.	即刻
incipient	/ɪˈsipiənt/	adj.	初始的
skid	/skid/	v.	滑动，打滑（空转），（侧向）滑移
illuminate	/iˈl(j)uːmineit/	vt.	阐明，说明；照亮
periodic	/ˌpiəriˈɔdik/	adj.	周期的；定期的
inconsistently	/ˌinkənˈsistəntli/	adv.	不一致地，不协调地
equivalent	/iˈkwiv(ə)l(ə)nt/	adj.	等价的，相等的；同意义的
vessel	/ˈves(ə)l/	n.	船，舰；脉管，血管，容器，器皿
increment	/ˈiŋkrim(ə)nt/	n.	[数] 增量；增加；增额；盈余
accumulator	/əˈkjuːmjuleitə/	n.	蓄电池；储电器；累加器；积聚者
chirpy	/ˈtʃəːpi/	adj.	快活的；活泼的；啁啾叫的
diffuse	/diˈfjuːz/	vt.	扩散；传播；漫射
		adj.	弥漫的；散开的

anti-lock braking system	防抱死制动系统
wheel-speed sensor	轮速传感器
hydraulic pressure	液压，水压，油压
impending brake	紧急制动

Notes to the Text

1. When the wheel locks, it stops rotating and the tire skids or slides over the road surface, thus, the vehicle requires a greater distance to stop than if the tires were not skidding.
   当车轮抱死时，车轮停止转动，轮胎在路面上侧移或侧滑，因而，这时的汽车相对于轮胎不打滑时需要一个较长的制动距离。

2. The function of an anti-lock, or anti-skid, braking system is to prevent the wheels from locking under hard braking.
   防抱死或防滑移制动系统的功能是防止紧急制动时车轮抱死。

3. The system uses a sensor that knows when one wheel (or a pair of wheels) is skidding. The sensor sends a signal to a computer, which signals a modulator valve.
   防抱死制动系统使用传感器来得知车轮何时滑移。传感器把信号输送给计算机，计算机给液压调节器的电磁阀发送信号。

4. A car with an ABS may require a longer distance to stop on loose or uneven surfaces than an equivalent car without anti-lock.
   相对于没有装备 ABS 的同等车辆来说，装备了 ABS 的车辆在不平整或松软的路面上行驶时则需要一个更长的制动距离。

5. Developed to improve the running performance of vehicles, ABS is designed on the principle that makes good use of the coefficient of wheel and ground.
   为提高汽车的行驶性能而研发的 ABS，其工作原理是充分利用轮胎和地面之间的附着系数。

Exercises

I. Answer the following questions according to the text.

1. What's the function of an anti-lock braking system?
2. Please name the major parts that make up an anti-lock braking system.
3. When the speed sensor detects the wheel lock-up tendency, how does it work?
4. What is the function of the accumulator?
5. Give a way to detect whether the ABS has gone wrong.

II. Choose the correct answer to fill in the blanks.

1. What's the primary advantage of anti-lock braking systems?_____.
   A. They allow you to stop easier
   B. They allow you to steer while braking
   C. They prevent locking
2. Developed to improve the running performance of vehicles, ABS is designed on the principle that makes good use of the _____ of wheel and ground.
   A. function   B. frequency   C. coefficient   D. index
3. The _____ is a computer-controlled braking system that helps prevent wheel lockup during braking.
   A. ABS   B. ITS   C. GPS   D. EBCM
4. The EBCM performs a control cycle: if the wheel is decelerating too fast, isolates the wheel circuit. What does the "wheel circuit" mean?_____.
   A. Master cylinder   B. Pressure chamber
   C. Wheel rim   D. Wheel cylinder
5. _____ regulates the pressure to the wheel brakes when it receives commands from the control unit.
   A. The hydraulic modulator assembly   B. The electronic control unit
   C. The solenoid valve   D. The ABS
6. Which component is not included in the ABS?_____.
   A. WSS   B. EBCM   C. HCU   D. EBD
7. If anything goes wrong, the ABS indicator on the instrument panel comes on, which implies the anti-lock function of the braking system has shut down. What does this sentence mean? _____.
   A. ABS is an active safety system   B. ABS is a passive safety system
   C. ABS is a self-leveling system   D. ABS is a self-checking system
8. Which statement about ABS is false?_____.
   A. Brake pedal pulsation will be felt as the solenoids modulate fluid pressure
   B. When starting a vehicle, an ABS light on the instrument panel will illuminate for a few seconds
   C. If the ABS light stays on, the ABS is not working
   D. If the ABS light stays on, the brakes do not exist

III. Translate the following abbreviations into corresponding Chinese terms.

1. ABS   anti-lock braking system   _____
2. AP   accelerator pedal   _____

3. BMC   brake master cylinder   _____

4. PKB   parking brake   _____

5. BTR   brake transmission ratio   _____

6. NPS   neutral position switch   _____

Ⅳ. Translate the following sentences into English or Chinese.

1. For the system to react quickly, the modulator/solenoid unit must have brake fluid under high pressure.

   _____

2. The control unit monitors the operation of the wheel sensors, solenoids, pump and faults; it shuts off power to the motor and solenoid.

   _____

3. 当车辆起动时,轮速传感器发出信号输入 EBCM。

   _____

4. 当 ABS 工作时,听到异响是正常的。

   _____

5. ABS 有在平坦路面上缩短制动距离的优点。

   _____

Ⅴ. The following picture shows an anti-lock braking system. Write out the terms according to the picture.

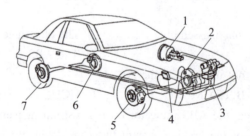

1. _____   2. _____   3. _____   4. _____

5. _____   6. _____   7. _____

Ⅵ. The following picture shows an anti-lock braking system. Look at the picture and label it correctly using the words and phrases given below.

steering wheel   break line

left brake   ABS system

master vacuum power section

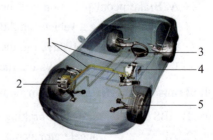

Unit 6 Safety Airbag System

Safety is foremost in the automobile manufacturers' minds. In order to guarantee optimal protection of vehicle occupants, lots of newer vehicles utilize airbag systems. An airbag is much like a nylon balloon that quickly inflates to stop the forward movement of the occupant's upper body. Fig.4-6-1 shows the safety airbag and Fig.4-6-2 shows the various safety airbag locations.

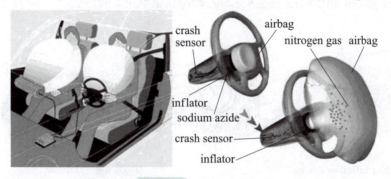

Fig.4-6-1 Safety airbag

As a matter of fact, airbags are designed to keep your head, neck and chest from slamming against the dashboard, steering wheel or windshield in a front-end crash. An airbag is an inflatable cushion, containing air or some other gas. Airbags are most commonly used for cushioning, in particular after very rapid inflation in the case of an automobile collision. See Fig. 4-6-3.

 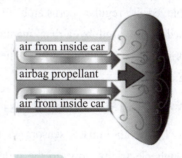

Fig.4-6-2 Various safety airbag locations   Fig.4-6-3 The way airbag works

1—side anti-collision airbag   2—rear occupant crash-proof airbag
3—driver anti-collision airbag   4—front occupant crash-proof airbag

An airbag system consists of impact sensors, an airbag inflation device and an airbag. The system can detect an impact, and send a signal that inflates the airbag.

The sensor is the device that detects an impact and tells the bag to inflate. The number of sensors used in a system depends on the design of the system. Some systems use only a single sensor and others use up to five. Normally sensors are located in the engine and passenger compartments. To prevent accidental deployment of the airbag, most systems require that at least two sensor switches be closed to deploy the airbag. Typically, ignition of the airbag only occurs when an outside sensor and an inside sensor are closed. See Fig. 4-6-4.

The inflation of the airbag is typically accomplished through an explosive release of nitrogen gas. An airbag inflation device includes the igniter, nitrogen gas, filters and sodium azide. The igniter is an integral part of the inflator assembly. It starts a chemical reaction to inflate the airbag. At the center of the igniter assembly is the squib. When voltage is supplied through the squib, an electrical arc is formed between two pins. The spark ignites a solid propellant, which burns extremely rapidly to create a large volume of gas to inflate the bag. See Fig. 4-6-5 and Fig. 4-6-6.

Fig.4-6-4　Crash sensor

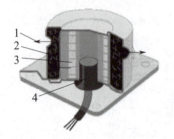

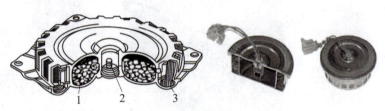

Fig.4-6-5　**Airbag inflation device**

1—nitrogen gas　2—filters
3—sodium azide　4—igniter

Fig.4-6-6　**Inflator**

1—sodium azide　2—igniter　3—filter screen

The bag itself is made of a thin, nylon fabric that is folded into the steering wheel, dash, seat or door. The powdery substance released from the airbag when it is deployed is regular cornstarch or talcum powder. These powders are used by airbag manufacturers to keep airbags lubricated and pliable while they are in storage. See Fig. 4-6-7.

Fig.4-6-7　Airbag

How the SRS Airbag Works

1) In an impact, sensors in the car detect the sudden deceleration. If the crash is severe enough, electricity flows to the inflator and causes ignition of the gas generator.

2) The gas generator then rapidly burns in the metal chamber. The rapid burning produces inert gases and small amounts of dust. The inert gases and dust are cooled and filtered during inflation of the airbag.

3) The inflating airbag splits open the trim cover. The airbag then rapidly unfolds and inflates in front of the occupant.

4) After inflation, the gas is vented through openings or open weave areas in the airbag.

These steps take place in a fraction of a second. Airbags deflate in under a second and may be pushed aside for occupants to exit. See Fig. 4-6-8.

Airbags have saved thousands of lives since their introduction in the early 1980s. Most cars had only a driver-side airbag and a passenger-side airbag years ago. Today, some cars go far beyond having dual airbags to having six or even eight airbags. The occupants in the front seat may be further protected by side airbags and side curtain airbags. The rear passengers may be protected by airbags in the rear of the front seat backs, side airbags and side curtain airbags.

In the future, we will further expand the number of vehicles equipped with 6 airbags by adding side airbags that protect the arm and chest areas and curtain airbags that protect the head area in side impacts. See Fig. 4-6-9.

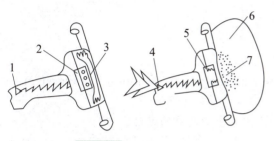
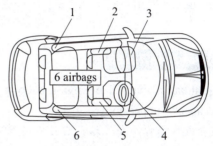

Fig.4-6-8　**Airbag inflates**
1,4—crash sensor　2,5—inflator
3,6—airbag　7—nitrogen gas

Fig.4-6-9　**Six-airbag system**
1,6—curtain airbag system　2,5—side airbag system
3—passenger airbag system　4—driver airbag system

New Words and Expressions

nylon	/ˈnailən/	n.	尼龙
inflate	/inˈfleit/	v.	膨胀，充气
inflator	/inˈfleitə/	n.	充气机，打气筒
occupant	/ˈɔkjupənt/	n.	乘坐者
nitrogen	/ˈnaitrədʒən/	n.	氮
sodium	/ˈsəudiəm/	n.	钠
azide	/ˈeizaid/	n.	[化]叠氮化物
squib	/skwib/	n.	雷管
arc	/ɑːk/	n.	弧，弧形，弧度
propellant	/prəˈpelənt/	n.	推进物
dash	/dæʃ/	n.	控制板
fabric	/ˈfæbrik/	n.	织品，布
cornstarch	/ˈkɔːnstɑːtʃ/	n.	玉米淀粉
talcum	/ˈtælkəm/	n.	[矿]滑石
crash	/kræʃ/	n.	碰撞
impact	/ˈimpækt/	n.	碰撞，冲击，冲突
deceleration	/diːˌseləˈreiʃn/	n.	减速，减速度
inert	/iˈnəːt/	adj.	惰性的
split	/split/	v.	劈开，(使)裂开
unfold	/ʌnˈfəuld/	vt.	打开，展开
vent	/vent/	n.	放气孔
		v.	放出，排出

airbag system	安全气囊系统	electrical arc	电弧
nylon balloon	尼龙气球	steering wheel	转向盘
impact sensor	撞击传感器	nylon fabric	尼龙布
inflation device	充气装置	talcum powder	滑石粉
airbag	气囊	airbag inflator	安全气囊气体发生器
passenger compartment	驾驶室	gas generator	气体发生器
nitrogen gas	氮气	push aside	把……推开，避开
sodium azide	叠氮化钠	side airbag	侧气囊
chemical reaction	化学反应		

Notes to the Text

1. An airbag is much like a nylon balloon that quickly inflates to stop the forward movement of the occupant's upper body.
   安全气囊很像尼龙气球，它可以迅速充气，阻止乘客上身向前的运动。

2. To prevent accidental deployment of the airbag, most systems require that at least two sensor switches be closed to deploy the airbag. Typically, ignition of the airbag only occurs when an outside sensor and an inside sensor are closed.
   为了防止安全气囊意外充气，大多数系统要求至少有两个传感器开关闭合才能给气囊充气。典型的安全气囊只有在外部传感器和内部传感器都闭合时，充气装置才能点火。

3. When voltage is supplied through the squib, an electrical arc is formed between two pins. The spark ignites a solid propellant, which burns extremely rapidly to create a large volume of gas to inflate the bag.
   当有电压提供给雷管时，会在它的两极产生一个电弧，点燃固体燃料，燃料燃烧，并快速产生大量氮气，充满气囊。

4. The powdery substance released from the airbag when it is deployed is regular cornstarch or talcum powder. These powders are used by airbag manufacturers to keep airbags lubricated and pliable while they are in storage.
   当安全气囊展开时，从安全气囊中释放出的粉状物质是细腻的玉米淀粉或者滑石粉，安全气囊制造商使用这些粉末来保持安全气囊储存时的润滑和柔韧性。

Exercises

Ⅰ. Answer the following questions according to the text.

1. What's the function of the airbag system?
2. What components does an airbag inflation device include?
3. What is the working process of SRS?
4. What does the inflator consist of?

Ⅱ. Translate the following passage into Chinese.

The sensor is the device that detects an impact and tells the bag to inflate. The number of sensors used in a system depends on the design of the system. Some systems use only a single sensor and others use up to five. Normally sensors are located in the engine and passenger compartments. To prevent accidental deployment of the airbag, most systems require that at least two sensor switches be closed to deploy the airbag. Typically, ignition of the airbag only occurs when an outside sensor and an inside sensor are closed.

_____
_____
_____
_____
_____
_____

III. Translate the following phrases into Chinese or English.

1. airbag system _____
2. airbag module _____
3. radiator support _____
4. solid chemical gas _____
5. center airbag sensor assembly _____
6. 气囊传感器 _____
7. 安全气囊气体发生器 _____
8. 气体发生器 _____

IV. Choose the correct answer to fill in the blanks.

1. Airbags are called _____ because they are designed to work in combination with safety belts.
   A. diagnostic units   B. supplemental restraints   C. inflators   D. bumpers
2. By what percentage do seatbelts reduce the risk of death for a person sitting in the front seat? _____.
   A. 40%   B. 50%   C. 60%
3. How far behind the steering wheel should you sit to avoid injury from an inflated airbag? _____.
   A. 8 in (20.3 cm)   B. 10 in (25.4 cm)
   C. 5 in (12.7 cm)
4. Where do typical car seatbelts apply most of the stopping force? _____.
   A. The shoulders and hips   B. The ribcage and pelvis
   C. The chest and abdomen
5. What kind of gas inflates an airbag? _____.
   A. Hydrogen   B. Helium   C. Nitrogen
6. What area of a car is designed to deform in a collision? _____.
   A. The doors   B. The interior   C. The crumple zone

7. By what percentage can airbags reduce the risk of dying in a direct frontal crash?_____.
   A. Twenty percent   B. Thirty percent   C. Fifty percent

Ⅴ. **The following is an anti-lock braking system. Write out the terms according to the picture.**

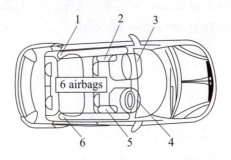

1. _____   2. _____   3. _____
4. _____   5. _____   6. _____

Unit 7 Cruise Control System

Cruise control (sometimes known as speed control) system is a system that automatically controls the rate of motion of a motor vehicle. The driver sets the speed and the system will take over the throttle of the car to maintain the same speed. The parts of cruise control system and their location are shown in Fig.4-7-1.

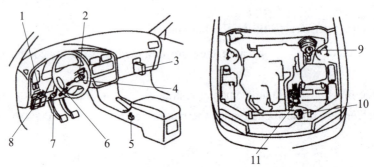

Fig.4-7-1 The parts of cruise control system and their location

1—terminal box No. 1   2—ignition switch   3—cruise control system electrical control elements
4—cruise control switch   5—parking brake switch   6—parking light switch   7—clutch switch
8—diagnostic communication link   9—brake fluid level warning light switch
10—neutral drive switch   11—cruise control actuator

Modern cruise control was invented in 1945 by the blind inventor and mechanical engineer Ralph Teetor. His idea was born out of the frustration of riding in a car driven by his lawyer, who kept speeding up and slowing down as he talked. The first car with Teetor's system was the Chrysler Imperial in 1958. This system calculated ground speed based on driveshaft rotations and used a solenoid to vary throttle position as needed.

The driver must bring the car up to speed manually and use a button to set the cruise control to the current speed. The cruise control system takes its speed signal from a rotating driveshaft, speedometer cable, speed sensor (found on the wheels) or from the engine's speed. Most systems do not allow the use of the cruise control below a certain speed (normally 55km/h) to discourage use in city driving. The car will maintain that speed by pulling the throttle cable with a solenoid or a vacuum-driven servomechanism.

Most systems can be turned off both explicitly and automatically when the driver hits the brake or clutch. Cruise control often includes a memory feature to resume the set speed after braking and a coast feature to reset the speed lower without braking. When the cruise control is in effect, the throttle can still be used to accelerate the car, but once the accelerator is released the car will then slow down until it reaches the previously set speed. See Fig.4-7-2.

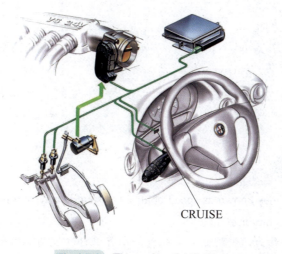

Fig.4-7-2　The cruise of Alfa Romeo

Some modern vehicles have adaptive cruise control (ACC) systems. These use either a radar or laser setup to allow the vehicle to keep pace with the car it is following, slow when closing in on the vehicle in front and accelerate again to the preset speed when traffic allows. Some systems also feature forward collision warning systems, which warn the driver if a vehicle in front gets too close. See Fig.4-7-3.

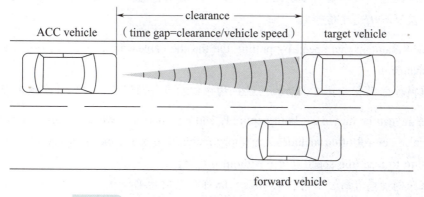

Fig.4-7-3　The principle of adaptive cruise control system

New Words and Expressions

cruise	/kruːz/	n./vi.	巡游,巡航
throttle	/ˈθrɒtl/	n.	节气门
driveshaft	/ˈdraivʃɑːft/	n.	传动轴
button	/ˈbʌtn/	n.	按钮
speedometer	/spiˈdɔmitə/	n.	速度表
vacuum	/ˈvækjuəm/	n.	真空
servomechanism	/ˈsəːvəuˌmekənizəm/	n.	伺服机构
coast	/kəust/	v.	滑行
accelerator	/ækˈseləˌreitə/	n.	加速器,加速踏板
radar	/ˈreidɑː/	n.	雷达,无线电探向和测距
laser	/ˈleizə/	n.	激光器
adaptive	/əˈdæptiv/	adj.	自适应的,适合的
cruise control			巡航控制
throttle position			节气门位置
adaptive cruise control（ACC）			自适应巡航控制

Notes to the Text

1. Cruise control（sometimes known as speed control）system is a system that automatically controls the rate of motion of a motor vehicle.
   巡航控制（有时也被称为速度控制）系统是一个可以自动控制机动车行驶速度的系统。

2. His idea was born out of the frustration of riding in a car driven by his lawyer, who kept speeding up and slowing down as he talked.
   他的想法源于他的律师差劲的驾驶技术,因为他的律师在说话的时候,不能稳住车速。

3. The cruise control system takes its speed signal from a rotating driveshaft, speedometer cable, speed sensor（found on the wheels）or from the engine's speed.
   巡航控制系统可以从转动的传动轴、速度表、转速传感器（安装于各个车轮处）或者发动机转速处获取车辆速度信号。

4. The car will maintain that speed by pulling the throttle cable with a solenoid or a vacuum-driven servomechanism.
   汽车可以通过电磁或者真空驱动的伺服机构来控制节气门绳索,以保证车速不变。

5. Most systems can be turned off both explicitly and automatically when the driver hits the brake or clutch. Cruise control often includes a memory feature to resume the set speed after braking and a coast feature to reset the speed lower without braking.
   当驾驶人踩制动或者离合器时,大多数系统都会及时地自动关闭。巡航控制一般具有记忆功能,使车速在制动后恢复到设定值,以及滑行功能,用于在不制动的情况下重置为较低的速度。

Exercises

I. Answer the following questions according to the text.

1. What is cruise control sometimes called?
2. How does cruise control work?

II. Translate the following phrases into English.

1. cruise control system　　　　_____
2. adaptive cruise control (ACC)　_____
3. logic probe　　　　　　　　　_____
4. accelerator pedal　　　　　　　_____
5. throttle position　　　　　　　 _____
6. transmission speed sensor　　　 _____
7. cruise control module　　　　　_____
8. cruise control switch　　　　　 _____
9. vehicle speed sensor　　　　　　_____

III. Write out the names of the following famous brands.

Column A

1. _____　2. _____　3. _____　4. _____　5. _____

6. _____　7. _____　8. _____　9. _____　10. _____

IV. Translate the following passage into Chinese.

　　Some modern vehicles have adaptive cruise control (ACC) systems. These use either a radar or laser setup to allow the vehicle to keep pace with the car it is following, slow when closing in on the vehicle in front and accelerate again to the preset speed when traffic allows. Some systems also feature forward collision warning systems, which warn the driver if a vehicle in front gets too close.

Chapter 5

Electric Vehicles

Unit 1 Introducing Electric Vehicles

1 Introduction

Automobile industry is the fundamental industry of national economy, it is closely related to people's life, and it has become an essential factor of modern society.

However, although providing us with fast and comfortable vehicles, traditional automobile industry consuming petroleum has already caused the economy's deep dependence on fossil energy resources and has made the conflict between energy production and consumption even worse.

24% of the world's total energy resource consumption is vehicle energy resource consumption.

As the number of vehicles is still increasing, the energy resource problem becomes more and more obvious and threatening.

Moreover, the air pollution and global warming caused by CO_2 has made a great influence on the environment in which we human beings are living.

In the circumstance of energy and environment crisis, increasing the efficiency of energy consumption and reducing the discharge of harmful waste are highly required.

However, it is very difficult to deal with this problem only by improving the performance of the engine. Developing new energy vehicles becomes the very direction of the development of automobile industry in the future.

Developing electric vehicles (EVs) is one of the effective ways of solving this problem. See Fig.5-1-1

a) Hybrid: Ford Escape HEV

b) Plug-in hybrid: Toyota Prius PHEV

Fig.5-1-1 Types of electric vehicle (continued)

c) Battery only: Tesla Roadster BEV   d) Fuel cell: Honda FCX hydrogen FCV

Fig.5-1-1　Types of electric vehicle

2　Advantages and Disadvantages of Electric Vehicles

Using electric vehicles is not a new concept. In the early 1900s, electricity was widely used in the US to run vehicles. Around this period, more than 50,000 vehicles running on electricity traveled across the US. However, as cheaper methods for production of gasoline were found, reliance on electric vehicles dwindled. There has currently been a revival of electric cars due to rising gas prices and environmental concerns.

◎ Advantages of Electric Vehicles

Compared with ordinary engine vehicles, EVs have the following advantages.

(1) High Level of Efficiency

The engine efficiency of engine vehicles is about 38%, while the ultimate efficiency is only 12% because of frequent braking, low-speed driving and signal waiting. But EVs suffer no loss of idling, and 80% of the e-power can be transfered from motor into vehicle motion. Besides, they can retrieve power when braking.

(2) Low Level of Environmental Pollution

Powered by batteries and supercapacitors, pure electric vehicles discharge no waste gas.

(3) Low Rate of Noise

The noise and vibration of the automobile depends on the engine and the driving condition. Compared to engine vehicles, EVs have much fewer vibration sources, no burning procedure, no mechanical motion, only noises from the air compressor, cooling fan and transmission mechanism. Thus their noise level is much lower than engine vehicles.

(4) Multiple Energy Resources Available

Not restrained by petroleum resources, EVs can acquire e-power from the public power grid. Thus any method to acquire e-power can apply to EVs, such as hydropower, nuclear power, thermal power, wind power, subterranean heat and solar power.

(5) Energy Feedback

According to the energy resource combination mechanism, we can easily retrieve the braking energy or potential energy when the speed is declining. Thus the continual mileage and the stability are going to increase. All the new EVs developed in recent years have energy retrieving systems, which can increase the continual mileage by 10% to 15%.

🎯 Advantages of Electric Vehicles Using Electricity as the Alternate Fuel

1) Electricity is readily available.

2) Since there is no internal combustion (IC) engine, the vehicle runs noiselessly, in fact, many times you won't even know that a vehicle has just passed you.

3) There are no emissions from EVs making them environmentally friendly.

4) Manufacturing EVs is very easy; you have to merely assemble various components of the vehicle. This is especially true for small motorcycles or mopeds.

5) EVs require less maintenance.

🎯 Disadvantages of Electric Vehicles

What are the disadvantages of electric vehicles? Some of the disadvantages include:

(1) They Have Their Limited Range, Some Need to Re-Fuel After Only 100 Miles

In EVs, a battery is used to store electricity, and it has to be charged from time to time. The normal working range of the battery is from 50 to 130 miles, thereafter the battery has to be recharged. When traveling a long distance, you may be at risk of the battery running out if there are no battery charging stations available on roads and highways. In some states like California and Arizona, shopping malls and some stores offer charging facilities, but they are not available everywhere. In the future, the trend of providing charging points is surely going to spread across other businesses and states. To compensate for this, you can choose a hybrid car, which can run on gasoline when the battery runs out.

(2) The Time It Takes to Recharge the Battery or Re-Fuel Can Be Over an Hour

It takes around 6 to 8 hours for the battery to get recharged completely. The battery of the EV rotates the shaft of the motor, which in turn rotates the wheels of the vehicle.

(3) They Can Be Expensive, Some Costing $50,000

To avoid emergencies due to discharging of the battery, companies are now manufacturing hybrid vehicles. Hybrids run on electricity as well as gasoline or diesel. This means you don't have to worry about the distance you are going to travel and the charging points. Although you will save on gas, the initial payment for EVs or hybrids is much higher than that of a gas-powered car. However, some still wonder about the practicality of such a car. Does it pay off?

(4) The Power Plants Producing Electricity Do Produce Pollution

Though the vehicle running on electricity does not produce pollution, the power plants producing electricity do produce pollution. The pollutants created by thermal power plants are one of the major sources of air pollution. The electricity generated from solar energy is totally pollution-free.

3 History of Electric Vehicles

"The electric vehicle", we may usually hear it recently, especially during the era of high price of gasoline today. However, the electric vehicle is not a recent development. In fact, the electric vehicle has been around for over 100 years, and it has an interesting history of development. Shortly after Joseph Henry's invention of the first electric direct current (DC) motor in 1830, engineers became interested in creating an electric-powered vehicle that would be a reliable source of transportation but the process was not perfected until much later, after the creation of rechargeable batteries by the French engineer, Gaston Planté, in 1859.

France and England were the first nations to develop the electric vehicle in the late 1800s. It was not until 1895 that Americans began to pay attention to the electric vehicles. Many innovations followed and interest in motor vehicles increased greatly in the late 1890s and early 1900s. And in 1897 the first commercial application was realized as city taxis. At the turn of the 20th century, America was prosperous with the motor vehicle. The years 1899 and 1900 were the high point of electric vehicles in America, as they outsold all other types of cars. Electric vehicles had many advantages over their competitors in the early 1900s. They did not have the vibration, smell and noise compared with gasoline cars. Changing gears on gasoline cars was the most difficult part of driving however electric vehicles did not require gear changes. It makes the control of electric vehicles simpler. While steam-powered cars also had no gear shifting, they suffered from long start-up times of up to 45 minutes on cold mornings. So the electric vehicle was the preferred choice during that period. But electric vehicles, shortcoming, limited range, led to a decrease in their popularity. With the invention of the electric starter for gas-powered cars, the reliability increasing, and the cheap price of gasoline, gas-powered cars took over the market and the EV industry vanished.

However, with the oil crisis of the 1970s, there was a need for alternative fueled vehicles to reduce the dependence on the oil and solve the problems of exhaust emissions from internal combustion engines, electric cars began to reemerge. During the period many vehicle manufacturers developed several electric vehicle models, see Fig.5-1-2, Fig.5-1-3 and Fig.5-1-4. Unfortunately, the low performance-to-price ratio of the electric vehicles made them very difficult to sell, and most of the vehicle manufacturers could not afford to make electric cars or could not make a profit, but to abandon electric vehicles. But now environmental pollution is becoming more and more serious, to solve it, humans have no choice but to devote more attention to study of the electric vehicles and make them more practical and improve the performance-to-price ratio to make them accepted by the public, and make benefits for the world verily. Subaru R1e, a kind of pure electric vehicle made by Fuji Auto, Tokyo Electric Power Company and NEC, represented the most advanced technology of pure electric vehicles. It weighs only 870 kg, and is driven by a motor of 40 kW supreme powers. And its top speed is up to 100 km/h. The battery can ensure 80 kilometers of the maximum trip range mileage. The battery charging system can be filled with 80% power in 15 minutes, so with less charging time, users no longer have to wait for hours of charging. And the life of the battery even up to 10 years makes the electric vehicles more acceptable.

a) 1914 Detroit EV: 80 miles range, 20 mph, NiFe batteries

b) 1980 commuter vehicles Comuta-Car: 30 mph, 40 miles range, PbA batteries

c) 1974 Zagato Elcar: 35 mph, 35 miles range, PbA batteries

Fig.5-1-2　Examples of low speed past production EVs

a) 1997 Chevrolet S10 EV: 95-mile range, NiMH batteries

b) 1998 Ford Range EV: 82-mile range, NiMH batteries

c) 1998 Solectria Force: 84-mile range, NiMH batteries

d) 2002 Toyota RAV4 EV: 94-mile range, NiMH batteries

Fig.5-1-3　Examples of long-range EVs still sold today

a) 1999 Chrysler EPIC: 79-mile range, NiMH batteries

b) 1999 General Motors EV1: 140-mile range, NiMH batteries

Fig.5-1-4　Examples of long-range EVs few to be found today (continued)

c) 1999 Honda EV Plus: 80-mile range, NiMH batteries   d) 2000 Think City: 55 mph, 45-mile range, NiMH batteries

Fig.5-1-4 **Examples of long-range EVs few to be found today**

4 Working Principle of Electric Vehicles

There is no doubt that most people are familiar with the gasoline engine vehicle: gasoline is pumped through the engine to create a series of explosions that produce the energy needed to move a vehicle. Electric vehicles have electric motors. These motors use electricity in place of gasoline to power the vehicle. They work when electricity is fed to the motor, creating a magnetic field. The magnetic field in the motor causes a tightly wound coil of wire to rotate. This rotation is used to spin the axle of the vehicle, hence turning the tires for motion.

5 Structure of Electric Vehicles

As for the motive power supplier, there are several kinds of motors suitable for electric vehicles like the brushless DC motor (BLDCM), switched reluctance motor (SRM) and exchange asynchronous motor. But at present the direct current series-excited motor is widely used in electric cars. This motor's "soft" mechanical properties are very similar to vehicle operating characteristics. It has many shortcomings like low efficiency, heavy maintenance workload; with the development of motor and motor controlling technology, it will be eliminated.

Compared to the gasoline engine, the battery is like the oil tank. It offers the electric motor electrical energy and the motor changes the electrical energy into mechanical energy making the car move and driving other devices to work. At present lead-acid battery is one of the most widely applied powers on the electric vehicle, but with the development of electric vehicle technology, the lead-acid battery, known for its low specific energy and long charging time, has been replaced by other batteries gradually, like the sodium-sulfur battery, the nickel-cadmium battery, the lithium battery, fuel cells, the flywheel battery and so on. These new types of electrical energy opened up broad prospects for the development of the electric vehicle.

The transmission transmits the motor driving torque to the car's driveshaft, and ensures cars move. Compared to internal combustion engine vehicles, for the motor can spin with load, the clutch is unnecessary. And the motor can change its direction of turning by circuit controlling; it can elide the reverse in the transmission.

The driving device is similar to traditional vehicles' including the wheel, tire, suspension, etc. It transmits the motor driving moment and acts on the ground. The steering device changes the direction of the car according to driver's willing. It includes the steering machine, the steering wheel, steering mechanisms, turning wheels, and so on. The braking device is also an important device of the cars. All the devices work cooperatively to ensure the vehicle performs normally. See Fig.5-1-5.

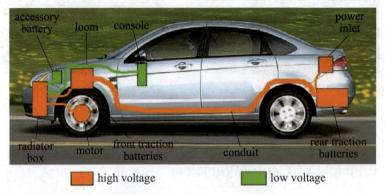

Fig.5-1-5 Construction overview

New Words and Expressions

fossil	/ˈfɔs(ə)l/	n.	化石；僵化的事物；顽固不化的人
crisis	/ˈkraisis/	n.	危机；危险期；决定性时刻
extensively	/ikˈstensivli/	adv.	广阔地；广大地
skyrocket	/ˈskairɔkit/	v.	（价格）飞涨；突涨，飞升
dwindle	/ˈdwind(ə)l/	vi.	减少；变小
revival	/riˈvaiv(ə)l/	n.	复兴；复活；苏醒；恢复精神；再生效
ultimate	/ˈʌltimət/	adj.	最终的；极限的；根本的
		n.	终极；根本；基本原则
thereafter	/ˌðɛəˈɑːftə/	adv.	其后；从那时以后
vanish	/ˈvæniʃ/	v.	销声匿迹，无影无踪
supreme	/suːˈpriːm/	adj.	最高的；至高的；最重要的

fossil energy	化石能源，矿物能源
energy production	能源生产；发电
production and consumption	生产和消费
air pollution	空气污染
global warming	全球变暖
plug-in hybrid	插电式混合动力
fuel cell	燃料电池
environmental concerns	环境问题
air compressor	空气压缩机
transmission mechanism	传导机制；传动机构；传动装置
rechargeable battery	充电式电池
pure electric vehicle	纯电动汽车
performance-to-price ratio	性价比
battery charging	电池充电
electric motor	电动机
switched reluctance motor	开关磁阻电动机
lead-acid battery	铅酸电池
nickel-cadmium battery	镍镉电池
sodium-sulfur battery	钠硫电池

Answer the following questions according to the text.
1. What industry is the fundamental industry of national economy?
2. How much of the world's total energy resource consumption is the vehicle energy resource consumption?
3. What problem becomes more and more obvious and threatening as the vehicle holding is still increasing?
4. What has made a great influence on the environment in which we human beings are living?
5. Please describe the advantages and disadvantages of electric vehicles.
6. Can you talk about the history of the electric vehicle?
7. Please describe the working principle of electric vehicles.
8. At present what batteries can be used on the electric vehicle?

Unit 2 Technology of Electric Vehicles

1 Present Technology of Electric Vehicles

To meet the practical application, the motor requires a high instant power and a high power density; a high torque at low speed for starting and climbing, as well as a high power at high speed for cruising; a very wide speed range with constant-power region; a fast torque response; a high efficiency over the wide speed range with constant torque and constant power regions; a high efficiency for regenerative braking; downsizing, weight reduction and lower moment of inertia; a high reliability and robustness for various vehicle operating conditions; reasonable costs. And there are four types of motor drives applied to electric vehicles. They are brushed DC motor drives, induction motor (IM) drives, permanent magnet (PM) brushless DC (BLDC) motor drives and switched reluctance motor (SRM) drives. By comparison, the DC motor drives asre likely to continue to be used in electric vehicles because DC motor drives are available at the lowest cost. Considering efficiency, PM BLDC motor drives are the best choice. SRM drives have the lowest weight among four types of motor drives for electric vehicles. If the choice of motor drives for electric vehicles is determined by three factors that are weight, efficiency and cost, it is clear that SRM drives are the best choice for electric vehicles. Except for the efficiency, weight and cost, SRM drives also have the ascendancy in the aspects of cooling, maximum speed, fault tolerance and reliability.

For the battery, as we all know, batteries are energy accumulators. It offers the motor electrical energy just like the oil tank. And it has many requirements, such as high specific energy to ensure the electric vehicles achieve the basic reasonable trip mileage. As to the charging time, the normal battery charging time should be less than 6h, the battery can adapt to the requirements of the fast charging. The battery can adapt to the requirements of the fast discharging, lower self-discharging and long-term storage. The battery can work steadily in room temperature conditions; does not need special heat and other heat management systems. The battery should be dry and clean, no electrolyte leakage and the shell of the battery should not cause spontaneous combustion or burning. When coming across accidents, it should not cause harm to the crew. Besides, the waste batteries could be recycled and regenerated. And the recycling life of battery is not less than 1000 times. So it needs high-performance batteries for electric vehicles. At present there are many suitable batteries like lead-acid, nickel-metal hydride, Zebra and lithium-ion and they have their own characteristics. Flooded lead-acid batteries are the cheapest and most common traction batteries available, usually discharged to roughly 80%. They will accept high charge rates for fast charging. Flooded batteries require inspection of electrolyte level and replacement of water. Nickel-metal hydride batteries are now considered a relatively mature technology. While less efficient (60% to 70%) in charging and discharging than even lead-acid, they boast an energy density of 30 to 80W · h/kg, far higher than lead-acid. When used properly, nickel-metal hydride batteries can have exceptionally long lives. The Zebra battery boasts an energy density of 120W · h/kg and reasonable series resistance. Since the battery must be heated for use, cold weather doesn't strongly affect its operation except increasing heating costs. And Zebras can last for a few thousand charge cycles and are nontoxic, with a good power density, and 80% to 90% charge/discharge efficiency. For lithium-ion, there are new variations on lithium-ion chemistry that sacrifice energy and power density to provide fire resistance, environmental friendliness, very rapid charging and very long life spans. Ensure the electric vehicles have enough trip mileage and long service life.

Fig.5-2-1 and Fig.5-2-2 show major components not in the radiator box and found on the radiator plate, respectively.

Battery chargers replenish the energy used by an electric vehicle much like a gasoline pump refills a gas tank. One significant difference is that an electric vehicle operator can fully charge the vehicle overnight, at home, rather than refueling at a gasoline station. The battery charger converts the alternating current distributed by electric utilities into the direct current needed to recharge the battery. Usually, it takes from several hours to overnight to recharge an electric vehicle battery pack. The time required to recharge electric vehicle batteries depends on the total amount of energy that can be stored in the battery pack, and the voltage and current available from the battery charger. See Fig.5-2-3.

a) Motor b) Motor to clutch and transmission adapter
c) Battery d) Console

Fig.5-2-1 Major EV components not in radiator box

Chapter 5 Electric Vehicles

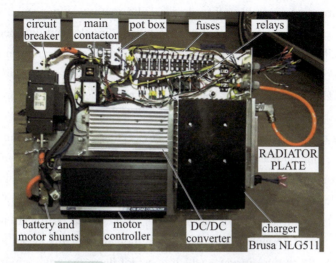

Fig.5-2-2　Components found on radiator plate

a) At home

b) At an RV park

c) At a public on-grid PV charging station in Vacaville

d) From an off-grid PV generator trailer

Fig.5-2-3　EV charging

2 New Technology of Electric Vehicles

　　The in-wheel drive system is an advanced environment-friendly drive system that no longer requires engine, transmission and driveshaft in existing internal combustion engines as it is equipped with electric motors inside each wheel. And the motor fitted on each wheel is worked through a power converter by detecting the driver's driving/braking intention. The system is extremely efficient as it transmits drive power directly to the tires by mounting the motor and speed-reducer right to the wheel itself. This allows a greater degree of freedom for the design of the car layout and interior cabin, traditional transmission is no longer necessary and it also helps save weight. And it has more freedom room to assemble other devices like increasing the amounts of batteries. The driving forces of the electric wheels can be controlled directly and independently, making its movement more flexible, convenient and reasonable and improving the performance on bad roads.

As we all know, after the energy in battery is used up, we have to spend a long time recharging it for the next time. The efficiency is low and consumes much electricity. So it is great to invent new types of battery which can use solar power to create electricity for the motor. Solar cell may be one of the choices. Solar cell is a solid-state electrical device that converts the energy of light directly into electricity by the photovoltaic effect. Assembling the solar panel at the vehicle surface where could accept the sunshine and convert it into electricity. So the vehicle could be charged wherever sunshine is besides during the movement. It can save electricity and make use of solar energy. Also, there are many new types of battery like fuel cell that converts the chemical energy from fuel into electricity through a chemical reaction with oxygen or another oxidizing agent. Hydrogen fuel cell is the most common cell, its product is water which does not harm the environment.

According to the shortcomings of the present electric vehicles, like short driving range, low specific energy of battery and long battery charging time, new technology would overcome all the shorts and could drive long distances up to hundreds of miles after charging and the battery is lighter and packages more electricity. New developments in battery recharging would decrease the time required to recharge electric vehicle batteries to as little as 10 to 15 minutes. Pulse battery chargers have demonstrated that a battery pack can be recharged in less than 20 minutes without damaging it. If this technology is fully deployed, electric charging stations similar to gas stations, would allow the electric vehicle operator to quickly recharge the battery pack. This new charger technology, coupled with advanced batteries with a range of 200 miles between recharging, will allow the electric vehicle operator the same freedom of the road currently enjoyed by today's operators of gasoline-powered vehicles.

3 Prospects for the Electric Vehicle in the Coming Decades

In 2008 there were less than 500,000 hybrid vehicles sold worldwide, with the market for plug-in hybrid electric vehicles (PHEVs) and battery electric vehicles (BEVs) still limited to conversions of current technologies or high-end vehicles manufactured by specialty producers. Although currently, the EV in its entirety represents a very small proportion of the total number of passenger vehicles in most jurisdictions, it is widely expected that the EV will experience rapid growth over the coming decades. In a 2009 study, JP Morgan estimated that by 2020 11 million EVs could be sold worldwide, including 6 million in North America. According to JP Morgan, this will mean that the EV will equal nearly 20% of the North American market and 13% of the global passenger vehicle market at that point in time. The transition to the EV away from the internal combustion engine is expected to be led by the hybrid gasoline-electric vehicle, with this followed by the PHEV, and then finally the full-scaled BEV. In the short-term, government incentives for the EV related to economic stimulus and international competitiveness, efforts to mitigate climate change, as well as a push by governments to improve energy security will be the major catalysts for the EV. The United States, for example, recently announced upwards of $2.5 billion in funding and grants for a variety of EV-related companies and initiatives, intending to have one million EVs on the road by 2015. China, meanwhile, is also focusing on the EV from the perspective of economic and energy policy. Notably, the government has made known its intent to position its auto manufacturing sector to be the largest global producer of EVs with a ten billion yuan ($1.46 billion) program to help its industry with automotive innovation in addition to supporting consumption of the EV through generous fiscal incentives. The importance of Japan in terms of the EV and the emphasis Japanese automakers are placing on the EV should also be recognized, both due to the leading role the country's auto manufacturers already have in the hybrid market as well as in terms of the country strength in battery technology development and production.

New Words and Expressions

cruising	/ˈkruːzɪŋ/	n.	巡航
		adj.	巡航的
ascendancy	/əˈsend(ə)nsi/	n.	优势；支配地位，统治权（等于 ascendency、ascendence）
mileage	/ˈmaɪlɪdʒ/	n.	英里数，里程
electrolyte	/iˈlektrəlaɪt/	n.	电解液，电解质；电解
replenish	/rɪˈplenɪʃ/	vt.	补充，再装满；把装满；给添加燃料
recharge	/riːˈtʃɑːdʒ/	vt.	再充电；再袭击；再控告
		n.	再袭击；再装填
		vi.	再袭击
interior	/ɪnˈtɪəriə/	n.	内部；本质
		adj.	内部的；国内的；本质的
transition	/trænˈzɪʃn/	n.	过渡；转变；[分子生物] 转换；变调
environment-friendly		adj.	有利环境的，生态型的
high power density			大功率密度
moment of inertia			[力] 惯性矩，转动惯量
be determined by			由……所决定
induction motor			[电] 感应电动机；异步电动机
permanent magnet			永久磁铁，永磁体
BLDC			无刷直流
have the ascendancy			对……占支配地位，对……占上风，占优势
fault tolerance			容错，故障容差，容错性
energy accumulator			蓄能器
self-discharge			自放电；自身放电
electrolyte leakage			电解质渗漏
lead-acid battery			铅酸电池
nickel-metal hydride battery			镍氢电池
discharge efficiency			放电效率
lithium-ion			锂离子
lithium-ion battery			锂离子电池
oxidizing agent			[助剂] 氧化剂，氧化物，有机氧化物
coupled with			加上，外加；与相结合
government incentive			政府激励，政府的刺激措施，政府的鼓励措施

Answer the following questions according to the text.

1. What types of motor drives are applied to electric vehicles to meet the practical application?
2. What can offer the motor electricity energy just like the oil tank?
3. What are the major components of the electric vehicle not in the radiator box?
4. What components are found on the radiator plate?
5. How long does it take to recharge electric cars with the new developments in batteries?

Unit 3 Hybrid Electric Vehicles

A hybrid vehicle is usually a vehicle with both battery electric and IC elements in its drivetrain. Like many of the concepts we have been discussing, the idea is not new. Hybrids have had a bad press in the EV community, perhaps because the best known and most successful commercially have been "plug-free" hybrids such as the Toyota Prius which ultimately get all their power from petrol pumped into the tank. This bad press is a mistake. Unless and until battery technology gets to the point that range ceases to be an issue, a good hybrid may sometimes be worth considering for some applications.

Hybrids may also be a way of easing the transition from IC to EV in a commercial and emotional sense: for some buyers, the security blanket of a fill-up-and-go IC drivetrain may be necessary to encourage them to buy into pure electric power.

1 Working Principle of the Hybrid Electric Vehicle

Hybrid electric vehicle power system is mainly composed of the control system, driving system, auxiliary power system, battery pack, etc. See Fig.5-3-1.

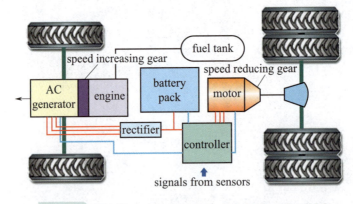

Fig.5-3-1 Working principle of the hybrid electric vehicle

2 Kinds of the Hybrid Electric Vehicle

So what kinds of hybrids are there? There are four classes that you can think of as a 2 × 2 matrix. Some hybrids ("Plug-in" hybrids) are, at their best, ordinary EVs with an extra IC engine just to get you there on the rare occasions that your journey is greater than the EV mode range. This sort of hybrid can be operated rather like a sailing yacht with an outboard motor, i.e. with the IC engine used as little as possible. For example, the Chinese-made BYD F3DM has an electric-only range of around 60 miles, so could be used as an electric vehicle most of the time by many drivers whose daily commute or school/shopping trips are less than this. Such a vehicle, used most of the time in EV mode, might in practice go hundreds of EV miles for every gallon of petrol used.

Other hybrids (like the Toyota Prius mentioned earlier) merely use the electric motor to smooth out the power demand on the IC engine, thus making it more efficient. These vehicles are sometimes referred to as "plug-free" hybrids (marketing speak for "you cannot charge the batteries from an external power source"). This sounds useless but curiously it does actually work. For example, the second-generation Toyota Prius was a 5-seater vehicle that could accelerate from 0 to 60 mph in just over 10 seconds. It had a 1500cc petrol engine putting out 76 bhp. The contemporary Volkswagen Golf Hatchback 1.6 S FSI weighed a similar amount, accelerated to 60 mph in much the same time but had a 1.6 litre engine putting out 113 bhp. The official fuel consumption figure for the Prius was 65 mpg, and the Golf was 41 mpg.

The reason it works is that you can use a smaller IC engine and run it closer to maximum efficiency, using the electric motor to make up the deficiency in power during hard acceleration.

Plug-free hybrids are better than nothing, but the improvement in efficiency over a good diesel is marginal. Many people regard them as green fashion-statements, essentially conventional cars with a transmission augmented by an auxiliary electric motor and batteries.

There is another way to classify hybrids apart from "plug-in" and "plug-free". "Parallel" hybrids use both the IC engine and the electric motor to drive the wheels (Fig. 5-3-2 and Fig. 5-3-3). By contrast in a "series" hybrid (Fig. 5-3-4 and Fig. 5-3-5), the IC engine does not drive the wheels directly; instead, it drives a generator that recharges the batteries. The batteries provide power to an electric motor which drives the wheels.

Indeed some EV owners have even built separate trailers with onboard generators to tow behind their cars on long journeys (Fig. 5-3-6 and Fig. 5-3-7).

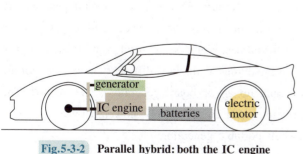

Fig.5-3-2 Parallel hybrid: both the IC engine and the electric motor can drive the wheels

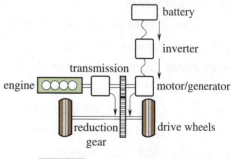

Fig.5-3-3 Parallel hybrid system

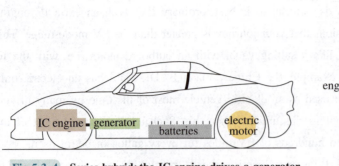

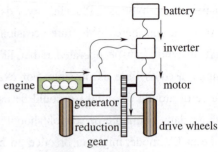

Fig.5-3-4 Series hybrid: the IC engine drives a generator and the electric motor drives the wheels

Fig.5-3-5 Series hybrid system

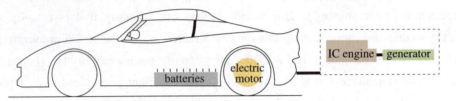

Fig.5-3-6 Range-extending trailer

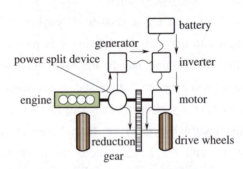

Fig.5-3-7 Mixed type hybrid system

Parallel hybrids are more complex but in theory, offer better performance. When you are accelerating hard, the control systems can tell the IC engine to forget about charging the battery and help the electric motor lay some rubber. Once you are in the cruise, the IC engine goes back to charge the batteries.

Series hybrids are simpler: conceptually they are ordinary EVs with an onboard generator to charge the batteries. A series hybrid doesn't need the complexity, weight and expense of a transmission that can mix power from two power sources. Nor does it need sophisticated control software to orchestrate the output from two power sources with very different power and torque curves. As a minimum, all you need to do is crank up an on-board generator when needed. The crazy BBC Top Gear trio demonstrated the principle with an absurd EV powered by a couple of lead-acid batteries supplemented by an off-the-shelf portable generator.

So there are actually four categories of hybrid: "plug-in series", "plug-in parallel", "plug-free series" and "plug-free parallel" (Fig.5-3-8).

In the real world, if you want a hybrid, the series hybrid is probably the right way to go. Let the different kinds of motor play to their strengths: IC engines are at their (limited) best running at constant speed, such as when running a generator. Electric motors are just far better at propelling a car.

One possible parallel hybrid layout that might be made to work is a conversion of a four-wheel drive vehicle that retains the IC engine but only drives one set of wheels and adds an electric drivetrain to power the other axle (Fig.5-3-9).

	Series	Parallel
Plug-in	Chevrolet Volt	BYD F3DM
Plug-free	Deltic diesel-electric	Toyota Prius

Fig.5-3-8 **Four categories of hybrid**

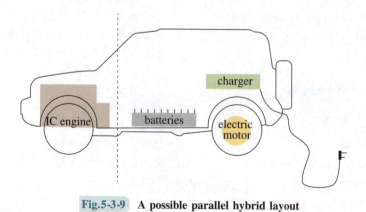

Fig.5-3-9 **A possible parallel hybrid layout**

Another intriguing possibility is the so-called "through-the-road hybrid"(TTRH) configuration. This involves adding in-wheel motors (like the protean example discussed earlier) to an existing IC-engined vehicle without modification to the existing drivetrain. This design enables the hybridisation of any existing vehicle resulting in 3 driver-selectable operating modes: IC engine only, electric only, electric + IC engine hybrid.

Accessories like heating, power steering, air conditioning and power brakes are a concern with any form of hybrid: if the IC engine is not operating much of the time, you will have to modify these components, but then what do you do on that long road trip when the propulsion battery is discharged 50 miles from home? In the end, hybrid drivetrains will always be heavier, more complex, more expensive and higher maintenance than either an EV or an IC-engined car.

New Words and Expressions

drivetrain	/ˈdraivtrein/	n.	动力传动系统，传动系统
ultimately	/ˈʌltimətli/	adv.	最后；根本；基本上，最终，终于
yacht	/jɒt/	n.	游艇，快艇；轻舟
accelerate	/əkˈseləreit/	vi.	加速；促进；增加
		vt.	使加快；使增速
marginal	/ˈmaːdʒin(ə)l/	adj.	微不足道的；边缘的
augmented	/ɔːgˈmentid/	adj.	增广的；增音的；扩张的
auxiliary	/ɔːgˈziliəri/	adj.	辅助的；副的；附加的
		n.	助动词；辅助者，辅助物；附属机构
onboard	/ɒnˈbɔːd/	adj.	随车携带的
		adv.	在船上；在飞机上；在板上
sophisticated	/səˈfistikeitid/	adj.	复杂的；精致的；久经世故的；富有经验的
absurd	/əbˈsəːd/	adj.	荒谬的；可笑的
		n.	荒诞；荒诞作品
off-the-shelf	/ɔfðəˈʃelf/	adj.	现成的；常备的；成品的
		adv.	现成地；无需作重大修改地
propel	/prəˈpel/	v.	推进；推动
propulsion	/prəˈpʌlʃn/	n.	推进；推动力
intriguing	/ˈintriːgiŋ/	adj.	有趣的；迷人的
		v.	引起兴趣（intrigue 的 ing 形式）
hybridisation	/ˌhaibridaiˈzeiʃn/	n.	混合淡化技术（等于 hybridization）
auxiliary power system			辅助电源系统，辅助电力系统，辅助动力系统
outboard motor			[船] 舷外发动机，舷外机，船外机，挂机
smooth out			消除；使平滑，解决
FSI（fuel stratified injection）			汽油直喷（燃油分层直喷）
series hybrid			串联式混合动力
parallel hybrid			并联式混合动力
mixed type hybrid system			混联式混合动力系统
mpg（miles per gallon）	/ˌempiːˈdʒiː/	abbr.	每加仑行驶的英里数
BHP（brake horse power）		abbr.	制动马力

Notes

燃油分层喷射（fuel stratified injection，FSI）技术是目前汽油发动机的关键技术之一。FSI 技术是将燃油直接喷射入气缸内，从而取代将燃油喷射入进气歧管的传统技术。

Answer the following questions according to the text.

1. What is the hybrid electric vehicle power system mainly composed of?

2. How many kinds of hybrid electric vehicles are there? What are they?

Appendix I

English Abbreviations for Automobile

Abbreviations	English Meaning	Chinese Meaning
AAP	auxiliary accelerator pump	辅助加速器泵
AAP	ambient absolute pressure	外界绝对压力
AAS	automatic adjusting suspension	自动调节悬架
AB	airbag	气囊
AB	air bleed	放气
ABDC	after bottom dead center	下止点后
ABS	anti-lock braking system	防抱死制动系统
ABS	anti-skid braking system	防滑制动系统
ABRS	airbag restraint system	安全气囊系统
ABV	air bypass valve	空气旁通阀
ABV	anti-backfire valve	防回火阀
A/C	air conditioning	空气调节
A/CL	air cleaner	空气滤清器
AC	automatic control	自动控制
AC	automatic clutch	自动离合器
AC	air compressor	空气压缩机
ACC	accessory	附属设备
ACC	air conditioning clutch	空调离合器
ACCS	air conditioning cycling switch	空调循环开关
ACRS	air cushion restraint system	（乘员）安全气囊式约束装置
ACS	air conditioning system	空调系统
ACG	alternating current generator	交流发电机
ACT	air charge temperature	进气温度
ACTS	air charge temperature sensor	进气温度传感器
ADM	advance module	点火提前角控制模块
AEC	automotive emission control	汽车排放控制
A/F	air-fuel ratio	空燃比
AFE	automobile fuel economy	汽车燃油经济性

（续）

Abbreviations	English Meaning	Chinese Meaning
AFS	air flow sensor	空气流量传感器
AIS	air injection system	空气喷射系统
ALC	automatic level control	车身自动调平控制
ALT	alternator	交流发电机
ANT	antenna	天线
AP	accelerator pedal	加速踏板
APP	accelerator pedal position	加速踏板位置
APS	absolute pressure sensor	绝对压力传感器
ASCD	auto speed control device	自动速度调节装置
ASIS	abort sensing and implementation system	紧急故障传感及处理系统
ASR	automatic slip regulation	侧滑自动控制
ASSY	assembly	总成
AT/ATM	automatic transmission	自动变速器
A/T	automatic transaxle	自动驱动桥
ATA	anti-theft alarm	防盗报警
ATDC	after top dead center	上止点后
ATF	automatic transmission fluid	自动变速器油液
ATS	air temperature sensor	空气温度传感器
AWD	all wheel drive	全轮驱动
AWS	all wheel steering	全轮转向
BA	brake assist	制动助力
BAS	brake assisted system	制动助力系统
BAT	battery	蓄电池
BAV	bleed air valve	泄气阀
BCM	body control module	车身控制模块
BDC	bottom dead center	下止点
B +	battery positive voltage	蓄电池正极电压
BLS	back-up light switch	倒车灯开关
BMC	brake master cylinder	制动主缸
BP	best power	最佳功率
BPA	bypass air	旁通空气
BPM	brake pressure modulator	制动压力调节器
BPMV	brake pressure modulating valve	制动压力调节阀
BSFC	brake specific fuel consumption	制动油耗率，制动单位油耗量

（续）

Abbreviations	English Meaning	Chinese Meaning
BTR	brake transmission ratio	制动传动比
BV	bypass valve	旁通阀
CAC	charge air cooler	进气冷却器
CAM	computer-aided manufacturing	计算机辅助制造
CAS	clear air system	净化空气系统
CB	circuit breaker	断路器
CCM	central control module	中央控制模块
CCM	cruise control module	巡航控制模块
CCS	cruise control switch	巡航控制开关
CCS	combustion control system	燃油控制系统
CES	clutch engaged switch	离合器接合开关
CDI	capacitive discharge ignition	电容放电式点火
CF	cooling fan	冷却风扇
CFI	central fuel injection	中央燃油喷射
CFI	continuous fuel injection	连续燃油喷射
CI	circuit ignition	线圈式点火
CI	compression ignition	压燃
CID	cylinder identification	气缸识别
CIL	clear indicating light	消除故障码指示灯
CIS	conventional ignition system	传统点火系统
CKPS	crankshaft position sensor	曲轴位置传感器
CMPS	camshaft position sensor	凸轮轴位置传感器
CPC	clutch pressure control	离合器压力控制
CPM	cycle per minute	每分钟循环数
CPP	clutch pedal position	离合器踏板位置
CPU	central processing unit	中央处理器
CR	compression ratio	压缩比
CRS	child restraint system	儿童安全保护系统
CSI	cold start injector	冷起动喷油器
CSS	cruise set speed	巡航设定速度
CTS	coolant temperature sensor	冷却液温度传感器
CTP	closed throttle position	节气门关闭位置

（续）

Abbreviations	English Meaning	Chinese Meaning
CVT	continuously variable transmission	无极变速器
	cylinder	气缸
CYP	cylinder position	气缸位置
DC	direct current	直流电
DEF	defogger	除雾器
DFI	direct fuel injection	直接燃油喷射
DFI	direct-fire ignition	直接点火
DI	distributor ignition	分电器点火
DIS	distribution ignition system	分电盘式点火系统
DID	direct injection diesel	柴油直接喷射
DIM	dash integrated module	仪表板集成模块
DLC	data link connector	诊断传输接头
DLS	distributorless ignition system	无分电盘式点火系统
DOHC	double overhead camshaft	顶置双凸轮轴
DMM	digital multimeter	数字式万用表
DS	detonation sensor	爆燃传感器
DTC	diagnostic trouble code	诊断故障码
DTM	diagnostic test mode	诊断测试模式
EAT	electronic automatic transmission	电控自动变速器
EACV	electric air control valve	电动空气调节阀
ECA	electronic control assembly	电子控制总成
ECC	electronic chassis control	电子底盘控制
ECI	electronic controlled ignition	电子控制点火
ECL	engine coolant level	发动机冷却液液面
ECM	engine control module	发动机控制模块
ECS	engine control system	发动机控制系统
ECT	electronic control transmission	电控变速器
ECU	electronic control unit	电子控制单元
EFI	electronic fuel injection	电子燃油喷射
EGR	exhaust gas recirculation	废气再循环
EI	electronic ignition	电子点火
EIS	electronic ignition system	电子点火系统
EIN	engine identification number	发动机识别代号
EMD	engine monitor display	发动机监控显示器

(续)

Abbreviations	English Meaning	Chinese Meaning
EPA	Environmental Protection Agency	美国环保局
EPS	electronic power steering	电动助力转向
ESAC	electronic spark advance control	电子点火提前控制
ESC	electronic spark control	电子点火控制
ESP	electronic stability program	电子稳定程序
ESS	engine speed sensor	发动机转速传感器
ETC	electronic temperature control	电子温度控制
F/A	fuel-air ratio	燃油空气混合比
FC	fuel consumption	燃油消耗量
F/F	front engine/front wheel drive	前置发动机/前轮驱动
FF	front engine front drive	前置发动机前轮驱动
FL	fusible links	熔断器
FLP	fault location panel	故障诊断仪表板
FR	front engine rear drive	前置发动机后轮驱动
FWB	front wheel brake	前轮制动
FWD	front wheel drive	前轮驱动
GAS. F	gas filter	汽油滤清器
GM	General Motors Company	通用汽车公司
GND	ground	搭铁
GP	gear ratio	传动比
GPS	global positioning system	全球定位系统
GSS	gear select switch	档位选择开关
GW	gross weight	总重量
HARN	harness	线束，配线
HHT	hand-held tester	手持式检测仪
HP	hydraulic pump	液压泵
HTC	hydraulic torque converter	液力变矩器
HSO	high speed output	高速输出装置
IAC	idle air control	怠速空气控制
IACV	idle air control valve	怠速控制阀
IAF	International Automobile Federation	国际汽车联合会
IATS	intake air temperature sensor	进气温度传感器
ICM	ignition control module	点火控制模块
ID	identification	辨认，识别
IFS	independent front suspension	前独立悬架
IMPS	intake manifold pressure sensor	进气歧管压力传感器

（续）

Abbreviations	English Meaning	Chinese Meaning
IRS	independent rear suspension	后独立悬架
ISC	idle speed control	怠速速度控制
ISO	International Standard Organization	国际标准组织
IT	ignition timing	点火正时
ITCS	ignition timing control system	点火正时控制系统
ITDC	ignition top dead center	点火上止点
KS	knock sensor	爆燃传感器
LCR	low compression ratio	低压缩比
LDC	lower dead center	下止点
LEV	low emission vehicle	低排放汽车
LED	light emitting diode	发光二极管
L-4	in-line four cylinder（engine）	直列式四缸（发动机）
LLC	long-life coolant	长效冷却液
LO	lubricating oil	润滑油
LOP	lubricating-oil pump	润滑油泵
LS	leaf spring	钢板弹簧
LSD	limited slip differential	防滑差速器
MAP	manifold absolute pressure	进气歧管绝对压力
MAF	mass air flow	质量空气流量
MAFS	mass air flow sensor	质量空气流量传感器
MAPS	manifold absolute pressure sensor	歧管绝对压力传感器
MAT	manifold air temperature	歧管空气温度
MCS	mixture control solenoid	混合气控制电磁线圈
MIL	malfunction indicator lamp	故障指示灯
MPI	multi-point fuel injection	多点燃油喷射
M/S	manual steering	机械式转向
M/T	manual transmission	手动变速器
N/C	neutral start switch/clutch switch	空档起动开关/离合器开关
NDS	neutral drive switch	空档驱动开关
NPS	neutral pressure switch	空档压力开关
N/V	ratio of engine speed to vehicle speed	发动机转速与车速之比
NSS	navigation satellite system	卫星导航系统
OBD II	on-board diagnostic II	第二代车载诊断系统
OCV	oil control valve	机油控制阀
ODI	oil drain intervals	换油期限
ODPSK	oil dipstick	（机）油尺，量油尺

Appendix I English Abbreviations for Automobile

(续)

Abbreviations	English Meaning	Chinese Meaning
OEM	original equipment manufacturer	原始设备制造厂
OFL	oil filter	机油滤清器
OHC	overhead camshaft	顶置凸轮轴
OHV	overhead valve	顶置气门
OSHA	occupational safety and health act	职业安全与卫生条例
OPS	oil pressure sensor	机油压力传感器
PCM	power train control module	动力系统控制模块
PCM	power control module	动力控制模块
PCV	positive crankcase ventilation	曲轴箱强制通风
PFI	port fuel injection	进气口燃油喷射
PMR	pump motor relay	油泵电机继电器
PS	power steering	动力转向
PSC	power steering control	动力转向控制
P/W	power window	电动车窗
RABS	rear anti-lock braking system	后防抱死制动系统
RAM	random access memory	随机存储器
RAR	repair as required	视情修理
RHD	right handle drive	右侧驾驶
RM	relay module	继电器模块
RPM	revolution per minute	转/分
RWD	rear wheel drive	后轮驱动
SAE	Society of Automotive Engineers	（美国）汽车工程师学会
China SAE	China Society of Automotive Engineers	中国汽车工程学会
SOHC	single overhead camshaft	顶置单凸轮轴
SPEC	specification	规格
SPI	single point injection	单点喷射
S/R	sun roof	遮阳板
SRS	supplemental restraint system	安全气囊
4S	sale, spare, service, survey	汽车销售、配件供应、维修服务、技术信息反馈（4S店）
SUV	sport utility vehicle	运动型多用途车
TA	intake air temperature sensor	进气温度传感器
TAP	throttle-alternator position	节气门开度位置
TB	throttle body	节气门体
TBI	throttle body injection	节气门体喷射

（续）

Abbreviations	English Meaning	Chinese Meaning
TC	turbocharger	涡轮增压器
TCC	torque converter clutch	液力变矩器离合器
TCS	transmission control switch	变速器控制开关
TCW	two-cycle water-cooled	二冲程水冷
TDC	top dead center	上止点
TDCL	test diagnostic communication link	自诊接头
TDCS	top dead center sensor	上止点传感器
T/N	tool number	工具编号
TPS	throttle position sensor	节气门位置传感器
TSB	technical service bulletins	技术维修通报
TS	temperature sensor	温度传感器
TS	transmission switch	变速器开关
TSS	transmission speed sensor	变速器速度传感器
TTS	transmission temperature sensor	变速器温度传感器
TWC	three-way converter	三元转化器
VAPS	variable assist power steering	可变式动力转向
VASC	vacuum advance spark control	真空提前点火控制
VATC	vehicle anti-thief system	车辆防盗系统
VC	valve control	气门控制
VCM	vehicle control module	车辆控制模块
VCRM	variable control relay module	可调控制继电器模块
VCV	vacuum control valve	真空控制阀
VEI	vehicle evaluation and improvement	车辆鉴定与改进
VIN	vehicle identification number	车辆识别代号
VSA	vehicle stability assist	车辆稳定性控制装置
VSS	vehicle speed sensor	车速传感器
VSV	vacuum solenoid valve	真空电磁阀
VTC	valve timing control	气门正时控制
VTV	vacuum transmitting valve	真空输送阀
VVT	variable valve timing	可变气门正时
WMI	world manufacturer identifier	世界制造厂识别代号
WOT	wide open throttle	节气门全开
WOT	wide open throttle switch	节气门全开开关
WSS	wheel speed sensor	轮速传感器
WV	weight of entire vehicle	整车重量,车辆总重
ZEV	zero emission vehicle	零污染排放车辆

Appendix II 科技英语知识

一、科技英语词汇的来源及特点

从词源学的角度来看，英语的大多数科技词汇都起源于古典的希腊语和拉丁语。这也是科技英语比普通英语更具国际性的一个基本原因。因为同一语系词汇的词素，绝大部分具有相同的语源，即使不是同一语系，也有同样可以追溯的国际词，例如：

诱导，感应	induction	（英语）	来源于拉丁语
	induction	（法语）	
	Induktion	（德语）	
磁铁的	magnetic	（英语）	来源于希腊语
	magnétique	（法语）	
	magnetisch	（德语）	

可以这样认为，希腊、拉丁词素是现代科学技术词汇的主要基础，而且也是今后创造新的科技词汇的重要源泉。拉丁语本身大部分来自希腊语，而其形式都经过不同程度的拉丁化。直接从希腊语中吸收的外来语，在科技英语中为数极少。

 科技英语中专业英语词汇的特点

科技英语以表达科技概念、理论与事实为主要目的；遵守科技英语的语法体系和翻译方法；特别注重客观事实和真理，表达准确、精练和正式。科技专业英语又是结合各自专业的科技英语，有很强的专业性，涉及的面更加狭窄，与专业内容配合更为密切。

专业英语与科技英语既有区别又有联系。专业英语的学习需要有一个良好的科技英语基础，同时也有其自身的词汇特点：

1. 专业英语中词汇的多功能性

专业英语中使用的大量词汇具有多功能性，这些词汇往往属于半专业性词汇。所谓半专业性词汇是指在各个学科领域里都经常使用的意义不尽相同的那些词汇，它们在专业文献中起着重要的修辞与语篇功能，常被用来表达作者的意图和观点。半专业性词汇其实都是基础词汇，不过将其意义扩展而已。像 eye、carrier、force、system、power、transmission、feed、run、work、energy 等既是基础词汇，又是半专业词汇。

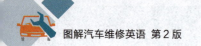

比如：在基础英语中 eye 作"眼睛"，在专业英语中可以根据不同场合分别表示"孔"、"环"、"镜"、"圈"、"窗"、"吊眼"等。

又如：carrier 在基础英语中作"运送者"解，牵涉化工方面可译作"载体"，牵涉机械方面可译作"托架"或"承载器"。

再如：solution 溶解（化学），解法（数学），还债（法律）；

circuit 电路（电工），巡回审判（法律），水准闭合环（测绘）；

adjustment 调节器（自动化），调解（法律），平差（测绘）。

2. 专业英语中词汇的转换功能

少量日常英语词义加以转义，即可赋予它们新的词汇意义，变成科技英语专业词汇。

如：光学词汇 scatter（散射）其实就是常用词汇 scatter（散布、分散）的转义；radioactivity（放射能）就是 radio 和 activity 二词的合成；semiconductor（半导体）就是由 conduct（引导）转义后再加后缀 or 和前缀 semi 派生而来。

有些专业词汇对于只通晓基础英语的人来说，可能是完全陌生的。例如，无机材料专业英语中经常会用上 soda-lime silicate（钠钙硅酸盐）、borosilicate（硼硅酸盐）、lead silicate（铅硅酸盐）、petrified liquid（固化的液体）、impervious to gases（不透气的）等这样一些专业词汇。

在汽车专业英语中还有如下词汇：

boot	（长筒靴）	引导，启动	collar	（衣领）	环、垫圈、法兰
nest	（窝、巢）	定位孔	bush	（灌木丛）	衬套、轴瓦
sleeve	（衣袖）	套筒、套管	reservoir	（水库）	容器，内存，油槽
energy	（活力、精力）	能、能量	moment	（瞬间、片刻）	力矩
power	（力、权力）	电能、电力，倍率，幂	base	（基础）	碱（化学），主要（医学）

3. 专业英语中词汇的复合功能

专业英语中常常用复合词来简单扼要地说明一个复杂的意思。常见的复合词很多，如：newtype（新型的）、lowtemperature（低温的）、fourphase（四相的）、workpiece（工件）、undersize（尺寸不足的）、fastmoving（快速运行的）、overheat（过热的）、in case of（在……场合下）、by means of（借助于）等。这些词比较容易理解，因为它们的词义基本上就是由它们的各个单词的含义合起来形成。

4. 专业英语中简易词汇的代表功能

为了节省时间和篇幅并使语言简洁，专业英语中经常出现一些缩略词，它们代表着特定的词义。这种缩略词，有的是常用符号，如：i.e.（that is），e.g.（for example），etc.（and so on）等；有的是专用符号，如：μ_r（relative permeability）等；有的是度量衡单位，如：h（hour），hp（horsepower），cm（centimetre），mL（millilitre），kg（kilogram）等。

Exercises

Ⅰ. Translate the following words into terms.

1. mouse（老鼠）　　　　　　　　　　_____
2. library（图书馆）　　　　　　　　　_____
3. drive（驱动、驾驶）　　　　　　　　_____
4. window（窗户）　　　　　　　　　　_____
5. probe（调查）　　　　　　　　　　　_____
6. package（包裹）　　　　　　　　　　_____
7. host（主人）　　　　　　　　　　　　_____
8. spring（春天）　　　　　　　　　　　_____
9. body（身体）　　　　　　　　　　　　_____
10. part（部分）　　　　　　　　　　　_____

Ⅱ. Translate the following words into Chinese.

1. psi(pounds per square inch)　　　　_____
2. A/C(air conditioning)　　　　　　　_____
3. ABS (anti-lock braking system)　　_____
4. BDC (bottom dead center)　　　　　_____
5. CMFI(central multi-port fuel injection)　_____
6. EFI (electronic fuel injection)　　　_____
7. IA(intake air)　　　　　　　　　　　_____
8. pre-combustion chamber　　　　　　_____
9. anti-freezing liquid　　　　　　　　_____
10. semi conductor ignition system　　_____

二　科技英语词汇的分类及构成

从语言学的角度来看，科技英语词汇主要是通过沿用生活词汇、类比、借用、派生、合成、缩略和混成等几种方式构成的。

词汇分类

1. 专业或技术词汇

专业或技术词汇是某个专业所特有的词汇，其专业性强，词义狭窄和单一。例如：

diode	二极管	substation	变电站，变电所
autotransformer	自耦变压器	capacitor	电容器
superconductivity	超导特性		

2. 次技术词汇

次技术词汇是很多专业和学科所共有的词汇，不同专业和学科往往具有不同的词义。例如：

power	幂，乘方；动力，功率，效率；电源，电力，功率，电能
bus	公共汽车；母线，总线
condenser	电容器，补偿机；冷凝器
power plant	发电厂；动力装置

3. 非技术词汇

非技术词汇在普通英语或非专业英语中使用较少，但实际却属于非专业英语的词汇。例如：

take in → absorb	find out → discover
look into → examine	turn round → rotate
make good use of → utilize	change → convert

🎯 词汇构成

1. 合成法

合成法由相互独立的两个或更多的词合成得到新词。

名词 + 名词（n. + n.）→n.　　　　　e.g. horsepower, bandwidth, power utilization

名词 + 形容词（n. + adj.）→adj.　　e.g. ice-cold, network-wide

名词 + 副词（n. + adv.）→n., adj.　　e.g. feedback

形容词 + 名词（adj. + n.）→n., adj.　e.g. low-pass, high-speed, short-circuit, newtype

形容词 + 名词 + ed（adj. + n. + ed）→adj.　e.g. forward-directed, small-sized

介词 + 名词（prep. + n.）→adj., n.　　e.g. bypass, overhead, on-line, overvoltage

2. 派生法

派生法是通过对词根加上各种前缀或后缀来构成新词。专业英语词汇大部分是用派生法构成的，比如：

由 semi-构成的词有 230 个以上：semiconductor（半导体），semimonthly（半月刊 n.）等；

由 thermo-构成的词有 130 个以上：thermo-chemical（热化学技术），thermo-electrical 等；

由 micro-构成的词有 300 个以上；

由 auto-构成的词有 260 个以上。

常用的前缀和后缀多达百个，可见派生法的构词能力是非常强的。作为一名专业技术人员，至少应掌握 50 个常用前缀和后缀。前缀（prefix）：词义变化，词类不变；后缀（suffix）：词义可能变化，词类一定会变。下面是一些常见的前、后缀：

名词前缀

前缀	含义	例词
auto-	自动，自己，自身	autocompensation, automation, autoexcitation
counter-	反，逆，抗，补	countermodulation, countercurrent
hydr(o)-	水，流体，氢（化）	hydroenergy, hydropower
hyper-	超，过	hyperfrequency, hyperplane
mini-	微，小	minicomponent, minipad
micro-	微，百万分之一	micromotor, microadjustment
semi-	半，部分，不完全	semiconductor, semiempirical, semielectronic
super-	超，上，特	superconductor, supergrid
ultra-	超，过度，极端	ultra-high voltage（UHV），ultraspeed
extra-	超，特	extra-high voltage（EHV）

名词后缀

后缀	含义	例词
-age	抽象概念，如性质、状态、行为等	voltage 电压，percentage 百分比，百分率
-ance, -ence	抽象概念，如性质、状态、行为等	resistance 电阻，difference 差别
-ency	抽象概念，如性质、状态、行为等	efficiency 效率，frequency 频率，emergency 紧急情况
-ion, -tion, -sion	抽象概念，如性质、状态、行为等	action 作用，automation 自动化，transmission 传输
-logy	学科，技术	technology 技术，dermatology 皮肤医学，iatrology 医学，electrotechnology 电工学
-ness	性质、状态、程度	hardness 硬度，deepness 深度，brightness 亮度，roughness 粗糙度
-ship	情况、性质、状态、关系、地位	relationship 关系，fellowship 伙伴关系 membership 会员资格，friendship 友好，scholarship 奖学金，学问，学识
-er, -or	物体名称	driver 驱动器，capacitor 电容器，conductor 导体，reactor 电抗器，breaker 断路器，disconnector 隔离器

形容词后缀

词缀	含义	例词
-able, -ible	能……的；可以……的	measurable 可测量的，convertible 可逆的
-ous	……的	continuous 继续的 electriferous 带电的 simultaneous 同时的
-ful	充满，有……的	powerful 强大的，useful 有用的
-less	无……的	colorless 无色的

副词后缀

词缀	含义	例词
-ly	以……方式	carefully 仔细地
-ward(s)	表示方式或动作的方向	backward 逆向，反馈 downward 向下地，向下 eastward 向东地，向东
-wise	按照……方式	clockwise 顺时针方向

动词后缀

词缀	含义	例词
-en	使……，变得……	broaden 加宽，harden 硬化，shorten 变短
-ify	转为，变为	diversify 使多样化，electrify 使……带电
-ize	使……变得……	standardize 使标准化，modernize 使……现代化

3. 词汇缩略

词汇缩略由词汇中的部分字母或由词组中每个词汇的首字母组成，可分为节略词，缩略词，首字词和缩写词。

（1）节略词：只取词汇前面几个字母或只由后面词根组成。

ad — advertisement	lab — laboratory	del — delete
flu — influenza	di(a) — diameter	exam — examination
dir — directory	deg — degree	dep — department
chute — parachute		

（2）缩略词：由词组中某些词的词头字母（有时多于一个）所组成，作为一个词按照正常的规则发音。

ROM — read only memory	只读存储器
RAM — random access memory	随机(存取)存储器
Radar — radio detecting and ranging	雷达

（3）首字词：与缩略词类似，区别在于每个实词只取第一个字母，且必须逐字母念出。

ABS — anti-lock braking system	防抱死制动系统
EFI — electronic fuel injection	电子控制燃油喷射系统
BDC — bottom dead center	下止点
CMFI — central multi-port fuel injection	中央多点燃油喷射

（4）缩写词：并不一定由某个词组的首字母组成。有些缩写词仅由一个单词变化而来，且大多数缩写词每个字母后都附有一个句点。

appx. — appendix	附录	fig. — figure	图
sq. — square	二次方	msg. — message	信息
amp. — amplifier	放大器	o.p. — operational amplifier	运算放大器

4. 混成法

混成法也叫拼缀法或紧缩法，即将两个单词按一定的规律进行剪裁，两个词各取一部分加以叠合混成一个新的单词或取一个词的一部分加另一个词的原型加以拼缀而成一个新的单词。由于混成词（blend）简略而又容易帮助联想理解词义，因而混成法在科技英语中频繁使用。

| positron — positive electron | 正电子 | negatron — negative electron | 负电子 |

5. 字母外形法

对一些形状与字母外形相似的物体，可以利用连字符把字母和名词连接在一起组成新词汇。

X-ray	X 射线	U-shaped magnet	马蹄形磁铁
Y-direction	Y 轴方向	H-frame structure	H 形框架结构
T-filter	T 型滤波器	Y-connection	Y（星）形联结

6. 人名法

对一些科学家、发明家所发现或发明的理论、方法、定理或定律、东西和物品等，用他们的名字组成新词。

| Ohm — 欧姆 | Ampere — 安培 | Volt — 伏特 | Coulomb — 库仑 |
| Hertz — 赫兹 | Watt — 瓦特 | Kelvin — 开尔文 | |

Exercises

Translate the following words into Chinese.

1. motel（motor hotel）_____
2. transistor（transfer resistor）_____
3. codec（code decoder）_____
4. biorhythm（biological rhythm）_____
5. superconductor _____ 6. subroutine _____
7. H-beam _____ 8. cross-bit _____
9. V-belt _____ 10. Cadillac _____
11. Cherokee _____ 12. aspirin _____
13. capacitor _____ 14. distributor _____
15. contractor _____ 16. O-ring _____
17. U-bolt _____ 18. nose cap _____
19. fire engine _____ 20. first aid _____

三 科技英语的句法特点

与日常普通英语相比，科技英语有所不同，其主要特点表现在：被动语态多；非谓语动词多；名词化结构多；复杂长句使用频率高。下面将逐一讨论这些特点及翻译方法。

一、广泛使用被动语态

科技文章侧重叙事、推理,强调客观、准确,其所强调的重点是"事物所发生的情况",即着重体现所述内容的客观性,因而大量采用第三人称叙述,使用被动语态。过多使用第一、第二人称,会造成主观臆断的现象。科技英语中的谓语至少三分之一是被动语态。在翻译此类结构时,行之有效的方式是将被动转为主动。例如:

1. Automobiles may **be manufactured** with computer-driven robots or put together almost totally by hand.
   汽车可以由计算机操纵的机器人来制造,或者几乎全部用手工装配。
2. Springs **are used as** cushions to absorb shock.
   弹簧被用作吸收振动的缓冲器。
3. Electrical energy **can be stored** in two metal plates separated by an insulating medium. Such a device is called a capacitor, and its ability to store electrical energy **is termed** capacitance. It **is measured** in farads.
   电能可以储存在被一绝缘介质隔开的两块金属板中,这样的装置被称为电容器,它储存电能的能力就被称为电容。电容的测量单位是法拉。
4. Such occupant protection systems **are also classified** as passive restraint systems, since the protective function is independent of any active contribution by the passengers.
   这类乘员保护系统也被称为被动约束系统,因为系统的保护功能是独立于乘客的任何努力而存在的。

二、广泛使用非谓语形式

每个英语简单句(或复合句的分句)中只能有一个谓语动词,如果需要叙述几个动作,先选其中主要动作当谓语,而其余动作采用非谓语动词形式,才能符合英语语法要求。汉语中则不存在这种结构,所以翻译时可酌情处理,或译成动宾结构,或另起一句翻译。

由于科技文章要求书写简练、结构紧凑,因而常常使用分词短语代替定语从句;使用分词独立结构代替状语从句或并列分句;使用不定式代替各种从句,"介词+动名词短语"代替定语从句或状语从句。这样,既可缩短句子,又比较醒目。英语中非谓语动词有三种:动名词、分词(包括现在分词和过去分词)和不定式。

(一)动名词

1. 用动名词短语取代时间从句或简化时间陈述句

The signal should be filtered before it is amplified.
The signal should be filtered before **being amplified**.
放大信号前,应先对其进行滤波。

2. 用动名词短语做主语

Changing resistance is a method for controlling the flow of the current.
改变电阻是控制电流的一种方法。
Conducting electricity means the flow of electrons through an object.
传导电流意味着电子在物体内的流动。

3. 用动名词短语做方式状语

The simplest example is a blacksmith's forging of a hot piece of metal by hammering the workpiece on an anvil.
最简单的例子就是铁匠在砧座上用锤子锻打红热的金属块。

（二）分词

过去分词短语替代从句中的被动语态；现在分词短语替代从句中的主动语态。

1. The power supply, which is shown in block-diagram in Fig. 1, is a single-phase switch-mode inverter.
   The power supply **shown** in block-diagram in Fig. 1 is a single-phase switch-mode inverter.
   图 1 中用框图表示的电源是一个单相开关逆变器。
2. The transistor, which is working with correctly polarities, can work as an amplifier.
   The transistor **working** with correctly polarities can work as an amplifier.
   工作于正确电源极性下的晶体管，作用就像放大器。

（三）不定式

用不定式短语来替代表示目的和功能的从句或语句。

1. The capacity of individual generators is larger and larger so that the increasing demand of electric power is satisfied.
   The capacity of individual generators is larger and larger **to satisfy** the increasing demand of electric power.
   单台发电机的容量越来越大，目的就是满足不断增长的用电需求。
2. What does a fuse do? It protects a circuit.
   The function of a fuse is **to protect** a circuit.
   熔丝的作用就是保护电路。

三、大量使用名词化结构

科技英语要求行文简洁、表达客观、内容准确、信息量大，常强调存在的事实，而非某一行为，所以大量使用名词化结构（表示动作意义的名词＋of＋名词）。大量使用名词化结构可以缩短句子的长度，译成汉语时则不宜套用英语的这种模式，而是需要根据汉语的表达习惯灵活处理，有时也可将其拓展成汉语的句子。

1. **The earth rotates on its own axis, which** causes the change from day to night.
   The rotation of the earth on its own axis causes the change from day to night.
   地球绕轴自转，引起昼夜的变化。

名词化结构 the rotation of the earth on its own axis 使复合句简化成简单句，而且使表达的概念更加确切严密。

2. Archimedes first discovered the principle <u>of displacement of water by solid bodies</u>.
   阿基米德最先发现固体排水的原理。

句中 of displacement of water by solid bodies 系名词化结构，一方面简化了同位语从句，另一方面强调 displacement 这一事实。

3. This shows that **the resistance of an electric conductor** is inversely proportional to its cross-section area.
   这表明，导体电阻值的大小与导体横切面的大小成反比。
4. This position was completely reversed by this man's **development of the utilization** of nitrogen from the air.
   由于这个人发明了利用空气中氮气的方法，这种局面就完全改变了。

四、省略句使用频繁

为了使句子更加精炼，在科技英语中大量使用省略句，其中省略成分主要有：状语从句中的主语、全部或部分谓语；定语从句中的关系代词 which 和 that、从句中的助词等；还常用介词短语替代从句。

1. If **it is possible**, the open-loop control approach should be used in this system.
   If **possible**, the open-loop control approach should be used in this system.
   可能的话，这个系统应该使用开环控制方法。
2. As **illustrated in Fig.1**, there is a feedback element in the closed-loop system.
   As **in Fig.1**, there is a feedback element in the closed-loop system.
   如图 1 所示，这个闭环系统中有一个反馈元件。
3. The device includes an instrument transformation and a relay system **which has** two circuits in it.
   The device includes an instrument transformation and a relay system **with** two circuits in it.
   这个装置包括一个互感器和一个有两个电路的继电器系统。

其他常用的省略形式

As already discussed	前已讨论	As explained before	前已解释
As described above	如上所述	If possible（necessary）	如果可能（必要）
If so	倘若如此	As previously mentioned	前已提到
When needed（necessary, feasible）	必要时	Where feasible	在实际可行的场合
Where possible	在可能的情况下		

五、复杂长句使用频率高

科技文章要求推理谨严、论证准确，为了完整、准确地表达事物内在联系，因此有时一个英语句子里包含不少短语和从句，来进行周密细致的限定和说明，而这些从句和短语又往往互相制约、互相依附，形成从句中有短语、短语中带从句的复杂语言现象。常见的句型是：It...that...结构。例如：

1. The reluctance motor operates synchronously at a speed **which** is determined by the supply frequency and the number of poles for **which** the stator is wound.
   磁阻电动机以某一速率同步转动，该速率是由电源频率和定子绕制的级数决定的。
2. The testing of a cross-field generator will be described in this section with chief reference to the tests **that** are normally taken on every machine **before** it leaves the makers works.
   交变磁场发电机的试验将在本节中叙述，它主要涉及每台电机在离开制造厂前应进行的试验。

3. It has been mentioned above **that** the electrons in a metal are able to move freely through the metal, **that** their motion constitutes an electric current in the metal and **that** they play an important part in conduction of heat.

   前面已经提到：金属中电子能自由地通过金属，电子的移动在金属中形成了电流，电子在热传导中起着重要的作用。

4. It therefore became necessary to adopt a pressurized cooling system where this had not previously been the case, and to increase the air flow through the radiator by fitting a coarser pitched (and potentially noisier) fan together with a radiator cowl.

   因此，采用一个压力冷却系统变得十分必要，而这在从前不曾有过，并通过将一个螺距更大的（且噪声可能更大的）风扇与一个散热器罩相配来增加通过散热片的空气流量。

六、大量使用后置定语

大量使用后置定语是科技文章的特点之一。常用的句子结构形式有：介词短语后置、形容词及形容词短语后置、副词后置、分词及定语从句后置。例如：

1. Although the experienced driver can undoubtedly drive much satisfaction from skilful use of the clutch and gearbox, there are many drivers **who would gladly dispense with the clutch pedal given a choice**.

   虽然经验丰富的驾驶人能够通过熟练操作离合器和变速器，来获得很大的满意程度，但如果有可能，许多驾驶人愿意省去操作离合器踏板的动作。

   此句中，定语从句 who would gladly dispense with the clutch pedal given a choice 修饰 drivers。

2. The forces **due to friction** are called frictional forces.

   由于摩擦而产生的力称之为摩擦力。（介词短语后置）

3. During construction, problems often arise **which require design changes**.

   在施工过程中，常会出现需要改变设计的问题。（定语从句后置）

4. The molecules exert forces upon each other, **which depend upon the distance between them**.

   分子相互间都存在着力的作用，该力的大小取决于它们之间的距离。（定语从句后置）

5. In radiation, thermal energy is transformed into radiant energy, **similar in nature to light**.

   热能在辐射时，转换成性质与光相似的辐射能。（形容词短语后置）

6. The force **upward** equals the force **downward** so that the balloon stays at the level.

   向上的力与向下的力相等，所以气球就保持在这一高度。（副词后置）

7. The heat **produced** is equal to the electrical energy **wasted**.

   产生的热量等于浪费了的电能。（单个分词，但仍保持较强的动词意义）

Exercises

Translate the following sentences into Chinese.

1. It is evident that a well lubricated bearing turns more easily than a dry one.
2. Some gas seems to have been released from the pipe.
3. The new cooling method is to be further improved.
4. If you use firebricks round the walls of the boiler, the heat loss can be considerably reduced.
5. Attention must be paid to the working temperature of the machine.
6. A direct current is a current flowing always in the same direction.
7. There are different ways of changing energy from one form into another.
8. It is necessary to interrupt the flow of power (by uncoupling) before gears are shifted.
9. The rotor arm distributes the surge to the segment linked to the right spark plug in sequence required by the firing order.
10. This shows that the resistance of an electric conductor is inversely proportional to its cross-section area.

四 科技英语的翻译 1

一、翻译的标准

翻译的标准，自有翻译以来，众说纷纭。有"信、达、雅"说，也有"忠实、通顺、美"说，有"神似"说，也有"化境"说。细较起来，这些说法都有共同点，即信息传真——饱满而准确，风格再现——译什么像什么，可读性强——增彩不增意。

科技英语的翻译标准又不同于一般的文学英语，有三条标准：准确、通顺和规范，即忠实于原文，准确、完整、科学地表达原文内容，语言通顺连贯，上下文衔接流畅，用词造句符合汉语习惯，符合学科领域规范，符合汉语专业词汇表达的独特语言形式，简练紧凑，通俗易懂。

二、翻译方法

科技英语的翻译是词汇、语句、段落、文章翻译的有机整体。一般包括理解和表达两个阶段，只有在正确理解原文的基础上，才能正确表达原文，使得译文既忠实于原文的内容，又用词正确得体，行文流畅通顺，符合译文习惯，避免逐字死译的生搬硬套。对于长句、难句的翻译，由于修饰语多、联合成分多、结构复杂，例如介词短语、分词短语、状语从句、定语从句、同位语、插入语等，通过一定的语法规则与句子主干结合在一起，使句子长而复杂，但具有严密、细致、紧凑的特点，能够非常准确地表达思想内容。而汉语句子倾向于短句，这样一来，在英语长句汉译时，既要从汉英差异出发，处理好句子结构形式上的问题，又要做到不忽视原文的文体特征，保留英语长句在表达思想方面严密紧凑的特点，不使译文松散脱节。下面就科技英语的语言特点介绍一些常用的翻译方法。

（一）引申译法

当英语句子中的某个词按词典的释义直译不符合汉语修辞习惯或语言规范时，则可以在不脱离该英语词本义的前提下，灵活选择恰当的汉语词语或词组译出。例如：

Jigang will fix this problem during the recent shut down of the finishing mill.
济钢会在最近的精轧机停产时解决这一问题。

词典中"fix"的意思为"固定、修理"，这里引申译为"解决、处理"。

（二）抽象译法

机械翻译是翻译科技英语的大忌，同时也违背了翻译的标准。因此，为达到忠实通顺的要求，抽象译法是我们经常用到的一种翻译方法。例如：

In order to get a cleaner emission, electronic fuel injection system is applied.
为了降低排放，应用了电子燃油喷射系统。

这里 cleaner emission 不能机械地翻译成"较清洁的排放"，这会令读者费解。因此，译成"降低排放"符合专业表达。

（三）词量增减译法

词量增减是指在英译汉时，根据汉语的习惯，在译文中增加一些原文中无其形而有其意的词，或减去原文中某些在译文中属于多余的词。

1. 增词法

增词法就是在译句中增加或补充英语句子中原来没有或省略了的词语，以便更完善、更清楚地表达英语句子所阐述的内容，从而使译文在语法及语言表达上能与原文在内容和形式上达到对等。

（1）A fuel injector is nothing but an electronically controlled valve.
喷油器是<u>通过</u>电磁阀控制的。

译文中增加了谓语动词，从而不会误解为：喷油器就是个电磁阀。

（2）Matter can be changed into energy, and energy into matter.
物质可以转化为能，能也<u>可以转化</u>为物质。（增补英语中省略的词）

（3）The best conductor has the least resistance and the poorest has the greatest.
最好的导体电阻最小，最差的<u>导体电阻</u>最大。（增补英语中省略的词）

（4）If A is equal to D, A plus B equals D plus B.
若 A = D，<u>则</u> A + B = D + B。（增加关联词）

2. 减词法

在英语句子中，有的词从语法结构上讲是必不可少的，但并无什么实际意义，只是在句子中起着单纯的语法作用；有的词虽有实际意义，但按照字面译出又显多余。这样的词在翻译时往往可以省略不译。

（1）The <u>world</u> of work injury insurance is complex.
工伤保险是复杂的。（名词省译）

（2）A wire lengthens while **it** is heated.
　　金属丝受热则伸长。（代词省译）

（3）Stainless steels **possess** good hardness and high strength.
　　不锈钢硬度大、强度高。（动词省译）

（4）Practically all substances expand when heated **and** contract when cooled.
　　几乎所有的物质都是热胀冷缩的。（连词省译）

（四）词性转换

英语翻译中，常常需要将英语句子中属于某种词类的词，译成另一种词类的汉语词，以适应汉语的表达习惯或达到某种修辞目的。这种翻译处理方法就是转换词性法，简称词类转换。由于英汉两种语言属于不同的语系，所以它们在语言结构与表达形式方面各有特点。要使译文既忠实于原意，又顺畅可读，就不能局限于逐词对等，必须采用适当的词性转换。

1. 转译成汉语动词

（1）**A change of** state from a solid to a liquid form requires heat energy.
　　从固态<u>变为</u>液态需要热能。（名词转译成动词）

（2）The term "laser" stands for amplification **by** stimulated emission of radiation.
　　"激光"这个术语指的是<u>利用</u>辐射的受激发射放大光波。（介词转译成动词）

（3）Both of the substances are not **soluble** in water.
　　这两种物质都不<u>溶于</u>水。（形容词转译成动词）

2. 转译成汉语名词

某些表示事物特征的形容词做表语时可将其转译成名词，其后往往加上"性"、"度"、"体"等。带有定冠词的某些形容词用作名词，应译成名词。

（1）The cutting tool must be **strong, tough, hard and wear resistant**.
　　刀具必须具有足够的<u>强度、硬度、韧性和耐磨性</u>。

（2）Both the compounds are acids, **the former** is strong, **the latter** is weak.
　　这两种化合物都是酸，<u>前者</u>是强酸，<u>后者</u>是弱酸。

（3）All structural materials behave **plastically** above their elastic range.
　　超过弹性极限时，一切结构材料都会显示出<u>塑性</u>。（副词转译成名词）

3. 转译成汉语形容词

（1）This experiment was a **success**.
　　这个试验是<u>成功的</u>。（名词转译成形容词）

（2）This man-machine system is **chiefly** characterized by its simplicity of operation and the ease with which it can be maintained.
　　这种人机系统的<u>主要</u>特点是操作简单、容易维修。（副词转译成形容词）

（3）It is demonstrated that dust is **extremely** hazardous.
　　已经证实，粉尘具有<u>极大的</u>危害。（副词转译成形容词）

4. 转译成汉语副词

（1）The mechanical automatization makes for a **tremendous** rise in labor productivity.
　　机械自动化可以<u>大大地</u>提高劳动生产率。（形容词转译成副词）

（2）A helicopter is **free** to go almost anywhere.
直升机几乎可以<u>自由地</u>飞到任何地方去。（形容词转译成副词）

（3）Rapid evaporation at the heating surface **tends** to make the steam wet.
加热面上的迅速蒸发，<u>往往</u>使蒸汽的湿度变大。（动词转译成副词）

（五）被动语态的翻译

科技英语主要是叙述事理，往往不需要说出主动者，或对被动者比主动者更为关心。此外，科技工作者为了表示客观和谦虚的态度，往往避免使用第一人称，因而尽可能使用被动语态。因此，在翻译英语被动语态时，大量语句应译成主动句，少数句子仍可译成被动句。

1. 译成汉语的主动句

- 原主语仍译为主语

当英语被动句中的主语为无生命的名词，又不出现由介词 by 引导的行为主体时，往往可译成汉语的主动句，原句的主语在译文中仍为主语。这种把被动语态直接译成主动语态的句子，实际是省略了"被"字的被动句。

（1）If a machine part **is not well protected**, it will become rusty after a period of time.
如果机器部件不好好<u>防护</u>，过一段时间后就会生锈。

（2）Every moment of every day, energy **is being transformed** from one form into another.
每时每刻，能量都在由一种形式<u>转换</u>成另一种形式。

- 把原主语译成宾语，而把行为主体或相当于行为主体的介词宾语译成主语

（1）Friction can be reduced and the life of the machine prolonged by **lubrication**.
<u>润滑</u>能减少摩擦，延长机器寿命。

（2）Modern scientific discoveries lead to the conclusion that energy may be created from **matter** and that matter in turn, may be created from energy.
近代科学的发现得出这样的结论：<u>物质</u>可以产生能量，能量又可以产生物质。

- 在翻译某些被动语态时，增译适当的主语使译文通顺流畅

由 it 做形式主语的被动句型：这种句型在科技英语中比比皆是，十分普遍，汉译时一般均按主动结构译出。即将原文中的主语从句译在宾语的位置上，而把 it 做形式主语的主句译成一个独立语或分句。

（1）**It is believed to** be natural that more and more engineers have come to prefer synthetic material to natural material.
愈来愈多的工程人员宁愿用合成材料而不用天然材料，<u>人们</u>相信这是很自然的。

增译逻辑主语：原句未包含动作的发出者，译成主动句时可以从逻辑出发，适当增加不确定的主语，如"人们""有人""大家""我们"等，并把原句的主语译成宾语。

（2）To explore the moon's surface, rockets **were launched** again and again.
为了探测月球的表面，<u>人们</u>一次又一次地发射火箭。

（3）Although the first synthetic materials were created little more than a hundred years ago, they **can be found** almost everywhere.
虽然第一批合成材料仅在 100 多年前才研制出来，但现在<u>人们</u>几乎到处都能见到它们。

2. 译成汉语的其他句型

- 译成汉语的无主句

英语的许多被动句不需要或无法讲出动作的发出者，往往可译成汉语的无主句，而把原句中的主语译成宾语。英语中有些固定的动词短语，如：make use of，pay attention to，take care of，put an end to 等用于被动句时，常译成无主句。

(1) In the watch making industry, the tradition of high precision engineering **must be kept**.

在钟表制造业中，**必须保持**高精度工艺的传统。

(2) **Attention has been paid to** the new measures to prevent corrosion.

已经注意到采取防腐新措施。

- 译成汉语的判断句

凡着重描述事物的过程、性质和状态的英语被动句，实际上与系表结构很相近，往往可译成"是……的"结构。

The voltage **is not controlled** in that way.

电压不是用那样的方法**控制的**。

- 译成汉语的被动句

英语的有些着重被动作的被动句，要译成被动句，以突出其被动意义。被动含义可用 "被""由""给""加以""为……所""使""把""让""叫""为""挨""遭"等表达。

The metric system **is now used by** almost all countries in the world.

米制现在**被**全世界几乎所有的国家**采用**。

(六) 定语从句的翻译

1. 只要是定语从句比较短的，或者虽然较长，但汉译后放在被修饰语之前仍然很通顺，一般的就放在被修饰语之前，这种译法叫做逆序合译法。例如：

(1) The speed of wave is the distance it advances per unit time.

波速是波在单位时间内前进的距离。

(2) The light wave that has bounced off the reflecting surface is called the reflected ray.

从反射表面跳回的光波称为反射线。

(3) Stainless steel, which is very popular for its resistance to rusting, contains large percentage of chromium.

具有突出防锈性能的不锈钢含铬的百分比很高。

2. 定语从句较长，或者虽然不长，但汉译时放在被修饰语之前实在不通顺的就后置，作为词组或分句。这种译法叫做顺序分译法。例如：

(1) Each kind of atom seems to have a definite number of "hands" that it can use to hold on to others.

每一种原子似乎都有一定数目的"手"，用来抓牢其他原子。(顺序分译法)

每一种原子似乎都有一定数目用于抓牢其他原子的手。(逆序合译法)

这句限制性定语从句虽然不长，但用顺序分译法译出的译文要比用逆序合译法更为通顺。

(2) Let AB in the figure above represent an inclined plane the surface of which is smooth and unbending.

设上图中 AB 代表一个倾斜平面，其表面光滑不弯。（顺序分译法）

设上图中 AB 代表一个其表面为光滑不弯的倾斜平面。（逆序合译法）

上面两种译法，看来也是用顺序分译法比用逆序合译法更为通顺简明。

3. 定语从句较长，与主句关联又不紧密，汉译时就作为独立句放在主句之后。这种译法仍然是顺序分译法。例如：

（1） Such a slow compression carries the gas through a series of states, each of which is very nearly an equilibrium state and it is called a quasi-static or a "nearly static" process.

这样的缓慢压缩能使这种气体经历一系列的状态，但各状态都很接近于平衡状态，所以叫做准静态过程，或"近似稳定"过程。

（2） Friction wears away metal in the moving parts, which shortens their working life.

运动部件间的摩擦力使金属磨损，这就缩短了运动部件的使用寿命。

4. There + be 句型中的限制性定语从句汉译时往往可以把主句中的主语和定语从句融合到一起，译成一个独立的句子。这种译法叫做融合法，也叫拆译法。例如：

（1） There are bacteria that help plants grow, others that get rid of dead animals and plants by making them decay, and some that live in soil and make it better for growing crops.

有些细菌能帮助植物生长，另一些细菌则通过腐蚀来消除死去的动物和植物，还有一些细菌则生活在土壤里，使土壤变得对种植庄稼更有好处。

（2） There is a one-seated which you could learn to drive in fifty minutes.

有一种单座式汽车，五十分钟就能让你学会驾驶。

Exercises

Translate the following sentences into Chinese.

1. We keep the battery in a dry place so that electricity may not leak away.
2. The speed of wave is the distance it advances per unit time.
3. Because energy can be changed from one form into another, electricity can be changed into heat energy, mechanical energy, light energy, etc.
4. Usually the capacitor is made up of plates of large area so that large electrical charges may be stored.
5. Electricity is such an important energy that modern industry couldn't develop without it.
6. It is evident that a well lubricated bearing turns more easily than a dry one.
7. This steel alloy is believed to be the best available here.
8. The resistance being very high, the current in the circuit was low.
9. The ABS is a four-wheel system that prevents wheels lock-up by automatically modulating the brake pressure during an emergency stop. By preventing the wheels from locking, it enables the driver to maintain steering control and to stop in the shortest possible distance under most conditions.
10. The rotor arm distributes the surge to the segment linked to the right spark plug in sequence required by the firing order.
11. This shows that the resistance of an electric conductor is inversely proportional to its cross-section area.

五　科技英语的翻译 2

（七）状语从句的翻译方法

在状语从句的翻译中，主要应注意状语从句的位置、连词的译法和省略以及状语从句的转译等。英译汉时状语从句的位置尤其重要。一般来说，汉语中，状语从句多半在主句前面，有时放在整个句子当中。此外，汉译英时连词常可以省略，这在时间、条件状语从句中尤为常见。

另一个值得注意的是，不要碰到 when 就译成"当"、碰到 if 就译成"如果"、碰到 because 就译成"因为"，而应酌情进行变化或简化。如：

（1）The computer will find the route <u>when</u> you send your signal to it.
　　　把信号输入计算机，它<u>就会</u>找到行车路线。

（2）<u>If</u> water is cold enough, it changes to ice.
　　　水温降到一定程度<u>便会</u>结冰。

另外，科技英语的翻译中，有时将时间状语从句转译成条件状语从句，将地点状语从句转译成条件状语从句。如：

（1）These three colors, red, green and violet, <u>then combined</u>, produce white.
　　　红、绿、紫三色<u>若合在一起</u>，就变成白色。

（2）<u>Where there is nothing in the path of the beam of light,</u> nothing is seen.
　　　<u>如果光轨迹上没有东西，</u>就什么也看不出来。

1. 时间状语从句的译法

● 译成相应的时间状语，放在句首

不论原文中表示时间的从句是前置或后置，根据汉语习惯，都要译在其主句的前面。

Heat is always given out by one substance and taken in by another <u>when heat-exchange takes place</u>.
<u>热交换发生时，</u>总是某一物质释放热量，另一物质吸收热量。

● 译成并列句

有的连词（如 as、while、when 等）引导时间状语从句，在表达主句和从句的谓语动作同时进行时，英译汉时可省略连词，译成汉语的并列句。

The earth turns round its axis <u>as it travels around the sun</u>.
<u>地球一面绕太阳运行，</u>一面绕地轴回转。

● 译成条件状语从句

When 等引导的状语从句，若从逻辑上判断具有条件状语的意义，则往往可转译成条件状语从句。

Turn off the switch <u>when anything goes wrong with the machine</u>.
<u>如果机器发生故障，</u>就把电门关上。

2. 地点状语从句的译法

● 译成相应的地点状语

一般可将地点状语从句译在句首。
Heat is always being transferred in one way or another, where there is any difference in temperature.
凡是有温差的地方，热都会以这样或那样的方式传输。

- 译成条件状语从句或结果状语从句

Where 或 wherever 引导的状语从句，若从逻辑上判断具有条件状语或结果状语的意义，则可转移为相应的状语从句。

（1） Where water resources are plentiful, hydroelectric power stations are being built in large numbers.
只要是水源充足的地方，就可以修建大批的电站。

（2） It is hoped that solar energy will find wide application wherever it becomes available.
可以期望，太阳能将得到广泛的利用，以至于任何地方都可以使用。

3．原因状语从句的译法

- 译成表"因"的分句

一般来说，汉语表"因"的分句置于句首，英语则较灵活。但现代汉语中，也有放在后面，此时往往含有补充说明的意义。

（1） Some sulphur dioxide is liberated when coal, heavy oil and gas burn, because they all contain sulphur compounds.
因为煤、重油和煤气都含有硫化物，所以它们燃烧时会放出一些二氧化硫。

（2） To launch a space vehicle into orbit, a very big push is needed because the friction of air and the force of gravity are working against it.
要把宇宙飞行器送入轨道，需要施加很大推力，因为空气的摩擦力和地球引力对它起阻碍作用。

- 译成因果偏正复句的主句

这实际是一种省略连词的译法，把从句译成主句。
Because energy can be changed from one form into another, electricity can be changed into heat energy, mechanical energy, light energy, etc.
能量能从一种形式转换成另一种形式，所以电可以转变为热能、机械能、光能等。

4．条件状语从句的译法

- 译成表示"条件"或"假设"的分句

按照汉语的习惯，不管表示条件还是假设，分句都放在主句的前部，因此英语的条件从句汉译时绝大多数置于句首。
Unless you know the length of one side of a square or a cube, you can not find out the square's area or the cube's volume.
除非已知一个正方形或一个正方体的边长，否则就无法求出这个正方形的面积或这个正方体的体积。

- 译成补充说明情况的分句

不少条件状语从句汉译时可置于主句后面，做补充说明情况的分句。
Iron or steel parts will rust, if they are unprotected.

铁件或钢件是会生锈的，<u>如果不加保护</u>。

5. 让步状语从句的译法

- 译成表示"让步"的分句

汉语中让步分句一般前置，但也可后置。

（1）<u>Though we get only a relatively small part of the total power radiated from the sun,</u> what we get is much more than enough for our needs.

<u>虽然我们仅得到太阳辐射总能量的一小部分，</u>但是，与我们的实际需要量相比，这已绰绰有余了。

（2）Energy can neither be created nor destroyed <u>although its form can be changed</u>.

能量既不能创造，也不能消失，<u>尽管其形式可以转变</u>。

- 译成表示"无条件"的条件分句

The imitation of living systems, <u>be it direct or indirect</u>, is very useful for devising machines, hence the rapid development of bionics.

对生物的模仿<u>不管是直接的还是间接的</u>，对于机械设计者都很有用处，因此仿生学才迅速发展。

6. 目的状语从句的译法

- 译成表示"目的"的后置分句

英语的目的状语从句通常位于句末，汉译时一般采用顺译法。

A rocket must attain a speed of about five miles per second <u>so that it may put a satellite in orbit</u>.

火箭必须获得每秒大约5英里的速度<u>以便把卫星送入轨道</u>。

- 译成表示"目的"的前置分句

汉语里表示"目的"的分句常用"为了"做关联词，置于句首，往往有强调的含意。

All the parts for this kind of machine must be made of especially strong materials <u>in order that they will not break while in use</u>.

<u>为了使用时不致断裂，</u>这种机器的所有部件都应该用特别坚固的材料制成。

7. 结果状语从句的译法

英语和汉语都把表示"结果"的从句置于主句之后，因此这类句子可采用顺译法。注意汉译时应少用连词，或省略连词。

Electronic computers work so fast <u>that they can solve a very difficult problem in a few seconds</u>.

电子计算机<u>工作如此迅速，</u>一个很难的题目几秒钟内就能解决。

（八）长句的翻译方法

其实，科技英语长句翻译和日常英语长句翻译一样，首先要抓住全句的中心内容，弄清楚<u>在逻辑上</u>哪些是主要的，哪些是次要的；然后进行全句的语法分析，找出主句和从句，并理解这些句子之间的关系；在这个基础上，按照汉语的表达习惯，把长句译成较短的汉语句子。科技英语长句的译法也可使用日常英语长句的翻译方法，即<u>顺译法、逆译法、分译法和综合译法</u>。

1. 顺译法

顺译法基本保留英语语序,在内容和形式两方面贴近原文。翻译时,应仔细阅读原文,抓住句子的主干部分,顺理旁枝,按原文所描述的动作的时间顺序翻译。例如:

If coolant leaks into a cylinder through the head gasket, or a cracked cylinder head, the cylinder will usually misfire when the engine is started, and the pressure gauge reading will drop during the leak test with no visible signs of external coolant leaks.

如果冷却液通过气缸垫或缸盖裂缝泄漏入气缸,则发动机起动时气缸中混合气不易燃烧。泄漏测试时压力表读数下降,但无明显的冷却液外漏迹象。

2. 逆译法

逆译法是当英语长句的表达顺序与汉语习惯不同时,可依据汉语的行文习惯,从长句的后面翻译的一种翻译方法。例如:

(1) The number of the young people in the United States who cannot read is incredible-about one in four.

大约有四分之一的美国青年人没有阅读能力,这简直令人难以置信!

(2) The very important oil industry, which has done much to rejuvenate the economy of the southern United States since the end of World War II, made considerable headway especially in the five states of Arkansas, Louisiana, Mississippi, Oklahoma and Texas.

第二次世界大战以后石油工业对振兴美国南部经济起了很大的作用。这个十分重要的工业部门特别是在以下五个州中取得了很大的进展:阿肯色、路易斯安那、密西西比、俄克拉荷马和得克萨斯。

3. 分译法

原句包含多层意思,而汉语习惯一个小句表达一层意思。为了使行文简洁,打破原文的复杂句式和结构,化长句为短句,将整个长句译成几个独立的句子,顺序基本不变,保持前后的连贯。

(1) Steel is usually made where the iron ore is smelted, so that the modern steelworks forms a complete unity, taking in raw materials and producing all types of cast iron and steel, both for sending to other works for further treatment, and as finished products such as joists and other consumers.

[初译] 通常在炼铁的地方就炼钢,所以现代炼钢厂从运进原材料到生产供送往其他工厂进一步加工处理并制成如工字钢及其他商品钢材的成品而形成一整套的联合企业。

[改译] 通常在炼铁的地方也炼钢。因此,现代炼钢厂是一个配套的整体,从运进原料到生产各种类型的铸铁与钢材;有的送往其他工厂进一步加工处理,有的就制成成品,如工字钢及其他一些成材。

(2) The loads a structure is subjected to are divided into dead loads, which include the weights of all the parts of the structure, and live loads, which are due to the weights of people, movable equipment, etc.

[初译] 一个结构物受到的荷载可分为包括结构物各部分重量的静载和由于人及可移动设备等的重量引起的活载。

[改译] 一个结构物受到的荷载可分为静载与活载两类。静载包括该结构物各部分的重量。活载则是由于人及可移动设备等的重量而引起的荷载。

4. 综合译法

综合译法就是将顺译法、逆译法和分译法等多种方法进行综合运用。例如：

In any internal combustion engine, burning fuel heats air which consequently expands, and in expanding exists a push to a piston which, in turn, rotates the engine crankshaft through a connecting rod.

在内燃机中，燃烧的燃料使空气受热并迅速膨胀，产生推力推动活塞，通过连杆推动发动机的曲轴。

Exercises

Translate the following sentences into Chinese. Pay attention to the features and translation methods of scientific English.

1. Manufacturing process may be classified as unit production with small quantities being made and mass production with large numbers of identical parts being produced.

2. Another solar electric technology is photovoltaics. It used silicon or other semiconductors to convert the sun's rays directly into electricity.

3. Various machine parts can be washed very clean and will be as clean as new ones when they are treated by ultrasonic, no matter how dirty and irregularly shaped they may be.

4. The global economy that boomed in the 1960s, growing at an average of 5.5 percent a year, and pushed ahead at a 4.5 percent a year in the mid-1970s, simply stopped growing in 1981 to 1982.

5. Electrical energy can be stored in two metal plates separated by an insulating medium. Such a device is called a capacitor, or a condenser, and its ability to store electrical energy is termed capacitance. It is measured in farads.

6. It therefore became necessary to adopt a pressurized cooling system where this had not previously been the case, and to increase the air flow through the radiator by fitting a coarser pitched (and potentially noisier) fan together with a radiator cowl.

Appendix Ⅲ

新能源汽车专业术语

1. 整车

BEV：全称 battery electric vehicle，纯电动汽车。
HEV：全称 hybrid electric vehicle，混合动力汽车。
PHEV：全称 plug-in hybrid electric vehicle，插电式混合动力汽车。
EREV：全称 extended-range electric vehicle，增程式电动汽车。
FCEV：全称 fuel cell electric vehicle，燃料电池汽车。

2. 驱动、行驶装置

辅助系统（auxiliary system），指驱动系统以外的其他用电操作的车载系统。
车载能源（on-board energy source），指变换器和储能设备的组合。
驱动系统（propulsion system），指车载能源和动力系的组合。
动力系统（power train），指动力电源与传动系的组合。
前后方向控制器（drive direction control），指通过驾驶人操作，控制汽车方向的装置。
电池承载装置（battery chassis），指为承载动力蓄电池而设置的装置，分为固定式和移动式。
电平台（electrical chassis），指一组电气相连的可导电部分，其电位作为基准电位。
动力电缆（power cable），指构成驱动用电动机动力电路的电线。
充电插孔（charging inlet），指在车身上安装的充电用插座或充电口。

3. 电气装置及部件

断路器（circuit breaker），指当电路异常时，切断电路的装置。
储能装置（energy storage），指能够存储电能的装置，包括蓄电池、超级电容、飞轮电池等。
带电部分（live part），指能够使电流通过的部分。
可导电部分（conductive part），指能够使电流通过的部分。
外露可导电部分（exposed conductive part），指能够使电流通过的部分。
主开关（main switch），指用于开、关动力蓄电池和控制其主电路的开关。
绝缘电阻检测系统（insulation resistance monitoring system），指检测动力蓄电池与车辆底盘之间绝缘电阻的系统。
维护插接器（service plug），指当维护或更换动力蓄电池时，断开电路的装置。

4. 指示器、信号装置

电池过热警告系统（battery overheat warning device），指当动力蓄电池温度超出限值时发出警告信号的装置。

电池液位警告系统（battery level warning device），指当动力蓄电池的电解液位过低，需要补充时发出警告信号的装置。

剩余电量显示器（residual capacity gauge），指显示动力蓄电池剩余电量的仪器。

电动机超速警告装置（motor overspeed warning device），指当电动机的转速超过限值时发出警告信号的装置。

电动机过热警告装置（motor overheat warning device），指当电动机的温度超出限值时发出警告信号的装置。

电动机过流警告装置（motor over current warning device），指当电动机的电流超出限值时发出警告信号的装置。

控制器过热警告装置（controller overheat warning device），指当主电路出现漏电时发出警告信号的装置。

可运行指示器（stand by indicator），指显示可以正常运行的装置。

制动能量回收指示器（electric retarder indicator），指显示电制动系统能量回收强弱的装置。

5. 行驶性能

放电能量（整车）（discharged energy），指电动汽车行驶过程中，由储能装置释放的电能。

再生能量（regenerated energy），指行驶中的电动汽车用再生制动回收的电能。

续驶里程（range），指电动汽车在动力蓄电池完全充电状态下，以一定的行驶工况，能连续行驶的最大距离。

能量消耗率（energy consumption），指电动汽车在经过规定的试验循环后，消耗的电网的电量与行驶里程的比值。

最高车速（1km）[maximum speed（1km）]，指电动汽车能够往返各持续行驶1km以上距离的最高平均车速。

30min 最高车速（maximum thirty-minutes speed），指电动汽车能够持续行驶30min以上的最高平均车速。

加速能力（acceleration ability），指电动汽车由某一速度到达另一速度所需的最短时间。

坡度起步能力（hill starting ability），指电动汽车在坡路上能够起动且1min内向上行驶至少10m的最大坡度。

动力效率（power train efficiency），指在纯电动汽车情况下，从动力系统输出的机械能与输入动力系统电能的比值。

爬坡车速（speed uphill），指电动汽车在给定的坡度上能够持续行驶1km以上的最高平均车速。

再生制动（regeneration breaking），指将一部分动能转化为电能并储存在储能装置内的制动过程。

6. 安全性能

误起步（unintended starting out），指车辆不在期望的情况下发生起步移动。

爬电距离（creepage distance），指在两个可导电部分之间沿固体绝缘材料表面的最短距离。

直接接触（direct contact），指人或动物与带电部分直接接触。

间接接触（in direct contact），指人或动物在基本绝缘失效的情况下与带电的外露可导电部分的接触。

基本绝缘（basic insulation），指带电部分上对触电起基本防护作用的绝缘。

附加绝缘（supplementary insulation），指为了在基本绝缘失效情况下防止触电而在基本绝缘之外使用的独立绝缘。

双重绝缘（double insulation），指同时具有基本绝缘和附加绝缘的绝缘。

加强绝缘（reinforced insulation），指为防止直接接触所提供的相当于双重绝缘防护等级的带电部分上的绝缘结构。

防护等级（protection degree），指按照 GB/T 4208 定义，对带电部分所提供的防护程度。

7. 质量

电动汽车整车整备质量（complete electric vehicle curb mass），指电动汽车按出厂技术条件装备完整（如备胎、工具等安装齐备），也是电动汽车在正常条件下准备行驶时，尚未载人（包括驾驶人）、载物时的空车质量。

电动汽车试验质量（test mass of an electric vehicle），指电动汽车整车整备质量附加试验所需质量之后的整车质量。

电动汽车最大总质量（max mass of an electric vehicle），指电动汽车整车整备质量附加最大允许承载质量之后的整车质量。

References

[1] THIESSEN F J, DALES D N. Automotive principles and service[M]. Reston: Reston Publishing Company, 1998.

[2] HEISLER H. Advanced vehicle technology[M]. Oxford: Butterworth-Heinemann, 2002.

[3] HALDERMAN J D, MITCHELL C D. Automotive brake systems[M]. Englewood Cliffs: Prentice Hall, 2004.

[4] RAE J B. The American automobile industry[M]. Boston: Twayne Publishers, 1984.

[5] 王锦俞,闵思鹏. 图解英汉汽车技术词典[M]. 北京:机械工业出版社,2008.

[6] 常丽,张红伟. 汽车专业英语[M]. 大连:大连理工大学出版社,2007.

[7] 黄星,黄汽驰. 汽车英语[M]. 3版. 北京:人民邮电出版社,2014.

[8] 粟利萍. 汽车实用英语[M]. 2版. 北京:电子工业出版社,2008.

[9] 王海林. 汽车专业英语[M]. 北京:机械工业出版社,2008.

[10] 甘辉. 汽车专业英语实用教程[M]. 北京:机械工业出版社,2009.